The Extreme Right in the French Resistance

THE EXTREME RIGHT IN THE FRENCH RESISTANCE

MEMBERS OF THE CAGOULE AND
CORVIGNOLLES IN THE SECOND WORLD WAR

VALERIE DEACON

LOUISIANA STATE UNIVERSITY PRESS BATON ROUGE

Published by Louisiana State University Press
Copyright © 2016 by Louisiana State University Press
All rights reserved
Manufactured in the United States of America
First printing

Designer: Barbara Neely Bourgoyne
Typeface: Whitman
Printer and binder: Maple Press (digital)

Library of Congress Cataloging-in-Publication Data
Names: Deacon, Valerie, 1981– author.
Title: The extreme Right in the French Resistance : members of the Cagoule and
Corvignolles in the Second World War / Valerie Deacon.
Description: Baton Rouge : Louisiana State University Press, [2016] | Includes
bibliographical references and index.
Identifiers: LCCN 2016005177 | ISBN 978-0-8071-6362-7 (cloth : alkaline paper) |
ISBN 978-0-8071-6363-4 (pdf) | ISBN 978-0-8071-6364-1 (epub) | ISBN 978-0-8071-
6365-8 (mobi)
Subjects: LCSH: World War, 1939–1945—Underground movements—France. |
Right-wing extremists—France—History—20th century. | Comité secret d'action
révolutionnaire—History. | Union des comités d'action défensive—History. |
France—History—German occupation, 1940–1945. | France—Politics and
government—1940–1945
Classification: LCC D802.F8 D37 2016 | DDC 940.54/8644—dc23
LC record available at https://lccn.loc.gov/2016005177

CONTENTS

ACKNOWLEDGMENTS

I owe many people considerable debts for the moral, emotional, intellectual, institutional, and financial support that made this project possible. Robert Young was the first to introduce me to the nuances of modern French history, and I am indebted to him not only for the intellectual foundation he provided but for his mentorship and friendship. His commitment to undergraduate teaching is unrivaled; one need look no further than the ongoing concern he has for his former students as evidence of this. I have always thought it hardly coincidental that my undergraduate mentor and my graduate supervisor, Bill Irvine, spent time together in France when they were young researchers. The two of them, different in so many ways, are extraordinary historians as well as extraordinary mentors.

Bill is both a generous scholar and a friend who has always taken my own moments of doubt in stride. While his work has been immensely influential, he has shared stories of being at the receiving end of academic rejection and pettiness, making my own struggles less painful. If he ever doubted my abilities, it was never obvious to me; this kind of confidence is priceless.

My colleagues at New York University are a continuing source of inspiration. Many of them have been kind enough not only to read my work but also to help me navigate the world of academic publishing. Herrick Chapman and Ed Berenson offered the warmest possible welcome to New York and to the Institute of French Studies at NYU. I have benefited more than I can express from their collegiality and their guidance. Jane Burbank and Fred Cooper also extended their kindness and hospitality to me in ways for which I will be forever grateful. Similarly, Andrew Lee and his family welcomed me into their home and have become dear friends.

My research was made possible in large part thanks to the archivists and staffs at the Archives de Paris, the Préfecture de la Police, and the Archives Nationales in Paris, as well as those at the Service historique de la Défense at Vincennes. I am particularly grateful to Lionel Dardenne at the Musée de la Libération in Paris, whose invaluable help allowed me to find the missing pieces of Maurice Duclos's life.

My academic and personal lives have also been enriched by the many brilliant friends I have made over the past decade. Katie Edwards, Laura Godsoe, and Alexia Yates were my dream team of women French historians. Jim Clifford, Ian Milligan, Tom Peace, Ian Mosby, Jason Ellis, and Dan Bullard were all part of the best cohort I could imagine. The world of academia has many flaws, but one benefit is that you never stop meeting new and wonderful people. All of these new and old friends deserve to have their names shouted from rooftops, but I will have to hope that they already know how appreciative of them I am.

Many thanks are in order to my family, particularly to Rod, who holds down the fort while I travel, research, write, and work.

Finally, my ultimate acknowledgment must go to my mother, Karen, without whom none of this would have been possible. She raised me singlehandedly, and it was thanks to her hard work that I was able to accomplish all that I have. She did not speak French, but she enrolled me in French immersion classes when I was six. She had not gone to university, but she did everything in her power to make sure I could. She was my closest friend and my most vocal supporter. Her death at age fifty left a chasm in many lives.

The Extreme Right in the French Resistance

INTRODUCTION

At the end of the Second World War, a shadowy figure known for his skills in gunrunning for groups of the extreme right was sentenced by a French court to twenty-five years of "national indignity" for his wartime activities undertaken in the name of the collaborationist French government. In 1948 he was sentenced to an additional four years in jail for his prewar activities, which included distributing, transporting, and importing contraband weapons of war; possessing and fabricating explosives; belonging to a criminal organization; plotting to change the form of government; and plotting to incite civil war. This man, Gabriel Jeantet, was so clearly guilty in the eyes of both courts that not even a letter from the well-known resister and future president of France, François Mitterrand, was enough to convince the judges otherwise. Thanks to the sentence of "national indignity," Jeantet was forbidden from voting, from holding office, and from participating in civil society more generally. Yet, less than five years later, Jeantet was awarded the Croix du combattant volontaire de la Résistance, an honor awarded to people who had served at least ninety days with an officially recognized resistance organization or those who had been wounded or killed in resistance action. As one arm of the recently reestablished French republican government punished Jeantet, another honored him. Taken together, their actions expose the sometimes tortuous elaboration of what it meant to resist the Germans during the Second World War in France.

It is difficult to clearly establish whether somebody like Jeantet was a resister, a collaborator, or both—in part because of the complexities of wartime behavior and in part because of the complex negotiation of identity that took place in France after the war. Since 1945, the categories of collaborator, resister, and *attentiste* (referring to those who did nothing while waiting to see which side would emerge victorious) have undergone many changes. Prompted sometimes by cultural productions (films, in particular), sometimes by deliberate official acts (e.g., the state's redefinition of who was considered a resister), sometimes by historical inquiry (the publication of Robert Paxton's book on Vichy France), these changes have been virtually ceaseless.[1]

Only in the last twenty years, however, have scholars started to take seriously the participation of the Right in the Resistance. Even in 2000, Dominique Veillon, a well-regarded historian of France, could write that "if certain matters concerning the Vichy regime are now clearer, thanks to Paxton's pathbreaking work, we are only just beginning to challenge the image of an idyllic Resistance, implacable and pure, which derived its legitimacy from a total and spontaneous condemnation of the Vichy regime from the outset."[2] Many earlier studies acknowledged the presence of the Right, but rarely did they offer a sustained investigation into the seeming paradox of antirepublican participation in what was seen as a republican phenomenon. However, it is this apparent contradiction that makes such a study all the more interesting. How did people who in the prewar years had actively sought to bring down the republican form of government choose during the war to resist, all the while suspecting that their resistance would result in the re-creation of the parliamentary system? Or, to highlight the paradox, why did these individuals not side with Vichy, which would seem to have been the logical choice for them?[3] Such questions have remained underexplored, though it is now common to read brief acknowledgments of the role the moderate Right played. Less common are full-length studies of the Right's role and serious discussions of members of the extreme Right in the Resistance.[4]

This book focuses on two prewar groups of the extreme Right, the Cagoule and the Corvignolles, and the members of those groups who decided to resist the German occupation of France. The two organizations shared similar characteristics before the war: anticommunism was at the forefront of each group's struggle; each was more or less antirepublican;

their politics were informed by anti-Semitism; each had a history of interaction with the royalist Action française; and most significantly, each group operated illegally, in the shadows of French society, in the 1930s. The reason for focusing on these particular groups of the extreme Right and for emphasizing their illegal nature is that when it came time to step into disobedience vis-à-vis the German occupiers, these men did not have far to step.[5] Unlike most other resisters, who faced enormous challenges in taking that step toward what was essentially subversive action against a legally constituted government, the men and women from the Cagoule and the Corvignolles already knew what it meant to operate secretly. Furthermore, the connections that these adherents had made in the 1930s by actively participating in groups that were so similar to one another had positive effects on their resistance activities.

To understand the nuances of wartime behavior, a brief introduction to the complexities of French history in the 1930s and during the Second World War is necessary. Gabriel Jeantet's path and that of others like him led to their participation in resistance activities of one kind or another—resistance to the German occupation of France from 1940 to 1944 but also, in certain cases, resistance to the legal, if not legitimate, government of France during this period, led by Marshal Philippe Pétain. For people like Jeantet—men and women who came from the far right of the political spectrum—the route to resistance was by no means a certain one. If the political, social, and moral situation in France in 1940 was, as has been suggested, notoriously murky, it was little more so than in the ten preceding years. The experience of the Second World War in France, with a crushing military defeat, the demise of the Third Republic, and the creation of the collaborationist Vichy regime, cannot be understood in isolation from the decade that came before.

Though the early 1930s were relatively calm in France, the rest of the world was already suffering from the effects of the Great Depression. France escaped the worst of the financial crisis in these years, but the delay was only temporary, and the Depression would last much longer in France than in other countries. Economic instability was matched by political uncertainty, as the many government coalitions of the Third Republic seemed paralyzed in the face of the financial challenges. The

decade started with a fragile consensus and a relaxation of political polarization, but by 1934 French society seemed ready once again to split
down the middle. Both the Left and the Right responded to these crises
with alarm. The most worrisome aspect of their response was that the
French republican model was no longer seen as a viable one.

The Left would not abandon the republican model entirely, though
the 1930s witnessed many left-wingers sliding toward the other end of
the political spectrum. The Popular Front experiment, the mid-decade
coalition between leftists and centrists that saw electoral victory in both
Spain and France, was enough to persuade many supporters of the Left
that there was still hope for the Republic. But the Right, including a
healthy segment of the parliamentary conservatives, was less and less
convinced that liberal democracy could remedy any of the problems
France faced. One reaction to the right wing's suspicion was the growth
of existing extraparliamentary leagues and the rise of new ones, in part
inspired by political events in Italy and Germany. Although some of these
ligues had been formed long before the 1930s—L'Action française, for
example, had been created in 1898[6]—they increased significantly in both
size and number in the mid-1930s. Each group had its own personality
and constituency, though they were all anti-Marxist, antiparliamentarian,
antiliberal, adept at using the media and other public avenues to advance
their cause, and frequent advocates of using violence as a means to an
end. The biggest and most influential leagues included François de la
Rocque's Croix de feu, Jean Renaud's Solidarité française, Marcel Bucard's
Francistes, Pierre Taittinger's Jeunesses patriotes, and George Valois's
Faisceau.[7] All of these leagues were invigorated in 1934, thanks to the
fragility of the government coalitions, successive government scandals,
and the removal of the Parisian prefect of police, who had been indulgent
toward the leagues while taking a hard line toward leftist groups.

This dismissal brought rightist groups, veterans' organizations, and
other disaffected people into the streets on February 6, 1934. The demonstrators all congregated outside the Chamber of Deputies in Paris,
demanding the overthrow of the government. This demonstration quickly
turned into a riot, as police tried to keep the protesters away from the
Chamber, and by the end of the day hundreds of people had been injured

and the police had fired on the crowds, killing thirteen protestors and fatally wounding six others.[8] In the following days, even more people were killed in violent demonstrations. The mobilization of the Right was ultimately a failure, but it did have significant consequences. Though it was unnecessary, as his government had survived several votes of confidence, Edouard Daladier resigned from his post as prime minister. "It was the first time in the history of the Third Republic that a cabinet had fallen in response to pressure from the street."[9] The leagues, by their very existence and their popularity, had shown just how little confidence people had in the Third Republic. Though there was considerable diversity among the various protestors in 1934, they were "competing for the support of broadly similar social constituencies, often sharing an overlapping membership, stealing each others' clothes but tailoring them to appear distinctive, misrepresenting each other in order to achieve strategic advantage."[10] Even the more peaceful protestors that day were not unhappy with the outcome: the fall of the center-left government, with the possibilities it opened for the creation of a new authoritarian regime, was welcomed even by veterans' organizations, traditionally understood to have been largely republican in orientation.[11]

More importantly, the Republic had shown itself vulnerable to pressure from the political extremes. Indeed, the fear that the extreme Right had made serious gains on February 6 and that France might be the next victim of a fascist coup was a catalyst for the Left to organize itself. The result of this mobilization on the left was a coalition of socialists, communists, and the Radical Socialists—the Popular Front—that achieved electoral success in 1936. This clear division between the rightist factions, engaging in extraparliamentary activities, and the Left, with its electoral dominance, heightened existing tensions in the country. The polarization of politics was further emphasized when the Popular Front government made the leagues illegal, leaving millions of rightists with no viable political alternative. The first chapters outline some of the choices rightists made in the face of this ban, but it was from this point on, from 1936 until the beginning of the war, that future resisters were unknowingly setting up social networks that would serve their anti-Nazi cause in only a few short years. While the Left, particularly the communist Left, had already had years of political experience and networking opportunities, it too learned valuable lessons during the latter 1930s. However, the real gains in political education came for those members of the extreme Right who had renounced parliamentary politics and had operated outside the boundaries of legality. The ban on the leagues encouraged many rightist activists to participate in secret, illegal organizations. These men and women benefited from the shroud of secrecy in the 1930s; the ability to exclude others, while enjoying the reciprocal confidence of other activists, and the creation of a society within an already complete societal structure have long been identified as powerful draws for secret political activity.[12] These skills, not to mention basic survival skills employed while being sought after by the authorities, would serve those members who chose resistance in 1940 very well indeed. Not only did these rightists establish lasting relationships among themselves, providing them with permanent bonds that transcended later divisions, but they were adept at hiding their activities, organizing for secrecy, using multiple identities, and so on—all skills that a successful resister desperately needed.

It was not entirely clear in 1940, however, that these men and women from the right would ultimately be inclined to take up resistance. On September 3, 1939, after Adolf Hitler had broken innumerable treaties and agreements, in addition to invading several sovereign nations, the government of France declared war on Germany. Alongside her ally Great Britain, France had tried to prepare herself for what was expected to be a long war. Since neither nation had been able to ensure that its military preparedness matched Germany's, in 1939 both nations needed to adopt a defensive position to hold Germany back until their military output reached a point where they could switch to an offensive strategy.[13] Until May 1940, then, the French and German armies faced off in what was called the Phoney War (*drôle de guerre*), in which both countries avoided provoking each other. Germany was busy elsewhere in Europe, and France was buying time, which created an odd situation of being at war, without any warlike activities. But the *drôle de guerre* was not "just a parenthesis between peace and war."[14] It heightened political polarization in France, particularly once the government banned the communist newspaper *L'Humanité*, dissolved the Communist Party, and began arresting prominent communists.[15] These moves were, of course, extremely popular among rightist activists, especially those ones who had recently spent time in jail for their own political activities.

Ironically, the declaration of war in 1939, while increasing the distance between the Right and the Left, also brought them closer in the way they thought about the possibility of war with Germany. For most of the late 1930s, the Left had been motivated by fear of Hitlerian aggression, but not to the point of being willing to act against it. By 1939, however, the Left, including a large segment that subscribed to a newer, unconditional form of pacifism,[16] had to admit that force might be required to stop Hitler. The Right, similarly, though for quite different reasons, had devoted considerable energy to trying to avoid war as well. However, "a rejection of the democratic principles and even a distinct preference for more authoritarian political systems—even fascist ones—did not necessarily entail an enthusiasm for the foreign policy goals of the Third Reich or an unwillingness to resist Hitler."[17] While rejoicing at the misfortunes of the communists in 1939, many rightists were also preparing themselves for what was coming.

Few people from either the far left or right were surprised when the German troops finally attacked France on May 10, 1940. Like the rest of the French public, however, they were astonished at the speed with which the German Army managed to overrun the country. Within days the French line was broken, and within a week the Germans had an open path to Paris. The speed and efficacy of the offensive, along with memories of the last war and rumors about German behavior in other countries, inspired terror in the French population. Millions of French people fled in front of the oncoming armies, causing chaos on the roads. The mobility of the French Army was severely limited by this exodus, and German planes found easy targets in the slow-moving, possessions-laden convoy of refugees.[18]

By the end of May, there were suggestions from both military and civilian officials that France had clearly lost the battle, if not the war. This sentiment was given an added boost at the beginning of June, when British and French troops were surrounded by the Germans on the shores of Dunkirk. The British government made the decision to evacuate its soldiers, whose backs were literally to the sea. This decision, highly contentious then as now, left the French Army greatly outnumbered, with about forty French infantry divisions and remnants of three armored divisions against fifty German infantry divisions and the remains of ten Panzer divisions.[19] As the government fled to Bordeaux to escape the German onslaught, calls for an armistice of some kind became more audible, for it seemed certain to some that the French Army would not be able to recover its footing. This decision to leave the capital only caused additional panic in the population, further adding to the numbers of refugees on the move, causing a "human flood."[20] By June 16 the prime minister, Paul Reynaud, had resigned—after much fighting with his own government and with his Anglo-Saxon allies—and the venerable hero of the First World War, Marshal Philippe Pétain, had been asked to form a new government. It came as no surprise when, on June 22, the Pétain government signed an armistice with Germany.

Explanations for France's defeat have run the full gamut, from moral degeneration to military incompetence. While some of these explanations are persuasive and others less so, there is no doubt that most French people were confronted with difficult choices after the defeat. The terms of the armistice dictated that France be divided into various sectors—an occupied zone in the north and an unoccupied zone in the south, as well as a small Italian zone of occupation, a zone along the coast that was off-limits to the French, and territory that was annexed directly to Germany. Although Pétain's government technically had control over all internal affairs, the Germans were very much present in the northern part of the country. Since Bordeaux, like Paris, was in the occupied zone, the French government moved to the spa town of Vichy and immediately voted to revise the constitution. When Pétain was given full powers to revise the constitution, he took the opportunity to issue a number of constitutional acts giving himself almost limitless power and the ability to suspend the parliament. Thus the Vichy government was born—authoritarian and antidemocratic. Pétain was, however, not the only game in town, so to speak. It immediately became apparent that while the Vichy government was the legal authority in France, one did not necessarily need to support Pétain and the Germans. Paris was full of collaborators, many of whom thought Pétain was not doing enough to support the Nazi goals for a new European order. London was home to several newly formed organizations, all of which were looking for recruits to carry on the fight against the Nazis. The French colonies' loyalty to the Vichy regime was not entirely assured, which meant that opportunities for action in those colonies were expanding. Newly created newspapers, especially in the south of France, called for resistance against the Germans, though they refused to denigrate Pétain. And, of course, there was always the option of biding one's time, waiting to see what would come in the months after the armistice.

While *attentisme*, waiting to see how events would play out, did not require too much thought, it did require a certain caution—it can sometimes be just as hard to mask opinions as it is to act on them—and the other choices were rarely taken lightly. This was especially true of those choices that led people to the wrong side of Vichy and the Nazis. Even the most dedicated resister would have thought long and hard before totally disobeying a legal government, especially one led by men who were known and respected. For this reason, a fair number of early resistance activities actually took place within the heart of the Vichy government. *Vichysto-résistants*, as these early resisters have come to be known, were often the first to protest against the German occupation of France but usually the last to criticize Pétain or his National Revolution, with which they often agreed.

Vichy was, relatively speaking, a fairly safe space for these resisters in the early days of the war. In fact, many people working at the heart of the Vichy bureaucracy were sympathetic to the goal of ridding the country of the Nazis, and since the early resisters refrained from attacking Pétain, there was little conflict between resisters and Vichyites. This is not to say that all resisters were willing to accept Vichy's legitimacy. Some major resistance groups, like the Musée de l'Homme or Libération (both north and south), immediately refused to accept the defeat of France and the armistice and thus refused to accept the authority of the state that was the architect of that armistice. It is important to acknowledge that many early resisters supported Pétain, even if they did not extend that support to his political colleagues, and were thus fairly comfortable coexisting with Vichy. This, however, would not be the case throughout the war.

Political changes within Vichy, changes in the course of the war, changes in the relationship between Vichy France and Nazi Germany, and changes within the resistance itself all meant that the relationship between the state and resisters would change too.

In many ways, life in France settled into something of a regular pattern after the defeat and armistice. People still went to work and to church, families still needed to be fed, farms to be cared for. At Vichy the government went about the task of reordering the nation to bring it in line with the precepts of the newly elaborated National Revolution—based on principles of work, family, and fatherland—and all kinds of people jostled for political power and acknowledgment. But Vichy was not unchanging, nor was it one ideological bloc.[21] The people who made up the French State lent to it their different political proclivities and attempted to fashion it in their own images. Philippe Pétain was, of course, the head of state in this new regime. His prime minister, Pierre Laval, was no less known to the French public than Pétain himself, as he had held the post, along with other high-ranking positions, several times in the 1930s. Laval had begun his political career as a socialist but by 1940 was committed to full collaboration between France and Germany, convinced as he was that the Germans would inevitably win the war against Britain. Even though Pétain himself had committed to collaborating with the Germans, many viewed Laval as an even more enthusiastic proponent of collaboration, and this perception allowed many early resisters to imagine that Laval, rather than Pétain, had authored various amicable agreements between France and Germany in the early days of the Vichy regime. These imaginings were further strengthened when Pétain had Laval removed from power in December 1940, which led some early resisters to believe that Pétain was only biding his time before taking a stand against the Germans.

Although the vast majority of early resisters waited to see what Pétain would do after the signing of the armistice before passing judgment on him and his regime, some saw the writing on the wall and realized they would be better served by leaving French territory to carry on the fight. French North Africa was initially seen as a possible base for future resistance activities, and it would later become so, but in 1940 it was not to the colonies that potential resisters would rush but rather to London. Great

Britain had already allowed other defeated European countries, including Poland, the Netherlands, and Belgium, to establish governments in exile on British territory. Moreover, after France's defeat, Great Britain was perhaps the only reasonable destination for resisters who had made the choice to escape occupied Europe. This is not to say that the decision to leave France for Great Britain was an easy one; rather, there were simply few other options. It was not even clear that Great Britain would win the war against Nazi Germany, but with few other nations willing to continue fighting, London became an important location for resistance activities.

On June 17, 1940, the future leader of the Free French Forces, Charles de Gaulle, flew from France to London upon receiving the news that Pétain had become the head of a new government and was seeking an armistice. De Gaulle, who had recently been promoted to the rank of brigadier general—the most junior general in the army—was relatively unknown outside immediate political and military circles, and within those circles he was not particularly well liked. Though he was given permission to broadcast his now infamous call to carry on the fight against the Germans on the BBC, many British politicians viewed him with suspicion. Winston Churchill, however, gave de Gaulle a chance to prove his usefulness, in part because he thought de Gaulle might be able to rally even more important French figures to the British side. By the end of the month, de Gaulle had been recognized by the British as the "leader of all the Free French, wherever they are to be found, who rally to him in support of the Allied cause."[22] But Churchill's hopes were initially misplaced, as de Gaulle did not easily win the hearts of other French men and women in England, many of whom decided ultimately to return to France. In fact, de Gaulle's creation of a true "force" of people determined to do something about the German occupation of France was at times tortuous.[23] Perhaps by sheer will or arrogance, both of which de Gaulle had in spades, the Free French Forces (Forces françaises libres) was created, starting with the couple hundred French men and women who had ended up in London that summer by choice or by chance.[24] By the summer of 1943, when recruitment to the FFL was halted, more than sixty thousand people were engaged in the organization.[25] The FFL had many different bodies attached to it, including an air force, a navy, and its own intelligence services, the Bureau central de renseignements et d'action (BCRA). This secret service was critical, not only because of its own work but also because of its liaisons with other resistance organizations. When it came time for de Gaulle to unite the disparate elements of the Resistance, the BCRA and its agents would play a central role.

It was thanks to these agents that de Gaulle even knew about resistance activity in France, and although he was quick to assume that those resisters would follow his orders—as the resisters in London did—he initially had no way of knowing how their activities might fit into his larger strategy. Late in 1941, Jean Moulin arrived in England to meet with de Gaulle. Moulin, who had been the prefect of Chartres when the German forces invaded France, had tried to commit suicide rather than give in to the German insistence that he sign a document falsely avowing that French colonial troops had been responsible for civilian atrocities. After being dismissed by the Vichy government, Moulin started to explore opportunities for resistance. Upon arriving in London, Moulin claimed to have extensive knowledge of the blossoming resistance in France; although the claim was not altogether accurate, he convinced de Gaulle of his usefulness.[26] De Gaulle sent Moulin back to France as his official delegate. His mission was to get the southern resistance movements to coordinate their activities and, more importantly, to recognize the authority of de Gaulle as the sole leader of the Resistance. This was an exceptionally complicated task, made more so by the outspoken personalities involved in these movements, but by the beginning of 1943 Moulin succeeded in getting three movements to form a single organization, the Mouvements unis de la Résistance (MUR). These three movements—Combat, Franc-Tireur, and Libération-Sud—were large resistance organizations, natural choices for initial unification. They were not, however, the only representatives of resistance in France.

In addition to the large movements (*mouvements*), there were hundreds of smaller networks (*réseaux*). Although they were fighting for similar goals, there were significant differences between the networks and the movements. The movements, many of which were created in 1940, were generally focused on propaganda and the dissemination of clandestine newspapers to counteract the skewed news pouring out of Vichy or even

Germany. It is fair to say that the movements were largely of a civic, or civil, nature, whereas the networks tended to be based in a more militaristic culture. There were different kinds of networks—intelligence, sabotage, escape—but most were formed explicitly to assist the actual war effort. The network was "an organization created in preparation for precise military work, essentially intelligence."[27] Since France was no longer a combatant country, this focus on the war effort meant that the networks tended to be linked to one of the Allied countries, working with the British Special Operations Executive (SOE), the British Secret Intelligence Service (SIS), the London-based but Gaullist BCRA, or the American Office of Strategic Services (OSS). This connection to formal intelligence services meant that members of these resistance networks were militarily engaged in the war and submitted to an official military hierarchy during it or were integrated into the traditional army at war's end.[28]

While Moulin's unification of Combat, Franc-Tireur, and Libération-Sud was impressive, it did not prove that de Gaulle had the confidence of all French resisters. This broad-based support was important for a number of reasons, not least because the Americans, having joined the war in 1941, refused to recognize de Gaulle as the sole authority to speak for the French. Moulin was thus sent back to France with the goal of creating a single Resistance body that would encompass both zones and include representatives from resistance movements and political parties. This was achieved with the creation of the Conseil national de la Résistance (CNR), which held its first meeting in May 1943. Although they were not always in agreement, the participants in the CNR did agree that de Gaulle should be recognized as the single head of a French provisional government. While this was not the last power struggle de Gaulle engaged in, it did signal his dominance and persuaded some resisters that it would be wise to throw in their lot with the Gaullist forces.

The success of de Gaulle's unification of disparate resistance organizations was in part due to events over which he had little control. The situation in France had changed over the course of 1942 and into early 1943, resulting in increased motivation to resist not only the German forces but also the Vichy regime. In April 1942, Pierre Laval returned to power at Vichy as the "head of government," leaving Pétain with a largely titular position, indicating that the nature of the regime had clearly changed. Laval's government was decidedly more interested in close collaboration with the Nazis than Pétain's had been, and to ensure that this path would be followed, Laval padded the government with like-minded colleagues. Thus the Vichy government was radicalized in many ways, including in its crackdowns on so-called enemies of the state, most notably Jews, communists, and resisters. In the meantime, the war raged on around France. Germany had invaded the Soviet Union the previous summer, the United States had joined the war in December 1941, and Anglo-American leaders were contemplating how to break into Nazi-controlled Europe. They finally made a major step toward this goal when a joint British-American force landed in Vichy-controlled North Africa in November 1942 (Operation Torch). However, this move had major (and unexpected) consequences in France.

Although the British and American planners had solid intelligence leading up to the landings that suggested there would be little-to-no resistance from the French Army in North Africa, this intelligence clearly had underestimated those soldiers' loyalty to Pétain, who had instructed them to defend against any Anglo-American aggression.[29] There was, then, quite serious bloodshed in North Africa, which only ended with a ceasefire agreed to by Admiral François Darlan, who happened to be in Algiers visiting his polio-stricken son. Darlan's agreement to the ceasefire was not entirely voluntary, but he had little choice, as he was virtually a hostage of the US forces. Although the agreement left a Vichy man—Darlan—in charge of French North Africa, causing a great deal of anger within the Resistance, he was soon dismissed from his post by the Vichy government for having signed the ceasefire agreement. This, however, was not enough to persuade Hitler that the French were not about to do a volte-face and strike a deal with the Allies, so on November 11 German forces moved to occupy the whole of France, removing the so-called free zone. It was clear who was in charge of France. Although the Vichy government remained in place, the occupation of the whole country changed everything. The resisters who had previously maintained their support for Pétain had to admit that he was no longer in control of the government. But even more significant was the increased threat to the Resistance. Many resisters were forced to adapt to these changing circumstances, with Laval's cronies in key positions at Vichy, the Germans now occupying all of France, and even the sense that the support of Britain and the United States was not guaranteed.

Early in 1943 Laval endorsed the creation of the Milice française, a paramilitary organization with clearly defined collaborationist goals. The Milice had grown out of the Service d'ordre légionnaire (SOL), which itself had grown out of the Légion française des combattants, once headed, as we will see, by Georges Loustaunau-Lacau. But the SOL was in many ways very different from the Légion: it attracted mainly activists who publicly celebrated their hatred of the Third Republic, communists, and Jews. Led by Joseph Darnand, the former *cagoulard*, the SOL quickly came to be seen as a French version of the Nazi SS.[30] The Milice, however, was even more radical in its collaborationist goals than the SOL had been; one of its primary objectives was to rid France of resisters. Darnand gave the Milice both a military and a political objective, both focusing on restoring "order" in the country. The *miliciens* under his command "could not tolerate the rise of resistance on their territory, finding this far more unbearable than the presence of the Germans and even believing it to justify closer cooperation with the latter."[31] Indeed, increased vigilance on the part of the authorities made life considerably more dangerous for resisters, who increasingly denounced both the Germans and Vichy. The Germans and their repressive apparatus were now located all over the country. Many people at the heart of the Vichy government who had taken initial steps toward involvement in resistance activities quickly found that it was no longer safe to stay put and had to make the transition from internal resistance to external.

Through all these changes, both within and outside the country, French men and women undertook a vast range of activities, ranging from collaboration to resistance, with many subtle variations in between.[32] While it is true that Vichy became increasingly dominated by authoritarian nationalists, there were men and women of all political stripes in both collaborationist and resistance circles. The paths to both were never straightforward, particularly those leading to resistance, but we should not overstate the element of rupture in 1940. The development of a large and active resistance in response to the Occupation did not appear out of thin air; it had its genesis in an earlier period. Some of the very first *résistants* were characterized by the very fact that their behavior continued from the interwar period. Although "the great majority of French people needed something other than the emotional charge of defeat and Armistice to provoke the kind of anger and defiance necessary for opposition,"[33] many people who began resisting in 1940 displayed attitudes and patterns of behavior formed in the 1930s. Moreover, many groups within the Resistance relied on tradition and old symbolism in their struggle against the German occupiers. While many resisters were fighting for a change, many were also fighting because the Nazi ideology was inconsistent or incompatible with their already established values. Olivier Wieviorka argues that "the Resistance doesn't constitute a rupture but is part of a continuity, as the groups, by their struggle to preserve their identity or values, finish by turning to look to the past rather than the future."[34] Wieviorka does not deny that the Resistance, by its very existence, did cause major changes in the end. However, he emphasizes how important it is not to overstate what seemed to be discontinuity and an overturning of traditional hierarchies and authority. One aspect of this continuity that is frequently forgotten is that many men and women who resisted the Germans had known one another in the interwar years and had received a political education of one kind or another in those tempestuous years.[35]

Fully exploring the legacy of the Right's participation in the Resistance has been challenging for a number of reasons. The largest stumbling block has been, and continues to be, the fact that many more rightists participated in the Vichy experiment—a natural home for antirepublican, anticommunist, and anti-Semitic tendencies—than in the Resistance. The fact that Vichy was unquestionably "of the Right" and far more appealing to many people on the right means that rightist resisters were always a minority in the Resistance. This minority status, which was actually shared by all resisters, given that many more French men and women did not participate in resistance activities, does not mean that rightists had a negligible impact. Nor does it mean that we cannot learn valuable things about the political culture that shaped these men and women and the motivations behind their decisions to resist during the war.

The issue of motivation has proven to be something of a challenge to exploring the extreme Right's role in various resistance activities. Many historians would likely feel more comfortable imagining the men of the extreme Right as *résistants* if Emmanuel d'Astier de la Vigerie's so-called marginality thesis had held true.[36] Although this sense that the first resisters were *inadaptés* still held some sway in the 1970s—for example, Jonathan King insisted that these men "would tend, whatever the circumstances, to be at war with the status quo, nature's rebels waiting for a cause"[37]—historians in the last thirty years have been far less willing to see maladjustment as a motivation for resistance. It is impossible to establish a single motivation for resistance during the war, as the reasons for disobedience were endless. This is also true of other roads taken by civilians from 1940 to 1944. Competing loyalties, familial pressures, the influence of social networks, self-preservation, ideological stances, and a host of other complicated reasons fed into the individual decision to resist, collaborate, or accommodate.

All of these choices were individual ones, which in part is what makes motivation so challenging to explore. We might find that a resister fought "for values in which he believed, a sense of adventure, the lure of leadership, the need to conform to a group or the desire to stand out, a strategy for taking power."[38] Similarly, Laurent Douzou notes that "entering into resistance" was unlike entering into religion or politics, for example, because the groups, rituals, and modes of action were unknown in 1940 and 1941. He argues that "in the beginning, one didn't enter into resistance in the sense that one was joining existing communities; one tried to lay the foundation of a hypothetical resistance to come."[39] For many years after the war, the decision to join the Resistance was seen by historians as having been motivated by patriotism (above all else, usually) and antifascism. This argument has, in fact, been given new life by Julien Blanc, who notes that for resisters, patriotism is explanatory, as they subsumed all other ideologies in order to accomplish their primary goal of ridding France of the Germans. Blanc goes on to state that the same does not hold true for collaborators, for example, as their action continued to be motivated by other sentiments (anticommunism, antirepublicanism).[40] While we need to take patriotism seriously as a motivation for resisters, we cannot rely on it entirely, given that it motivated both the Resistance and supporters of Vichy.[41] Relying on such essentialisms might suggest that the defeat and the Occupation should have made all French people respond in the same way.[42] Since this clearly was not the case, many historians have tried to problematize resistance activity, while retaining some idea of patriotism, particularly since many resisters themselves rely on patriotism to explain their participation.

Finding other sources of motivation that can explain a wide variety of actions is not easy, though. Many definitions of resistance by their very nature exclude the participation of the extreme Right. According to an early definition offered by François Bédarida, "The Resistance was clandestine action undertaken in the name of the nation's liberty and human dignity by volunteers who organized to fight against the domination, and more often the occupation, of their country by a Nazi or fascist regime or its satellite or ally."[43] Using Max Weber's "ideal type," which helps elaborate an abstracted concept comprising essential characteristics, Bédarida argues that there are four central elements of resistance: a will to fight; a clandestine combat that has been freely chosen; a politico-ethical logic; and a didactic memory. Of particular interest to us is his third element, the political and ethical logic of resistance. He notes that the political is quite diverse, ranging from nationalism to internationalism, from classic conservatism to antifascism, and includes the combat of democracy against dictatorship, defense of the *patrie*, religious factors, and revolutionary hopes.[44] As useful as this definition may be, it clearly does little to explain the participation of the extreme Right. Perhaps their revolutionary hopes would place them within this definition, but it seems unlikely that Bédarida is referring to their hopes. Defending the *patrie* was certainly motivation for many of them, but such a concept poses the same risk as patriotism, in the sense that its ability to explain resistance, as opposed to collaboration, is limited. As Paul Jankowski asks, "Could resisters and collaborators start out with identical motives, resemble each other, end up by accident alone on opposite sides?"[45] Jankowski, like most other historians, concludes that accident is not a particularly plausible motivation. He places great importance on already established loyalties and associations among resisters and argues that "the rootless, the drifters, the criminals and idlers, the *marginaux*, discolored collaboration while barely tarnishing resistance."[46] The sense that most resisters had strong societal ties is not unique to Jankowski. As other historians have noted, and as we will soon discuss in greater detail, important social and familial factors need to be accounted for in considering what led an individual one way or another.

What stands out in many discussions of resistance and motivation is the idea that the decision to resist was fundamentally based on republican ideology. Georges Fournier writes that "it seems incontestable that the Resistance is mostly situated in a direct line from a republican heritage, or, if we prefer, from a republican culture."[47] Even though most historians are willing to admit the variety of motivations and values that led to resistance activity, almost all seem to suggest, whether implicitly or explicitly, that republicanism was central to the Resistance. For example, Robert Tombs compares the urban revolt of 1944 with those of the nineteenth century and notes a parallel with the revolt of 1870–71. He argues that "in both cases political radicalism was combined with intense patriotism and mass resentment caused by the hardships and humiliation of defeat. This widened potential support and created a temporary working alliance between different political tendencies." This supports the argument that people of many different political stripes were participating in the Resistance, but he notes that this temporary alliance was "in the name of the nation, the republic and the liberty of Paris."[48]

Given that there are numerous examples of *résistants* who cannot, properly speaking, be called republican or be said to have acted in the name of the Republic, it seems misleading to continue to speak of the Resistance exclusively in terms of its republican heritage. Some historians argue that it is preferable to speak of "resistances" to allow for the wide and diverse range of action and thought. H. R. Kedward notes that this allowance is particularly important given that the Resistance as a whole "became an alternative society, a parallel universe."[49] This is not to say that it is impossible to speak of a culture that fostered the Resistance; indeed, the republican heritage of which many historians speak was created by the same culture that created the Resistance. But this culture was not hegemonic: it had, and continues to have, room for changes, subversion, and divergent paths.

The culture that defined the contours of the Resistance and allowed for its creation and growth was not, strictly speaking, republican, but it did grow out of the years following the Revolution of 1789. I would suggest that the Resistance represents yet another variation of the French political tradition of insurrection. In its various permutations, this tradition was both Revolutionary and revolutionary, both leftist and conservative.[50] Although it was largely elaborated by the Left, including Jacobins, the Carbonari, and Blanquists, throughout the nineteenth century, this tradition was appropriated in the early twentieth century by far more conservative forces. Patrick Hutton suggests that "in terms of direct influence, however, Blanquist ideology made its most immediate impact on the political Right. . . . As a contribution to revolutionary thought, this legacy of the Blanquists, unsavory as it may be, ought not to be minimized. For in many ways, it was the Right, refurbished with a militant nationalist ideology and a belligerent political style, which emerged as the more revolutionary force in France in the years between the first and second world wars."[51]

One central feature shared by the Resistance and many of these other insurrectionary groups on both the left and the right was the fact that they were largely goal oriented. Adherents (or participants, in the case of the Resistance) were often grouped together in politically ambiguous organizations. The reason for the unusual cooperation between people with varying political sentiments was often necessity, but that does not diminish the importance of that cooperation. For instance, the French Carbonari, or *charbonnerie,* formed in opposition to the government of Louis XVIII, were bound together, as Alan Spitzer explains, by the ideological cement of their political methods.[52] Spitzer further elaborates this idea and argues that revolutionary tactics sometimes constituted a *political* alternative. He writes that French Carbonarism "was the temporary convergence of various political tendencies at a point where an illegal opposition seemed desirable to all of them."[53] Despite these different political tendencies, there were similarities between the members of the

Carbonari.[54] Like the *résistants,* in particular those on the right, the Carbonari shared some central political characteristics but perhaps differed in the way they imagined such politics becoming a reality.[55]

Drawing from his experience as a member of the French Carbonari, Louis Auguste Blanqui created several similar organizations, bringing people together in "a comradeship of dedicated revolutionaries, bound by rites of initiation, a code of secrecy, and a commitment to the conception of a revolution as a coup d'état."[56] The Blanquists, like the Carbonarists, managed to sustain cooperation based on a particular conception of revolution and the shared goal of allowing such a revolution to occur. The essence of this conception of revolution was "the certainty that political violence was a legitimate, honorable, and peculiarly effective mode of social change."[57] In practical terms, this strategy of insurrection also included a reliance on secrecy and the notion that people would join the revolution once it was under way but that it needed initially to be led by an elite of professional revolutionaries.[58]

Taking into account this French political tradition of insurrection allows us to see that the Resistance was not a revolution but was certainly inspired by a revolutionary spirit.[59] It also forces us to acknowledge that this revolutionary spirit could actually be shared by those on both the left and the right, particularly if it was goal oriented. These parameters of resistance actually fit quite well, it seems, with Pierre Laborie's definition of resistance, which he notes is so fluid and complex that it is impossible to truly describe it in a way that encompasses all of its varied aspects. Laborie, while recognizing the plurality inherent in the Resistance, suggests several things to consider as we attempt to elaborate which elements were necessary for resistance. His definition is broadly as follows:

> The willingness to do harm to an identified enemy, the occupier, or those in the service of the occupier by putting themselves in a situation of war and in organizing to prevent by all means possible the realization of their objectives. . . .
>
> The consciousness of resisting, that is to say, participating in the collective and coordinated expression of an intransigent refusal, by a voluntary choice, by responsible adherence to clearly affirmed objectives, by accepting in fact and in principle the necessity of armed struggle, with an accurate awareness of the risk and the meaning of the struggle. . . .

Engagement in action that is fundamentally linked to transgressive practices.[60]

Laborie's definition privileges the intentions of resisters and their goal, consciously developed, to rid France of the enemy. Achieving this goal did not necessarily require republican values or a concern for human rights writ large to motivate resistance activity.

This is not to suggest that the Resistance was theoretically arid or that it was elitist. Yet, such an argument allows us to take seriously the many contradictions within the Resistance and may prevent our privileging of the Resistance that did emerge from republican circles. Although often repeating that the vast majority of the resistance organizations were left-leaning, many people during the war commented on the difficulties inherent in trying to categorize them politically. One report from the *réseau* Brutus in 1943 noted that it was almost certain that most resistance efforts were originating in leftist and republican circles, but its author also commented that

> it is difficult to politically classify the resistance movements: the activist generally joined the first organized group of which he heard, and there he met people who in all other aspects of life aside from the fight against the invader had perspectives that were different from his own. This is a truth that too often escapes the heads of these movements, who believe to have behind them a group ready to follow them into whatever kind of postwar political action, while these people often don't even know their names, and they are engaged in serving one well-defined goal, that of liberation.[61]

It is not difficult to see the truth in this statement. In the early days of the war, when there was no formal Resistance to speak of, many future resisters turned to their already established social networks to find out about the possibilities of resistance and from there may indeed have joined the first group they could find.

As the war and the Occupation dragged on, more and more possibilities for resistance presented themselves, and political divergences became more noticeable. However, there was still a great deal of cooperation based on the common goal of ridding France of the German invaders. Methods might differ, ideologies certainly did, but the goal was the glue, so to speak, of many organizations. Moreover, this goal was revolutionary not only because it meant the overthrow of an existing power structure but also because it very rarely (so rarely, in fact, so as to be virtually nonexistent) included the restoration of prewar politics. There has been some excellent scholarship on the postwar goals of many of the resistance groups;[62] unsurprisingly, however, nothing has been written about the goals of the right-wing *résistants*. The fact that their goals were not left-leaning does not mean that they were not revolutionary. Most reports to London during the latter part of the war suggest several key elements of change upon which the French were supposedly banking. Some of these changes included a new republic, one that would be stronger and no longer *des camarades*; a new constitution; the reestablishment and safeguarding of individual and public liberties; judicial reform; reform of public instruction; suppression of private trusts; suppression of paternalism; reconstruction of the French economy; a new army and navy; and the creation of international and European organizations.[63] The vast majority of these suggestions are vague enough to fit comfortably in a plan coming from either the Left or the Right, and it is important to keep in mind that many resisters from both sides of the political spectrum blamed the corrupt ways of the Third Republic for France's defeat and subsequent occupation. It is no surprise that most of them had revolutionary goals for the war's end. As one report pointed out, the distinctions between leftist and rightist political tendencies made little difference from an economic or social point of view but "showed more clearly in the plans for the constitution (one part desiring an authoritarian regime, dismissive of parliamentarianism, and the other part clearly aspiring toward a true political democracy, with a hatred of fascism)."[64]

The same author, who is unnamed, goes on to stress the revolutionary goals of all resistance perspectives:

> Despite these differences, we can still talk of a "spirit of the resistance movements," which translates into the political field through a myth of Revolution . . . we find among the activists of the movements, alongside the will to apply tough penalties for traitors or those who profited from collaboration, a violent desire for radical change from the prewar in all domains: moral, constitutional, economic, social. This revolutionary accent constitutes the political

force of the movements, creates among them a certain unity despite profound doctrinal divergences, and happily fortifies the political climate of Gaullism.[65]

Although both the Left and the Right were fighting for dramatic changes, all of which were revolutionary to some degree, it is wrong to assume that the desire to reinstate the republic was a natural effect of its suppression in 1940. Not only did many people rally to the French State and its National Revolution, not only did elements of the extreme Right, which had never wanted a republic in the first place, fight against the Occupation, but reports from France during the war also suggest that French people desired a stronger, more authoritarian government. None of these people necessarily wanted to see a republican government come to power at the war's end. One report from 1943 notes that

> the totalitarian idea has progressed, though not the spirit of pro-Nazism. Many young people are inclined toward a totalitarian government, with order and authority and stability in the government of tomorrow. Among the youth who rally to a totalitarian formula different from that of the Germans and Italians, many come from old, more or less paramilitary resistance groups organized by Vichy and are now enrolled in the formations of the Resistance, after the dissolution of the official organizations. There is no doubt that at least one-third of these people see de Gaulle as the leader of the totalitarian government that they imagine and that at least half would rally to General de Gaulle as the leader of a government of this kind.[66]

The story of the extreme Right in the Resistance is a complicated one, made even more so by all its different components—the politics of the Right in the 1930s, the defeat and the Occupation, the different reactions of the Right to these events, the Resistance and the many tensions within it, the postwar reestablishment of the republican government, the rise and fall of rightist political fortunes, the creation of a Resistance myth in France, and the challenges to that myth. Not a single one of these topics is simple, and each has its own considerable historiography. This work is an attempt to draw some of these themes together to explore the seeming paradox of the extreme Right in the Resistance and to add to our understanding of the resistance against the German occupation.

It is unsurprising, but noteworthy, that these rightist activists tended to make similar choices once they committed themselves to resistance. The story of these activists after 1940 takes place largely in the milieu of the *réseaux*, rather than in that of the *mouvements*, of the Resistance. The resisters who joined a network were generally unconcerned with winning the hearts of their fellow citizens and were more focused on task-based resistance. It is not hard to see how the two kinds of resistance would attract particular types of people, and the activists on the extreme right in the 1930s, given their fundamental desire for action, were better suited to work in a network. Also, all of these resisters had adhered, in one way or another, to a hierarchical organization in the interwar period—whether it was the army or the military-inspired Cagoule—and would have felt comfortable in such an environment. Their decision to work closely with the Allies was not always regarded in a positive light by fellow resisters or by others in occupied France. This was particularly true for resisters who left France. The decision to leave France was not seen as a positive choice for people who wanted to "do something" to liberate the country, and those people who did live in England, for example, were often resented by those who stayed behind and dealt with the German occupation on a day-to-day basis.[67] While the relationship between the internal and external resistance is a complicated one, it is somewhat moot in the story of these resisters. Though they were mostly engaged in gathering military intelligence for the Allies, most of the activists in this study stayed in France for as long as they could. With the exception of Maurice Duclos, who went immediately to London, they felt that they were accomplishing quite a bit on native soil and stayed until they were deported or forced to flee. As we will see, they also experienced much of the same anxiety in their dealings with the external resistance as others, as few relationships were uncomplicated during the war.

As we explore the story of these men and women, from their prewar activities with the Cagoule and the Corvignolles to their postwar reintegration into French society, several themes should become apparent. While they came from similar backgrounds, these resisters walked down very different paths. It is always worth remembering that for each resister who came from these groups, many more lived out the war silently, adapting to the circumstances as they saw fit. One of the central goals of this study is to show that the Resistance was not monolithic and that the political groupings of the interwar period were similarly diverse. The extent to which political ideology guided the actions of these men and women varied, and we should not assume that day-to-day political activities are predictors of later behavior. While our approaches differ, Kevin Passmore's important contributions to the study of conservatives in France are, in some ways, confirmed by the people studied here. He adopts a valuable stance against essentializing political categories and notes that when he discusses conservatives, he is the one defining the parameters of *conservatives*. Passmore rightly notes that the subjects of his study share a common political culture, but it is reworked depending on context. It is here that the subjects of this study fit with his research, as he reminds us that because of the complexities of identity, "the motives of people within a movement are never reducible to the category: no-body acts simply as a liberal or as a fascist, but also as a mother or father, Catholics or Protestants, or as an anticlerical, bourgeois, or aristocrat, and much more."[68] Similarly, Passmore argues that the conventional use of categories obscures varying levels of commitment to political groups, as well as the connections between different groups. The men and women of this study, then, confirm Passmore's statements about the multiplicity of options, motivations, and activities available to the members of two groups on the extreme right.

Even when these men and women behaved similarly, however, their activities in those instances are not always represented equally. Some of these resisters' names are now familiar to the French public, but this should not suggest that they are all remembered in the same fashion. Georges Loustaunau-Lacau will always be remembered primarily as a conspiratorial figure; Maurice Duclos as a resistance hero; Georges Groussard as a man of unshakable and sometimes unpopular convictions (and one who, additionally, looked very much like the popular actor Erich von Stroheim). The ways in which these resisters have been remembered have depended less on their wartime activities and more on their relationships with other resisters, notably with the Gaullists, who fundamentally shaped the way resistance would be remembered after the war. In particular, it may become increasingly obvious throughout this book that an acceptance of de Gaulle's leadership meant a much easier reintegration into postwar society. For some of these resisters, this acceptance was fairly easy; after all, de Gaulle's politics were not always so different from those of these men and women on the right. For others, de Gaulle would never serve as a leader. And for still others, his star, though it might have shone brightly during the war, would fade dramatically in later years as he made decisions that were antithetical to the thinking of the extreme Right.

By its very nature, a history of resistance is not straightforward. Though their expertise in illegality and their connections with one another made these men and women ideally suited for resistance, their politics meant that resistance, whether against the Nazis or Vichy or both, was not necessarily undertaken lightly. Demonstrating a refusal of the German occupation was one thing. Of all the political groups that nurtured anti-German sentiment throughout the 1920s and 1930s, the extreme Right did it with the most passion. International cooperation and pacifism were not, generally speaking, key interests of the extreme Right. But undertaking a clandestine fight against Philippe Pétain and the Vichy government was a whole different story. Most of these rightist activists knew Pétain from the prewar years, and most venerated him for his performance in the First World War, as did the vast majority of the French population in 1939.[69] The politics of Vichy tended to match the politics of these men and women, and many hoped that Pétain's National Revolution would be successful. One might easily assume that in resisting both the Nazis and Vichy these men were forced to reevaluate their political positions. While some did, certainly, others did not. This is the story of the "other" resistance—the participation of the men and women of the extreme (and illegal) Right in the Resistance and the challenges they faced both during and after the war.

HISTORIOGRAPHY AND TERMS

The historiography of the Resistance has undergone many important changes since the war's end in 1945, both within and outside France. Generally speaking, early scholarship in France focused on the Resistance rather than on the nature of the Vichy regime. The reasons for this particular focus are numerous, including restrictive archival policies that made it impossible to access documents relating to the government and its domestic and foreign policies. It was also a product, however, of a historiography that was subject to the demands of its audience. For complex reasons, the French were rather more interested in the history of a heroic resistance (histories that were in many cases written by the historical actors themselves) than in the ignominious history of the wartime regime.[1] This trend changed over time, thanks to changing expectations, the opening of archives, and the influence of foreign academics who were interested in different questions. In other parts of the world, notably in the United States, the trend in scholarship about wartime France was almost entirely the opposite. American historians simply were not very interested in the Resistance, ignoring it almost entirely in favor of histories of collaboration or various aspects of the Vichy regime.[2] For these reasons, in 1992 Tony Judt was able to rightly note that while the previous thirty years had seen increasingly sophisticated scholarship on Vichy, there had been no similarly mythbreaking work on the Resistance. "The historiography of the subject," Judt noted, "still echoes, however indistinctly, the early official accounts, which treated the war years as though they consisted largely of the activities of a national Resistance and the repression it elicited."[3]

While this no longer holds true, and scholarship has become far more sophisticated, two points are worth making about the recent developments. First, while historical research has become more nuanced and now tries to represent the diversity of resistance experiences, this has not necessarily translated into similar nuances in how the public perceives the Resistance. A small pamphlet published in French in 2010 and then quickly translated into many other languages continued to portray resistance as a "natural" choice for all resisters because they cared about human dignity and social democracy.[4] While there is no doubt that many, if not most, resisters cared about dignity, such a representation does not take into account the fact that some resisters cared about dignity for only a select few or that even the word *democracy* left them with a sour taste. Second, this historiography is as important to understanding the Resistance as the facts of resistance are. Our sense of what it meant to resist or not to resist has been shaped by an ongoing conversation among historians. Their contributions have served to highlight some elements of the French Resistance and obscure others.

Henri Michel, himself a former resister, noted early on the presence in the Resistance of all sorts of people. In 1962 he wrote that we might find cooperating in the same resistance organization a "revolutionary syndicalist and a former activist of an extreme Right league, a Masonic professor and a Dominican father, a professional soldier and a conscientious objector."[5] At a time when rigorous studies of the Resistance were only just beginning to appear, the acknowledgment of diversity seemed promising, as Michel noted that the Right was represented in London and in the movements, for example, Ceux de la Libération (CDLL), which was created by members of the Right. His comments about the presence of the Right were qualified, however: "But this did not constitute a current of thought and action of the right, except around General Giraud in Algiers."[6] It was as if the presence of the extreme Right had to be confined somehow, as if its unsettling presence needed to be pushed to the margins of the Resistance for fear of shattering a fragile unity.

This unity rested on the idea that the Resistance was of a leftist political nature and that in addition to fighting to liberate France, the *résistants* were also fighting for a new political order. Peter Novick wrote that resistance was an individual phenomenon and thus it is difficult to generalize about it, which is ultimately true. Yet Novick, too, diminished the importance of diversity in the Resistance by arguing that it was not unfair to say that it was "of the Left," mainly because the Right was enlisted so quickly to the side of Vichy and because it was the Left that suffered most during the war. In 1968 he argued that "unity was highly prized in the Resistance, and many right-wing *résistants* paid lip service to socialist ideals rather than cause internal dissension."[7] Novick, however, rested this argument on two assumptions that require further scrutiny. The first assumption is that politics were important enough to the Resistance to cause dissension if there were divergences of opinion, which is unlikely, particularly in the initial period of resistance to the Occupation, when there was no formal resistance, so to speak. The second is that it is not entirely true that right-wing *résistants* were subject to any kind of gag order, whether formal or informal. Many continued to express the same political opinions that they had held in the prewar years.

Though these early studies did not capture the full extent of resistance diversity, they were pioneering nonetheless. There are many understandable reasons why researchers focused on certain elements, while ignoring others, not the least of which is the availability of sources. As Julien Blanc notes in his very thorough study of one resistance *réseau*, the Musée de l'Homme, there was something of an archival desert after the war. Blanc makes the excellent point that it was the very nature of some resistance acts that if they were done well, there would be no trace; this was particularly true of the *réseaux*, which were far less document oriented than other organizations. The paucity of archival sources detailing the early years of the war should thus not lead us to believe that there was no resistance.[8] Yet there is also a political dimension to this scholarship that cannot be overlooked. The political Right was discredited after the war not only because of the perception that it had weakened the French republic in the interwar period but also because of the easy association most French people could make between the Right and the collaborationist Vichy regime. For many years it was inconceivable, both to scholars and to the public, that a person on the right or the extreme right of the political spectrum could have legitimately been a resister. Though scholars came to see that there was a fairly conservative element to many resistance organizations, there was still a certain hesitancy to address the participation of the extreme Right in the struggle to liberate France. Early scholars, though, were doing the very important work of laying the foundation for later studies, both in writing histories of the Resistance and in gathering important archival material and oral testimonies in the postwar period. Henri Michel, who directed many early resistance studies, felt strongly that the histories of resistance needed to be written as soon as possible after the war. He was worried that later historians who had not participated in the Resistance would be incapable of understanding the Resistance because they (like many of his contemporaries) lacked *l'esprit résistant*. In addition to this, Michel had a practical reason for privileging the participation of former resisters in the creation of their own histories. He was concerned that many of the documents created during the war, given the reliance on codes, pseudonyms, and other secrets, would be incomprehensible to outsiders.[9] Because this early work was being done in the climate of suspicion vis-à-vis rightist wartime activities, few rightist resisters were invited to contribute to the creation of resistance histories in the 1960s.

The elaboration of the wartime resistance story continued quite steadily through the 1970s and 1980s, but it was really in the 1990s that resistance history became far more inclusive. In a series of six colloquia from 1993 to 1996, a collaborative effort was made by the Institut d'histoire du temps présent, various French universities, and the Belgian Centre de recherches et d'études historiques de la Seconde Guerre mondiale to begin more intensive and consciously diverse research into the political and social history of the Resistance. Using new approaches, stemming particularly from a desire to explore the Resistance "from below," and recently opened archives, the participants contributing to the colloquia and the subsequent publication of the proceedings focused on five themes, which were meant to give the project unity. The major themes of the project were the concept of resistance; the temporality and chronology of the Resistance; places and spaces and how they were both influenced by and influenced the Resistance; the resistant phenomenon in terms of political cultures, rituals, and myths; and representations and memory.[10] In many ways this project was very successful. It opened many avenues of investigation that had previously been largely ignored. Readers of the proceedings were able to learn about the participation of different social groups in the Resistance, including workers from various industries, the middle classes, nobles, and the Catholic community. The scholarship also questioned why urbanites demonstrated their refusal of the German occupation much earlier than their rural counterparts and why cities lent themselves so well to clandestine struggles. A whole issue of the proceedings was devoted to resistance in northern Europe, another entirely to history and memory. The relationships between the various resistances of the interior, between the interior and exterior resistance, and between the Resistance and the Allies were all exposed in much greater detail than they had previously been. Though we can appreciate how these studies expanded the historiography of the Resistance, which had become overshadowed by scholarly work on Vichy, the Holocaust, and the military aspects of the Second World War, there was still something missing from this project. As Claire Andrieu points out in her short analysis of these conferences, the spontaneous inclination of most researchers has led them to study the Resistance of the Left, most often found in the movements, leaving the Resistance of the Right and the history of the *réseaux* poorly understood.[11]

Even in the thousands of pages that make up the proceedings of the abovementioned colloquia, the closest any scholar comes to investigating men and women of the Right is Claude-Isabelle Brelot's article on French nobles in the Resistance, though not all nobles were politically right-leaning. In the mid-1990s, scholars started to more seriously investigate resistance on the part of the republican Right. Olivier Wieviorka's 1995 study of Défense de la France and the behavior of its founder, Philippe Viannay, was one such investigation. Défense de la France was founded in October or November 1940 largely by Viannay, who eschewed the Gaullist option and the military perspective of the *réseaux*. This movement was centered on a journal and was focused on a rather intellectual resistance. Its members, as described by Wieviorka, were "mostly bourgeois and these environments were defined by their patriotism, a rightist, though republican, sensibility, a display of Catholicism corresponding to real faith."[12] Part of what makes this group interesting is its support for

Pétain. While rejecting collaboration, Défense de la France remained convinced that Pétain was resisting many of the German *diktats*. In fact, the group often supported the measures taken by the Vichy government in terms of interior politics, differing only on the timing of such measures. Wieviorka argues that "the *maréchalisme* of Viannay is explained by several factors. His familial culture, marked by anti-Semitism, conservatism, and Catholicism, hardly predisposed him to reject Pétain."[13]

This rightist, clerical, and anticommunist resistance organization relied on prewar attitudes to justify its activities. Wieviorka points to the defense of a classic patriotism centered on Alsace-Lorraine and the denunciation of Nazism based on Germanophobia as two central aspects of Défense de la France's involvement in the Resistance.[14] Furthermore, these attitudes were not new, according to Wieviorka. He notes the presence of such continuities between the interwar period and the Resistance and identifies several of them. The sense that Germany was a hereditary enemy was common to many conservatives, including Viannay. And powerful memories of the Great War were passed along in the interwar years from parents to children.[15] In addition, Wieviorka notes, Défense de la France members were frequently knowledgeable about Nazism and its reality because of interwar concerns about Germany.[16] All these factors explain, in part, why the members of Défense de la France, although rather conservative and supportive of Pétain, chose to engage in resistance activities.

The same year that Wieviorka's book was published also saw the publication of Richard Vinen's study of the many right-wingers and Pétain supporters who participated in the Resistance and thus found a space for themselves in postwar politics.[17] The book itself focuses on general Fourth Republic politics and how the period can be seen in terms of successful conservatism. Within this larger discussion, Vinen makes it clear that many of the characters on the postwar political stage retained their prewar convictions throughout the experience of Vichy and the Occupation. He writes:

> Historians have recognized that the Resistance contained some men with right-wing backgrounds, but they have usually assumed that they were isolated individuals who eventually assimilated the generally left-wing culture

of the Resistance. Examination of the origins of the PRL [Parti républicain de la liberté] suggests that there was in fact a coherent and self-conscious group of *modérés* in the Resistance, and that certain aspects of right-wing ideology, notably anti-Communism, not only survived the Resistance, but were strengthened by it.[18]

In 1945 the PRL was the only significant party to actually describe itself as right-wing.

The PRL, as Vinen explains, made much of its Resistance credentials (as did most parties, for that matter) but combined them with a rigidly rightist platform. The leader of the PRL, Michel Clemenceau, had been deported during the war, General Giraud was elected with PRL support, and two of its most prominent leaders, André Mutter and Joseph Laniel, had been members of the Conseil national de la Résistance. In fact, Mutter had been a member of the Parti social français (PSF) and then a leader of the rightist resistance network CDLL. Mutter was certainly not the only member of the CDLL to have come from the more extreme Right. In the testimonies gathered by the Comité d'histoire de la deuxième guerre mondiale, the theme of rightist political participation is oft repeated. One M. Marin proudly proclaimed to his interviewer that he had been active with the Action française since his early teenage years and that he "took his lessons about patriotism from Maurras."[19] Many other members had been involved with the PSF in the 1930s, although not all had been as active as Mutter. Of Mme Madeleine Regnault, an interviewer commented that "she had known Colonel de la Rocque very well before the war; without her saying so, it seems clear that she belonged to the PSF. It was friends from the PSF who, in October of 1940, sent her the first mimeographed circular beseeching the French to continue to resist the occupant; thus these friends were not following the instructions of Colonel de la Rocque, who was insulting de Gaulle and inviting people to follow Pétain."[20] She too joined the Resistance very early on.

Although Mutter himself described the CDLL as "a movement of the Right in which we detested politics,"[21] he later set out to turn the group into a true right-wing political party. Vinen describes the outcome of that attempt, which was the PRL, as rather extreme even among the Right.

He argues that the ideology of the PRL was dominated by anticommunism and writes that "some of the most virulent anti-Communists in the PRL were those Resistance veterans who had seen Communist tactics at first hand."[22] The PRL was also heavily involved in the campaign to give amnesty to Vichy supporters. Vinen rightly points out that there was not always a clear distinction between Pétainism and the Resistance.[23]

Although Vinen's book was groundbreaking in the sense that it repositioned conservatism in a period that has often been seen as one of failed reform, most of his discussion centers on rather standard conservative political groups, whose links to the Resistance are, it seems, no longer in doubt. What is more relevant to my examination of the extreme Right is Vinen's discussion of groups and people who acted to defend the reputation of Pétain and his supporters. Particularly interesting is Vinen's contention that such a defense changed the nature of the extreme Right in the postwar years. He argues that Pétainist apologia changed the Right vis-à-vis the issue of legality. Traditionally, the extreme Right despised the *pays légal* and had hoped to overthrow the Third Republic by means of a coup.

In the postwar period, however, right-wingers who defended the Vichy regime relied on the argument that Vichy was not a product of a putsch but of a parliamentary Third Republic vote. Right-wingers could take shelter behind the legality of the Vichy regime and would argue that they could not (or should not) be punished for actions that were technically legal from 1940 to 1944. This, according to Vinen, led to an increasing enthusiasm for the Republic, on which legality was founded.[24] Although this enthusiasm may have seemed opportunistic both to contemporaries and to later historians, I would argue that suspicion of the Right's claim to embrace legality does not fully explain the integration of the Right into postwar politics. Because of this emphasis on legality, but also because of the Fourth Republic's anticommunism and its closer relationship with the United States, the redefined extreme Right was easily able to fit into the new political system, at least for a time. Moreover, the early rightist argument concerning the legality of Vichy would later show up in serious academic studies of the regime, as it is undeniable that republican politicians voted in favor of granting full powers to Pétain.

In their article "Les premiers résistants face à l'hypothèque Vichy

(1940–1942)," Laurent Douzou and Denis Peschanski state quite clearly, as does Vinen, that there were both ideological and institutional links between Vichy and the Resistance, even though each is often defined by how it was perceived by the other.[25] They argue that we simply cannot ignore the fact that the majority of the first resistance groups and their leaders were *maréchalistes*. Using General Cochet as one example, Douzou and Peschanski note that he, like many other resisters, placed patriotism at the center of his motivations for resistance, and that he never denied the necessity and principles of the National Revolution, but felt that it should be implemented on French foundations.[26] This sense that Vichy was quite popular early in the war was strengthened both by academic studies of popular opinion in wartime France and by some archival resistance materials.[27] In early reports sent to London by resistance agents in France, we can see that changes made by Philippe Pétain were not always unwelcome, even to de Gaulle and his followers. Gilbert Renault (a.k.a. Rémy or Raymond) encouraged de Gaulle to work harder to improve his reputation in France and argued that "it is evident that the major reforms undertaken by Vichy would be excellent if applied on a solid base. They want to end flagrant abuses. Alcoholism needs to disappear, and family life needs to be reborn. *These reforms are popular.* It is to be expected that the anti-Jewish campaign in France will become more widespread. We should judge the Jews fairly: there are many who have legitimately acquired their French citizenship. But the majority of foreigners must be permanently removed from our country."[28] Even in 1944 this commonality between the Resistance and the French State existed. In a report discussing what the French did and did not want at the end of the war, one agent noted, somewhat regretfully, that the French people did not want Jews to hold important posts. "It's a new but certain and serious fact in the past three years," he wrote. "If the Hitlerian and Vichyssoise propaganda didn't succeed in giving the French a taste for persecution and ostracism of Jews, it nonetheless succeeded in making the Jews radically disgusting to the French."[29]

These studies from the 1990s moved scholarship to a point where historians would largely agree not only that resistance was diverse and thus that it is problematic to attempt to ascribe a political character to the

Resistance as a whole but also that participation in resistance activities did not necessarily indicate a condemnation of Vichy or its policies and that in fact the Resistance often sounded a common note with Vichy.[30] Julian Jackson also points to such groups as Défense de la France and the Centre d'action des prisonniers, which had been fervently Pétainist before 1943, to show rightist involvement in the Resistance. However, like many scholars, Jackson qualifies this information by arguing that the Resistance "might have despised the Third Republic, but it was committed to Republican democracy."[31] As we will see, this was not the case for all members of the Resistance.

As all of these historians would agree, these links between Vichy and the Resistance can only really be found in the early years of the war, before the regime radicalized and moved further and deeper into authoritarianism. Following the lead of Jean-Pierre Azéma and Denis Peschanski, more scholars have started to explore the paradox of these *vichysto-résistants*, resisters who moved from active participation in the regime to participation in the Resistance. Johanna Barasz, who worked under the supervision of Azéma, and Sébastien Albertelli, another former student of Azéma's, have written a collaborative piece on General Cochet and his uneasy participation in the Resistance.[32] Albertelli and Barasz note that Cochet, although he supported Pétain and the National Revolution, did not fit in the ranks at Vichy particularly well, especially after the radicalization of the regime in 1943. Nor did Cochet fit easily in the Gaullist circles in London. Perhaps this explains why Cochet was unable to secure a place in France's national memory after the war as either a Vichyist or a resister. Barasz has also written a similar article about General de La Laurencie, whose experience, she argues, sheds light on the many uncertainties the Resistance faced vis-à-vis Vichy in the early years of the war.[33] However, it could be argued that de La Laurencie and, to a certain extent, Cochet both held to a more traditional conservatism (like that of Frenay or de Menthon) rather than a truly extreme rightist position.

Robert Belot's *La Résistance sans de Gaulle*, published in 2006, is one of the most recent books to add to our understanding of alternative resistances. According to Belot, the idea for his study came from reading memoirs of the war from the years 1945–47. He was surprised to find that most of the authors used the books as a way to express a certain malaise and to testify to feelings of deception and frustration. Many of the memoirs expressed a sense of political failure that they often ascribed to de Gaulle, leading Belot to investigate further. He argues that this path of inquiry is not easy, because "it calls for a rethinking of the three founding assumptions, considered to be above questioning, around which the resistant memory was formed: its apoliticism (presupposed), its unity (dreamt), and its Gaullism (invented)."[34] By admitting that the Resistance was not as apolitical, unified, or Gaullist as it might seem, Belot attempts to complicate resistance historiography by looking at the previously unlabeled world of *proto-résistance* and the various ideological routes many resisters took during the years of engagement.

As his title suggests, the book centers on the many different kinds of connections, or lack of connections, resisters had with de Gaulle. Belot reminds us of the challenges de Gaulle faced in trying to encourage commitment to his project, not the least of which was convincing the French to act against Pétain.[35] Belot argues that, with a few rare exceptions, the first "resistance" in interior France was that of "patriots" who believed in Pétain's double game and the preparation of revenge from within the new regime.[36] Belot sets about mapping the various itineraries of these anti-Gaullist or a-Gaullist patriots and showing how their stance toward de Gaulle changed over the course of the war. He begins with an example of evolution from anti-Gaullism to pro-Gaullism, in the case of Gabriel Cochet, and moves on to investigate the move from a-Gaullism to conditional Gaullism in the case of Henri Frenay. Belot sees two major tendencies in the world of vichysto-patriotism, anti-Gaullism and a-Gaullism. He notes that within the first tendency we can also identify two subcategories, those who evolve toward Gaullism and those who stay true to their anti-Gaullism. He writes, "One could assume that the durable anti-Gaullist bias was rooted in a strong initial commitment to the Vichy regime in its first phase and that it remained unchanged even when these men had turned against Vichy."[37] Using the examples of General de La Laurencie and Georges Groussard, Belot delves deeper into these subcategories before moving on to look at groups within Vichy, such as the army and the secret services, which also represented early resistances.

Like Belot, Bénédicte Vergez-Chaignon also traces the paths of the *vichysto-résistants* throughout the war, though she focuses more extensively on the postwar experiences of these men and women than does Belot. Much of her book is devoted to the wartime activities of men who had been linked to Vichy at one point or another, but it seems that the creation of a Resistance myth is what ultimately grabs her attention. She argues that having been vilified as terrorists during the war, the Resistance needed to be seen in the postwar period as having been the legitimate choice.[38] This desire for legitimacy, together with the sense that the only way to have been a resister was to begin acting in 1940 and follow de Gaulle in his mission, led to the Gaullist predominance in the resistance story. Vergez-Chaignon argues that the Resistance lost any nuance in the postwar period through an unwieldy attempt to balance justification and celebration of its activities.[39] Through many postwar crises—neo-Pétainism, the Algerian War, May 1968—and the dialogue that accompanied these crises, it became impossible, Vergez-Chaignon argues, to conceive, both practically and morally, of a man having been a Pétainist and a resister. This, of course, has changed recently, and she notes that it was the revelations about François Mitterrand's past with the extreme Right and Vichy that forced people to start reexamining the issue of *vichysto-résistants.*[40]

This loosening of taboos can also be attributed to work highlighting a variety of reactions to the French defeat and occupation within Vichy. Simon Kitson's work reminds us that Vichy's secret services often engaged in counterespionage against Axis agents in the unoccupied zone and in the empire.[41] While there were several such services, Kitson sees Georges Groussard's Centre d'informations et d'études (CIE) as a similar type of organization and argues that "Groussard's organisation was short-lived and sometimes its help was more a hindrance, but it did recommend some officers for service in the BMA [Bureau des menées antinationales]."[42] The BMA did have a secret anti-German mission, though it was also created to protect the army from communists and British and Gaullist agents. Kitson recognizes that these secret services cannot be called resistance organizations, but he notes that there was a degree of resistance and that the number of Nazi spies arrested and imprisoned by these groups was not insignificant. The very existence of these groups and their anti-Axis missions also reminds us that Vichy was never a homogeneous government, a reminder that serves us well when we examine someone like Groussard, who never claimed that everyone at Vichy was anti-German but wanted it to be clear that some people were very interested in resuming the fight against the Nazis. Kitson's study fits in with other recent works on the inclination toward resistance within the Vichy administration, like that of Robert Belot, who also acknowledges the "para-resistance" of the secret services and the activities of the armistice army, which he sees as particularly honorable, given that those men had vowed loyalty and obedience to the state.[43] Or François-Georges Dreyfus's book, which also notes the varying tendencies both at Vichy and within the Resistance.[44]

Writing the history of the *vichysto-résistants* has been no small feat. Overcoming the assumptions about what the Right did and did not do during the war was only one of the many challenges that have faced researchers seeking to broaden and nuance our understanding of what it meant to resist. Joanna Barasz writes of her decision to work on *vichysto-résistants* that she chose a research subject that in effect "did not exist." She goes on to say that there was no "organization, no institution, not even an identifiable group *a priori.*"[45] In some important ways, the study of the extreme Right in the resistance is the same. There is definitely a section of the French population (about which scholars have written fairly extensively) labeled the "extreme Right," though this label is itself problematic. Moreover, because of the roads these men and women took in 1940, they do not end up in one group, one network, or one movement. Finding their traces in the Resistance requires flexible research methods and does not always result in as full a picture as we might wish.

Political historians of France have long been fascinated by the divide between the Right and the Left and the development in the twentieth century of an active and radical right wing. The growth of the leagues in the interwar period and the links, whether real or imagined, between the leagues and their fascist counterparts in Germany and Italy led historians of France to hotly debate the question whether France had its own fascistic tendencies or was "allergic" to such political developments. This debate, which became repetitive in so many other ways, inspired discussions of what historians of France truly mean when they refer to the Left, the Right, or "neither left, nor right."[46] William Irvine writes that traditional political taxonomies suggested that

> those on the Right identified, with various degrees of conviction and intensity, with some or all of the following: clericalism, nationalism, militarism, racism of one form or another, unabashed defense of the existing social order, and a suspicion of, or even intense hostility toward, parliamentary democracy. The political principles of the Left were in general the negation of those of the Right: anti-clericalism, internationalism and pacifism, anti-militarism, profound or even revolutionary changes to the social order, an unconditional defense of parliamentary democracy, and unqualified hostility to racism in any form.[47]

Part of the problem with this taxonomy, however, is that it obscures the reality of behavior on both the left and the right during the Third Republic. There are numerous examples of both rightists and leftists behaving as though they belonged to the other camp or maintaining ideological stances that were indistinguishable from those of their counterparts on the opposite side of the political spectrum. For example, all the political parties in interwar France maintained very similar perspectives on gender and race.[48] And the person most explicitly identified with the construction of the ideological parameters of the new Vichy regime, Gaston Bergery, began his career as a man of the Left, a central member of the Ligue des droits de l'homme.[49] As Diane Labrosse notes, Bergery's "seminal role in the creation of the Pétainist state speaks to the French political upheaval of the late 1930s, when party lines and ideological adhesions were broken and re-formed in an unpredictable manner."[50]

Though this book uses the terms *rightist* and *extreme Right* to classify the men and women in question, the terms are used as a matter of convenience to a certain degree. These men and women did share important characteristics, like nationalism, anticommunism, and a disdain for republican politics. Many of the people in question venerated the military, or to be more precise, an idealized version of the military, one of their own imagining. Many of them were anti-Semitic, a trait they shared with many other French people on both left and right. They all shared a sense of a deep France—a timeless nation that existed outside politics. Like the activists of many of the interwar leagues, the men and women who joined the Cagoule or the Corvignolles were brought together not because they all shared exactly the same doctrinal inclinations but because they were able to set aside whatever differences they had to achieve the goals of the groups.[51] For the Cagoule, the overarching goal was the replacement of the republican government with a more authoritarian one, ideally made up of *cagoulards*. For the Corvignolles, the goal was to combat communism but also to effect profound social and political change. The members of both groups were willing to act illegally to achieve these goals, a trait that sets them apart from other rightist critics of the Third Republic, who either abandoned their activism or participated in legal channels of activism once the antiparliamentary leagues were made illegal.

The fact that members of these groups participated in the Resistance is not surprising in and of itself. They were, after all, fiercely invested in a strong and independent France; many of them were anti-German (a lingering sentiment from the First World War); and the defeat of France's army, an institution so valued by these men and women, was a bitter pill to swallow. What is surprising about their resistance is that the goals for which they fought so violently in the 1930s—at risk to their liberty—were achieved with the creation of the Vichy regime. The goals that overrode all their other political concerns in the 1930s were achieved, and yet they still chose to resist the Germans and Vichy even if some of them remained *maréchalistes* at heart. The participation of these men and women in the Resistance highlights the complexity of political decision making in the 1930s and 1940s, the ways in which multiple identities shaped the behavior of people in the face of national crisis, and the various choices that were available to the French in 1940.

In the pages that follow I trace the paths that were open to men and women from the extreme Right who chose resistance over collaboration or a mixture of the two. Many rightists opted to begin their journeys in the heart of Vichy, where, even if they set up resistance organizations immediately, they did so believing that they had the support of Pétain. As the war went on and the Vichy regime became ever more hostile to resistance activities, most of these people left and resumed their activities in exile. There they joined colleagues who had fled in 1940 to the shores of London, a third option that was attractive in some ways to men and women of the Right, given Charles de Gaulle's early political ambiguity and his refusal, when discussing the war's end, to commit to the re-creation of a republican government. I end the book by examining the postwar lives of these people and the ways in which they were, or were not, able to reintegrate into French political life and how their resistance activities have been remembered and forgotten.

The examples of resistance presented in these pages are unique in the larger resistance narrative. These activists, all of whom came to the Resistance from the right wing, were never apolitical; their political perspectives were never silenced; they always had reservations about the communist resistance; they were not fighting for a return to republican politics; they did not necessarily condemn Vichy; and most of them have been excluded from the postwar memory of those years. What also makes these men unique, however, is their success in resisting the German occupation. Unlike many of their fellow *résistants*, many of them lived to see the liberation of France and the end of the war. This success can be explained in part by their having worked for so many years in the shadows; the step into secrecy in 1940 was no step at all for most of these resisters. The lessons learned and the connections they made in the 1930s allowed these men to live through the dark years—not comfortably, and certainly not with any measure of security, but they survived.

THE CAGOULE

In late 1937 the French minister of the interior, Marx Dormoy, announced that the police had uncovered a "genuine plot against republican institutions." In addition to making a spate of arrests, the police also searched the many Parisian properties belonging to the conspirators. Over the course of one year the police found more than 7,000 grenades, about 30 machine guns, 230 German and Italian automatic weapons, 150 handguns, more than 150 hunting rifles, 300,000 cartridges, and more than 150 kilos of explosives in these homes and businesses.[1] These discoveries sent shock waves throughout France and had journalists scrambling to figure out what kind of group could have amassed such a stockpile. But the stockpile did not come as a complete surprise. Strange crimes had been occurring throughout 1936 and 1937 and remained unsolved, as the police and the public had few ideas about who was responsible for them. No one had claimed responsibility, and the police had few leads to follow; thus the discovery of the many weapons depots might have struck the general public as simply another element in an ongoing criminal drama. Yet these discoveries were different. The police did know who they were looking for; they even knew the name of the secret organization that had collected the weapons: the Comité secrèt d'action révolutionnaire (CSAR). More colloquially, the group was called the Cagoule ("the hooded ones"), a moniker coined by Maurice Pujo of the monarchist journal *Action française*, to mock what he saw as a puerile political organization.

Though Pujo mocked the group, the Cagoule had indeed been responsible for some of the most public and notorious crimes in the previous two years. The group had been, and continues to be, described as a terrorist organization because it used many of the same techniques as latter-day terrorists.[2] While there is no question that there are significant similarities between the group and other terrorist organizations, that label does not fully capture the extent of the Cagoule's activities or the intentions behind the group's crimes. The Cagoule engaged in acts of destabilization much as terrorists do, but its principles of provocation were somewhat unique.[3] Rather than taking responsibility for their crimes, members of the group made it look as if someone else were responsible. The Cagoule was hoping to create a fearful population while simultaneously setting itself up as the only organization that could save France from chaos. The very first *cagoulard* crime, in the Parisian working-class suburb of Clichy on March 16, 1937, demonstrates these strategies of provocation perfectly.

Because of the ban on the rightist extraparliamentary leagues, the former Croix de feu was forced to reestablish itself as a legitimate political party, the Parti social français (PSF).[4] In a bold move, the PSF decided to hold one of its first meetings in Clichy, which prompted the local Popular Front committee to stage a counterdemonstration. Few meetings could inspire an animosity such as that between the leftist Popular Front forces and the militant rightists of the leagues, and this clash was no exception. As the situation quickly got out of hand, the police were called in to restore order and ended up firing on the crowd. By the end of the day, five people had been killed and some two hundred wounded, prompting many leftists to call Léon Blum, the head of the Popular Front government, the "murderer of Clichy workers."[5] The leftist government had been forced to call in the police to restrain its own supporters, and the government was thus blamed for the result. Although the communists (and other leftists) blamed the government for this fiasco, the reality was that members of the Cagoule had fanned the flames of this already tense situation. Frédéric Monier writes that "the responsibility of certain elements from the CSAR in these events is undeniable."[6] He points in particular to the *cagoulard* Jacques Corrèze, who, according to several witnesses, participated in the demonstration and played a central role in provoking the police to open fire on the demonstrators. Other people, however, have accused the CSAR of intervening on a much larger scale. Philippe Bourdrel writes that the police later found in the houses of the Cagoule leaders armbands with "CGT," the initials of the Confédération générale du travail, a confederation of trade unions, printed on them and others with "SFIO," the insignia of the Section Française de l'Internationale Ouvrière, the French Socialist Party. Apparently, the *cagoulards* had been wearing these armbands while provoking the police. Bourdrel argues that this was "all that was needed to create confusion in a working-class gathering, to organize clashes between the police and the protesters."[7] The Clichy demonstration provides an excellent example of the modus operandi of the Cagoule. In general, the group was determined to commit crimes that could be blamed on the Left, especially the communists, so that the French public would "realize" how dangerous leftist activists were and turn to the Cagoule for protection.

The next *cagoulard* crime was, in fact, the only exception to this rule. In May 1937 members of the group assassinated a young woman by the name of Laetitia Toureaux. This murder, a first on the Paris Métro, was described as the perfect crime, as it remained (and remains) officially unsolved. In the time it took for the train to leave one station and arrive at the next, Toureaux was stabbed in the neck with a dagger, and her assailant managed to flee. She died before she could identify her killer. The police were unable to solve the murder, and it is only thanks to recent archival work that we have any proof at all that the Cagoule was behind the crime.[8] Though political in a broad sense, this murder was highly personal for the killers. Toureaux had not only been the mistress of Gabriel Jeantet, a committed *cagoulard,* but she had been a spy for the police and for a private detective agency. Her killing was not consistent with the group's overarching goals.

The next *cagoulard* murders were far more political than Toureaux's assassination. On June 9, 1937, several members of the CSAR, led by the notoriously brutal Jean Filliol, murdered Carlo and Nello Rosselli in full daylight. The Rosselli brothers were prominent Italian antifascists, and Carlo had fled to France in 1929 to escape the political oppression of Mussolini's regime. Carlo had founded the influential antifascist movement Giustizia e Libertà and the newspaper of the same name in the late 1920s, and he and his brother were both active in their denunciation of fascism. In 1936 Carlo Rosselli was galvanized into action by the outbreak of the Spanish Civil War. He left France for Spain to fight alongside the Republican forces but was wounded and forced to return home to recuperate. After a second tour in Spain, Rosselli returned home, unaware of what was awaiting him. Because of his wound, which was not healing well, and a childhood health condition that continued to plague him, Carlo Rosselli decided to leave Paris for the Norman spa town of Bagnoles-de-l'Orne in May 1937. He was joined there by his brother, who traveled from Italy, and his British wife, Marion Rosselli (née Cave). After they spent several days together, Marion Rosselli was set to return to Paris and was driven to the train station by the brothers. After dropping her off, Carlo and Nello drove to the nearby town of Alençon to spend the afternoon there. On the return drive to Bagnoles-de-l'Orne, they came across what appeared to be some motorists with a broken-down car and pulled over to lend a hand.

Mussolini had taken out a contract on the Rosselli brothers' lives and had directed several of his senior army officers to make a deal with the CSAR to exchange semiautomatic weapons for the "suppression of troublesome persons."[9] The stranded motorists, who turned out to be members of the Cagoule, shot both brothers and disposed of their bodies in a nearby wood. Carlo died immediately, but Nello did not and was finished off with a dagger, which was left at the scene of the crime. This dagger, of Italian make and of fascist design, led the fascist press to link the assassination to conflicts within the antifascist community. According to the press, leaving the dagger behind was a clear, and clumsy, attempt to make it look as if the crime had been committed by fascists. However, it quickly became clear that the Cagoule was behind the crime. In 1938 Marion Rosselli identified the *cagoulard* Fernand Ladislav Jakubiez as someone who had come to the couple's home posing as a carpet salesman and asked questions about Carlo.[10] The police also identified similarities between the Rosselli crime scene and those in the cases of Toureaux and Dimitri Navachine, a Russian economist murdered by the Cagoule earlier in the year.[11] The dagger marks were almost identical, and the bullet shells were the same, but the police could not come up with a motive to show that the same person, or people, had been responsible for all of the crimes. After the war, however, there was no doubt that the Cagoule had killed the Rosselli brothers, as members of Mussolini's inner circle testified about the reciprocal relationship that had been established between the fascist regime and the CSAR.[12]

Murder was not the only violent activity engaged in by the Cagoule in the summer of 1937. Its members also experimented with some of the explosives the group had stockpiled, first to destroy planes that the French government had secretly promised to Spanish Republicans, then moving on to larger targets. On the night of September 11, two bombs exploded in the two most influential employers' organizations of the period. In what were referred to as the Étoile bombings because of the location of the crime in Paris, the offices of the Confédération générale du patronat français and the Union des industries métallurgiques et minières were bombed and two security guards killed. The author of this crime was a young *cagoulard*, René Locuty, who had a particular talent for working with explosives. Driven to the two locations by François Méténier and Jean Macon, he left a package at each building, delivered directly to the custodians before they left for the night.[13] The explosions rocked the entire neighborhood. Much like the Clichy demonstration, these bombings were based on a certain principle of provocation. Who would think to blame a group of the extreme Right for such bombings? Indeed, suspicion was immediately directed toward the extreme Left, which was ideologically opposed to employers' organizations. This displacement of suspicion onto the political Left was exactly what the Cagoule was hoping for. A fearful society and a destabilized government were necessary to achieve certain goals that the group had established early on.

Born after the failure of the extreme Right manifestations of February 6, 1934, the Cagoule was essentially made up of men who were disillusioned with the extraparliamentary leagues' inability to transform ideology into action. This disillusion eventually led to mass resignations from many organizations, but this trend was felt most deeply by the monarchist Action française (AF). Eugen Weber notes, "Convinced that the Republic could have been overthrown that day, young men like Guillain de Bénouville and Jacques Renouvin, both of whom soon drifted to the Cagoule before finding their way into the Resistance, left the Action Française, persuaded that Maurras did not really believe in the revolution."[14] What began as individual resignations from the AF soon turned into a veritable flood of activists fleeing the group in search of stronger leadership and better opportunities for action. Most of these activists, some of whom would join the CSAR, came from the 17th cell of the Camelots du roi, the AF's shock troops. Led by Jean Filliol, the leader of this particular team, the men demonstrated their anger by resigning en masse. In his interview with the police in 1937, Michel Bernollin, another future *cagoulard*, testified that he had belonged to the 17th cell and that he had been encouraged to leave the group in support of Filliol. "When he [Filliol] left the league following some political divergences," stated Bernollin, "I also submitted my resignation at the same time as ninety-five other comrades."[15]

For the two years following the resignations, these men seem to have disappeared from the political scene. It is hard to trace the activities of the rank-and-file members of the Cagoule after they left the leagues; but the leaders' paths are somewhat clearer. Initially some of the men, notably Eugène Deloncle and Jean Filliol, joined a short-lived organization called the Parti national révolutionnaire et social (PNRS). While this group was never really active, it was where the initial ideas for a clandestine group were born.[16] Sometime in 1936, such a group was indeed created; it was modeled after the French military, particularly in the way the leadership was grouped. Eugène Deloncle, considered by all to be the driving force behind the Cagoule, was the head of the group, in charge of the Premier Bureau; Dr. Felix Martin headed the Deuxième Bureau, which directed intelligence operations; the Troisième Bureau, in charge of operations and instruction of new recruits, was led by Georges Cachier; and the Quatrième Bureau, in charge of transport and supplies, was directed by Jean Moreau.[17] These men, along with other notables, such as Jacques Corrèze, Jean Filliol, Gabriel Jeantet, François Méténier, and Aristide Corre, formed the nucleus of the Cagoule.[18] The military-style organization did not end with the leadership, however. Active members and less involved adherents were grouped according to a similar kind of hierarchy.[19] At the most local level, the CSAR was organized in cells, either "light," with 7 men, or "heavy," with 12 men. Three cells formed a unit, usually made up of 20–30 men. Three units formed a battalion (60–80 men); three battalions made up a regiment (250 men); three regiments, a brigade (750 men); and at the most expansive level, three brigades made up a division of about

2,000 men.[20] The cells were the most important of these groupings, both because it was only at that level that members would meet and become familiar with their fellow *cagoulards* and because the cell represented the main combat group. As we will see, this pyramid type of organization, in which each member knew only a handful of other members, was useful both in the 1930s and during the Second World War.

By 1937 the Cagoule had essentially finished recruiting. Some people were recruited into the CSAR because they had been members of already established groups that were integrated into the Cagoule, but the majority of the recruitment took place by word of mouth. This was a personal and direct approach; existing members of the CSAR would approach friends, family, or strangers who seemed sympathetic to their cause and invite them to meetings. This task was facilitated by the 1936 law that ordered all the leagues to be dissolved immediately, leaving those vehemently opposed to joining an actual political party with no outlet for their activism. The direct method of recruitment worked well for the Cagoule, as is evidenced in the police reports from 1937. For instance, Gaston Jeanniot, a mechanic, was approached by one of his clients after discovering that they had similar political opinions. This client was Pierre Proust, already a member of the CSAR, who brought Jeanniot into the fold of the group by offering to rent a basement for "storage" purposes and inviting the mechanic to meet other like-minded people.[21] Similarly, Charles Nicod testified in 1938 that "in September or October of 1937 a stranger came to my house and asked me if I was satisfied with the Solidarité française, and I was asked to join a secret group intended to oppose a communist coup."[22] This testimony and others like it indicate that the CSAR was not interested in acting with other groups and indeed may have been trying to undermine the *ligues* by recruiting their members. Philippe Bourdrel, in his journalistic account of the Cagoule, maintains that the group was subversive in this respect. He writes that "the activists appeared everywhere, canvassing in all the rightist Leagues and among veterans."[23]

As with any group that operates outside the boundaries of legality, it is very difficult to establish just how large or small the Cagoule actually was. Obviously, its leaders had a stake in making the group seem larger and more powerful than it perhaps was. Also, the fact that recruitment was done so informally increases the difficulty of establishing firm numbers. Frédéric Monier's study of the group, which is one of the most reliable examinations, looks to the *cagoulard* trial for information.[24] The instruction period of the trial enabled investigators to establish that the *cagoulards* in Paris were made up of two divisions. Monier uses this information to conclude that the Cagoule had at least three thousand active members, but this number does not include members in the suburbs of Paris or in the provinces, nor does it include the members who were charged with missions other than those of a combat nature.[25] Given the success some of the *ligues* had in recruitment, the Cagoule's membership may have been much higher than three thousand,[26] since there was no other option for extraparliamentary political action by 1937. The CSAR stood alone in this sense.

The CSAR was also unique in its true dedication to violent and direct action against the Third Republic. The ultimate goal of the group, of course, was the overthrow of the government and the establishment of a new regime with *cagoulards* at its head. Aristide Corre, the unofficial archivist of the group,[27] clearly outlined what steps were necessary to achieve this goal: "There is no other solution but terrorism. But a scholarly, studied, and transcendent terrorism that only hits the leaders of the regime, but hits them without relief or respite, always, at any hour, in any circumstance. The kind that makes, through terror, all governing impossible and forces them to step down."[28] Corre and other leading *cagoulards* saw their activity as revolutionary; they did not envisage a return to any kind of real or mythical past. Though their plans for the future were not particularly well elaborated, they, like many other activists of the extreme Right in the 1930s, knew that a future government needed to be different from those that had come before. Of the difficulties that the Cagoule faced in creating this future, Corre wrote: "Hitler waited no less than ten years between his Munich coup and his accession to power. Mussolini himself had to wait more than three years after the formation of the fascists. The Russian revolutionaries fought for forty-plus years, interspersed with bloody attempts to realize their catastrophic, for all that, ideal. We are going through a period of trial and waiting, a hard period, a rough one."[29] He knew that all revolutionaries suffered for their cause and that the *cagoulards* were no different in this regard. They were, however, most firmly on the right, unlike many other revolutionaries.

The group was clearly antirepublican. Like many other nationalists in the 1930s, Corre seemed to have great love for an Eternal France, a nation that had been besmirched by the Revolution of 1789 and fully corrupted by the Third Republic. Corre described hearing the festivities in 1939, during the 150th anniversary celebrations of what Corre called "the dreadful and fatal 'Grande Révolution,'" and said, "I cried with shame, disgust and fury."[30] Corre's complaints about the state of affairs in France were always mixed with sadness, pity, and anger that such a grand civilization could find itself in such a degraded position. He tended, of course, to blame the government for the decline of France, but he also found a number of other scapegoats both within and outside France's borders. Obviously, the active participation of the Left in the Popular Front government was the main cause of concern for the *cagoulards*. Corre, in a temper after the arrests of his fellow *cagoulards*, warned, "Gentlemen of the governmental rabble, radical and Masonic, you haven't yet finished trembling."[31]

Yet it is a mistake to assume that the group was simply reacting to the Popular Front and the more leftist aspects of democracy. Even the more conservative members of the government did not escape Corre's scorn. On the eve of the death of Gaston Doumergue, who was a conservative member of the Radical Party and suspected of being a closet supporter of the *ligues*, Corre wrote, "In our opinion, he simply saved this dreadful regime and protected Freemasonry against just reprisals."[32] Even Pétain, long suspected of actually having been a member of the Cagoule,[33] was criticized in a similar vein. In 1939 Corre wrote, "Pétain? They are using him once again just like they used him in 1934 to save the Radical Party, Freemasonry, and the crooks."[34] It is clear that the dislike of republicanism was not confined to the Popular Front.

Another fairly prominent trait of the group was its anti-Semitism. Corre's personal anti-Semitism is quite clear in his diaries. He wrote, "The Jew is the enemy that must be cut down because he is first of all the framework of the regime and secondly because he is a Jew."[35] Corre quite obviously felt that the Jewish population, along with the Freemasons, was the secret power behind the Third Republic. "The Jews, however, here

have the top position in society," he wrote; "they are everywhere, they
control everything, they dominate everything, they make us go to war
for them."[36] Corre not only hated the Jews, he had plans for them. Discussing Céline's *Bagatelle pour un massacre*, Corre outlined his opinion of
the book and the necessary steps to take against the Jews. "This is a book
that we must spread profusely. I hope that they think about it in Paris. It
is necessary to root out this scum from our country, which they defile
and suck dry, and we will share the spoiled fruits of their plunder."[37] The
plan may sound familiar; Corre certainly did not protest when the Nazis
began burning synagogues in Berlin.

This anti-Semitism does not come up often in the testimony of the arrested *cagoulards*, although a couple of sources reinforce Corre's writings.
Two brothers, Jean and Elie Doquin de Saint Preux, actually ended their
relationship with the CSAR because of their Jewish ancestry. Jean told the
police that he had been brought to the group by Filliol, who had informed
him that "this organization had for its primary goal the anticommunist
struggle, but also, if successful in overturning the current regime and
instituting an authoritarian regime, a military dictatorship, I believe, the
suppression of leftist leaders and an unrestricted anti-Semitic fight."[38]
This view was seconded by his brother, Elie, who told the police that the
group had planned to suppress the leaders of the Left "and the Israelites,
whatever they are."[39]

Furthermore, in a lengthy letter from the governor-general of Algeria
to the French minister of the interior listing some of the more prominent
active members of the Cagoule in Algeria, there is a clear indication of
the anti-Semitic character of the group. Beside each member's name the
governor-general provided a short description of his or her activities in
Algeria. The most common description reads, "notorious anti-Semite."
Sometimes the notes are more descriptive. For example, Edouard Chanut
is described as a "prototype of a diehard anti-Semite."[40] Several of the men
are described as having also been members of an organization called the
Unions Latines, which the governor-general characterized as an anti-
Semitic group passionately devoted to Franco. The Unions Latines, much
like the Cagoule, took their politics to the streets in violent displays and
had dominated municipal politics in the Algerian Department of Oran in

the 1920s. Their success derived from the fact that they "directly addressed settler concerns, harnessing a political program steeped in colonial fascist themes: Anti-Semitism, algérianité, and appeals to a Latin racial hegemony."[41] Other men were simply "active anti-Semites," like Marcel Bellier, whom the governor-general also described as a "determined adversary of all republican governments."[42]

Thus, while we cannot say that the Cagoule had an anti-Semitic policy per se, it is quite clear that many of the members, both within the nucleus of the group and in lesser positions, were themselves anti-Semitic.[43] The anti-Semitism of the group is important, not so much because it formed a central aspect of its official politics but because it was almost taken for granted. As in the Action française, from which many cagoulards came, anti-Semitism in the Cagoule was of a "traditional" sort and seems not to have informed the group's activities. Most members did not even bother to mention anti-Semitism in their interviews with the police. Much like a number of their ideological perspectives, the anti-Semitism of the group varied from member to member but was also used flexibly by the leaders. When it seemed that anti-Semitism could help the leaders achieve their goals, whether in recruitment or mobilization of activists, it was unveiled and virulent. At other times it was rather less central and only provided a backdrop for more pressing concerns.

Also striking was a certain elitism within the membership of the Cagoule. Corre himself was unsympathetic to the workers of France, a sentiment that, of course, had something to do with their purported leftist leanings but also with their very nature. Of the workers Corre wrote, "What politics! Their views are at times miserable, at other times stupid; what base maneuvering of these crowds of slaves that deserve only the cudgel. You would not like the look of them, full of hatred, their laziness and a life of vice written all over their faces."[44] These comments, surrounded as they were by other, more implicit antiworker remarks, are further evidence of Corre's disdain for the working class.

The Cagoule's elitism is also indicated by the actual makeup of the organization. Of course, the extensive membership lists are unavailable for perusal, so it is difficult to make strong generalizations. However, the information about the seventy-nine cagoulards who were put on trial in 1948 tells us quite a bit about what kind of men joined the Cagoule. The majority of these men did not belong to what could be considered the working class. More than 10 percent of these members, including Deloncle, were engineers. Corre's profession was given as author. These seventy-nine men included two doctors, several insurance agents, many men involved in commerce, an architect, and various other professionals. In fact, the only representatives of more manual work were several mechanics. We cannot assume that these men represent *all* the members of the organization, but their social positions are significant.[45] Many leaders of the Cagoule lived in the tony 16th arrondissement, then as now one of the wealthiest parts of Paris.[46] They were rich, privileged men who dined at expensive restaurants, had vacation properties outside France, courted many women, and generally lived quite well. They were unconcerned with the working classes, except for their belief that those classes needed to be turned away from socialism.

Hatred of the Left was clearly the defining characteristic of the organization. Anticommunism was shared by all the members of the organization and was no secret, as it was one of the first aspects of the group to be made public. Every member of the group who risked the punishment of death by speaking to the police about the secret organization emphasized the CSAR's primary goal of combatting communism. Gerard Le Roy testified that "Durand came to recruit me for a secret anticommunist group that had weapons to defend itself."[47] André Revol similarly told the police, "It was in October or November 1936 that, introduced by a comrade, I agreed to join a secret group that had as its sole goal resistance against a communist coup d'état. I took an oath of loyalty, discipline, and secrecy to the Comité secret d'action révolutionnaire."[48] Over and over again, the police were told the same thing: these members had joined the CSAR to fight against a potential communist insurrection. Moreover, these members and other French citizens were, in late 1937, quite convinced that a communist coup was imminent. Certainly many rumors were circulating indicating that this was the case, and members of the Cagoule had warned the French Army that they had legitimate information proving that the communists were planning some kind of action.

In an ostensible response to this information, the Cagoule ordered a full mobilization of all of its Parisian troops on November 15, 1937. The *cagoulards*, all of whom were committed to their anticommunist action, even if unaware of the Cagoule's larger goals, quickly and quietly met, armed themselves, and waited for orders. These orders never came, and the men dispersed early the morning of the sixteenth. Not only did the communists not make a single move that night, but the Cagoule never received confirmation that the army would back up any preventative action, and Deloncle was unwilling to go through with his plans without the army's support.[49] In reality, none of the *cagoulard* leaders ever expected the communists to act. The rumors that had been circulating had almost certainly been put forth by the Cagoule to provide a pretext for their own insurrection.[50] In his diary, Aristide Corre had written a full two weeks before the Cagoule's mobilization in November 1937, "After all, it matters little to us whether the communists undertake or don't undertake their coup. What we want is that at some point they have the intention to do so in order to justify, at least in appearance, our preventative operation."[51] Corre became even more candid after the failed *cagoulard* action. On the one-year anniversary of that fateful November night, Corre reminisced about the group's movements. He explained his own perspective thus: "I was always absolutely convinced that the reds were incapable of doing anything. It meant always starting from this assumption, all the while pretending to believe otherwise, so that it would be easy, in the aftermath, to make the French people see the danger from which we saved them."[52] Although the anticommunism of the members was genuine, in November 1937 Corre and the other leaders were simply practicing another form of provocation, aiming to scare the French public into believing that the communists were about to take over and then present the Cagoule as the only option to restore order. But the leaders of the Cagoule were unaware that the police had been slowly but surely closing in on their organization. The Étoile bombings had intensified the search for those responsible for the spate of unsolved crimes. The public and violent nature of the bombings led Commissaire Charles Chenevier to step up his investigation of these crimes, which ultimately led to the infiltration of the group and its downfall.[53] In the weeks that followed the failed mobilization, the police arrested as many *cagoulards* as they could.[54]

Although the police were not particularly forthcoming about the discoveries they made after uncovering the Cagoule plot, the press and
the public were fascinated with the whole affair. Few people, however,
had any sense of what kind of organization the CSAR truly was. The
newspaper accounts range in their descriptions from calling the CSAR
a fascist group to denouncing the members as puerile adventurers. The
communist newspaper *L'Humanité* was one of the first to break the news
of the Cagoule conspiracy, and it is not difficult to imagine what its official
position was. Under the headline "Encore des armes fascistes et ce n'est
pas fini!," P. L. Darner wrote:

> Yes, these traitors were planning a civil war to encourage a foreign war and
> help an invasion . . . nobody is laughing any more at revelations about fascists'
> armaments, I think? Secret defense league, defense against the revolution?
> Come on! Against whom would those antitank bullets that the minister of the
> interior was showing yesterday in the halls of the Chamber be used—against
> whom if not against the army of the Republic? And what about those bombs,
> similar to those of recent attacks . . . ? It's clear! Germany, Italy armed these
> traitors. And with what abundance![55]

Much like *L'Humanité*, the socialist newspaper *Le Populaire* was also concerned that the actions of this extraparliamentary group were not being
taken seriously enough. Even before *Le Populaire* could report anything
conclusive about the group or its dangers, Jean-Maurice Herrman warned
the readers that "the 'cagoulards' are not, we have seen, a joke, nor a
creation of the imagination."[56] Both newspapers impressed upon their
readers that the CSAR was clearly dangerous, funded by foreign money,
seeking to overthrow republicanism, and planning to institute some kind
of fascist government after a prolonged civil war. O. Rosenfeld wrote in
Le Populaire that "this association is made up of men from parties of the
Right and the extreme Right, as well as the most active elements from
certain dissolved leagues. . . . It is organized on the model of the 'carbonari,' but naturally is very modernized and militarized. . . . And the goal
of the conspiracy? There is no possible doubt: overthrow the Republic to
establish a fascist regime. These rebels were ready to commit a 'putsch'
and to provoke civil war."[57]

Other newspapers were more restrained in their assessment of the situation but still wondered what the true nature of the group was and how serious the threat to the Republic could be. *L'Œuvre,* another left-of-center paper, left the matter to its readers to decide. "What were the slogans of these 'secret revolutionary militias' if not the struggle against 'communism,' the 'Jews,' and the 'socialists'? To which political program do these words correspond? The reader will decide."[58] These leftist papers clearly point to the fascist model as the one that the Cagoule was following, but other publications were not so sure that fascism played as big a role. The two papers that represented the republican Right, the *Journal des Débats Politiques et Littéraires* and *Le Temps,* approached the notion of a *cagoulard* plot with a good deal of skepticism. Both newspapers tried to indicate to their readers that the Cagoule had actually posed very little danger to the Republic. The *Journal* reported that "it seems that all these weapons and munitions were simple war souvenirs that the owners, alarmed by the searches, wanted to get rid of."[59] As incredible as it may seem, the paper actually tried to persuade people that the hundreds of German and Italian automatic weapons found in the *cagoulard* basements were simply souvenirs from the war. *Le Temps,* while not as skeptical as the *Journal,* argued that "there was a bit of childishness and a lot of ignorance in the projects and the plans of the conspirators whose games the police have just intercepted, and maybe the 'communiqué' of the minister of the interior neglected to highlight this aspect of the 'affair' that is producing so much noise."[60] The author of that article wondered how the Cagoule could actually think that it would succeed against the army, the police, and the public.

The newspapers even further to the right, like *L'Écho de Paris* and *L'Action française,* were generally convinced (much as lower-ranking *cagoulards* themselves were) that the persecution of the CSAR was intended to distract the public from the actual threat posed by the communists, who many fervently believed were plotting their own coup.[61] Although the AF had previously denounced its former members, AF journalists became more sympathetic as more and more *cagoulards* were arrested. Though unexpected, this sympathy makes a certain amount of sense in retrospect. The AF was the only league of the early twentieth century that we can say definitively had an influence on the Cagoule. The AF doctrine, one of the most coherent of all those proposed by the antiparliamentary leagues, was based on ideas of reason, simplicity, order, tradition, will, and social unification.

However, to a younger generation of activists, the Action française was also moribund. We have already explored *la grande dissidence* and the departure of many former AF members and future *cagoulards*. These dissidents may have concluded that Maurras had lost the vital spirit for action, but presumably they would have initially been attracted to the AF because of compatible political sympathies. It is impossible to say how much of the Maurrasian philosophy the *cagoulards* retained after their split from the group. However, we cannot ignore the influence the monarchist organization would have had in the formative years of these activists. The Cagoule and the AF shared many central characteristics. The anti-Semitism of Corre and other *cagoulards* was very similar to that of the old monarchist organization. Anti-Semitism of what we might call a traditional, or catholic, nature was a hallmark of both groups. Neither organization ever assumed the more racial and virulent anti-Semitism of, say, the Nazis. In addition, the nationalism of both groups took a similar form. Even the language that Corre used to describe the way France, the *pays réel*, was being destroyed seems to have been taken directly from the writings of Maurras. A third inheritance of *la maison mère* was its elitism.[62]

The Action française was generally unconcerned with mass politics, and the Cagoule entirely so. In fact, even the primary goal of both groups always remained the same: to rid France of parliamentary democracy. It was, fundamentally, only the methods of the organizations that were in opposition. Upon their departure from the old royalist organization, the men of the CSAR took with them many political lessons. The *cagoulards* dismissed the royalist privileging of ideology over action but borrowed from the AF a certain rhetoric of nationalism, a particular anti-Semitism, and a strong sense of elitism. In addition to all this, Maurras taught his students an excellent lesson in the manipulation of societal fears. The Cagoule's use of the communist "threat" was very similar indeed to Maurras's use of anti-Semitism, both of which provided a unifying element that could mask many internal contradictions. As Maurras commented, "All seems impossible without this providential anti-Semitism. With it all falls into place and becomes simplified."[63] Similarly, the notion of a communist threat greatly contributed to the Cagoule's achievements.

Few historians would agree with the assertion that the Action française was a fascist organization. Eugen Weber maintains that the AF "combined and almost reconciled the popular radicalism of nationalism with the reactionary elitism of the royalists."[64] Yet historians have generally concluded that the Cagoule was, at the very least, inspired by fascism. Certainly the group had ties to fascist countries, but these relationships were not as straightforward as one might imagine. As we have seen, the Cagoule received help from Italy, and Corre often wrote of his admiration for that country. Aside from the Rosselli deal, which Corre discussed several times in his diary, there were several other instances of Italy supplying the organization with weapons and what appears to have been moral support. Corre quite candidly wrote that "in Italy, an agreement with the Italian authorities assures us of the delivery of automatic weapons, grenades, and the rest, all in excellent condition."[65] Corre always referred to his Italian contacts as "our friends" and only once criticized the Italians, specifically for being poor soldiers. Corre himself summed up his attitude toward Italy by commenting that "in Italy we are even better off than in a friendly country."[66]

According to Corre, the Cagoule also received weapons from Nazi Germany, but under conditions that might have surprised many. He wrote at the end of 1937 that "it was under the cover of Spain that we were able to acquire the first shipment of machine guns in Germany. The Germans did not prove immediately inclined to sell us weapons."[67] In fact, Corre bragged quite extensively about the way in which the Cagoule "tricked" Germany into selling the organization automatic weapons. It seems that the CSAR operatives went to Germany posing as businessmen concerned with the fate of Spain and wishing to help Franco, and persuaded the Germans that they could offer safe passage for the weapons through France.[68] Of course, these weapons never made it to Spain and ultimately made up a large part of the CSAR's stockpiles.

Aside from several mentions of getting weapons from Germany, Corre did not write about any further dealings with the Nazis in 1937. The rest of his observations about Germany were written in 1938 and 1939 and were much more detached; they had no bearing on the Cagoule but were instead general commentaries on Hitler and his various political moves. Like many of his contemporaries, Corre seems to have recognized the danger that Germany posed to France. He wrote, "We find ourselves at the same point as we were in 1913, with the terrible German menace hanging again over our heads. A menace infinitely more serious than before because today's Germany, more compact and significantly readier and more formidable than before, has taken up her very same ambitions."[69]

Although Corre may have noticed and even admired Germany for being orderly, powerful, and prepared to do anything to achieve its goals, he was not impressed by Hitler. He believed that the western democracies were making too much of the Nazi leader. Commenting on the press coverage of Hitler's every move, Corre wrote, "It was pretty much their stupid band that made Hitler and is still serving him, hoisting him onto a pedestal and gathering a crowd around him."[70] He went on to ask, "Is Hitler's speech important?"[71] Corre felt that the only reason the Nazi leader was important was because nonfascist countries were paying undue attention to him. In fact, Corre was quite sympathetic to the populations of Austria and especially Czechoslovakia when Hitler invaded those states. Of course, his sympathy was mitigated by his belief that those countries should have had stronger governments to repel the invading forces and maintain national sovereignty.

Although these examples of cooperation, to whatever extent, between the Cagoule and fascist countries might indicate a close relationship, that really was not the case. In fact, even the question whether the Cagoule was fascist seems to hinder rather than help any investigation of its political leanings. Although the Cagoule shared some outward similarities with groups like the Falange in Spain, and some ideological similarities both with that group and fascists in Italy, these are not enough to prove the fascistic nature of the CSAR. The topic of fascist movements in France has been just as hotly debated as that of fascism in general, often without effect. As John Sweets has pointed out, the various ways of interpreting the situation in France have swung from describing France as a nation free of fascists to describing the country as one full of fascists.[72] But the

CSAR possessed certain characteristics that set it apart from most other political models, the most significant being its total disregard for mass politics. Unlike fascist organizations, which relied in many ways upon mass participation, and earlier insurrectionary groups, which intended to provoke *popular* insurrection, the Cagoule had no such goals. It hoped only for a passive acceptance of its coup by the general population. In the absence of any popular support, which they did not even attempt to gain, the *cagoulards* relied instead on a certain agent provocateurism to achieve their goals.[73] Like latter-day political terrorists, the Cagoule actively sought to destabilize and divide French society to the point where resistance to a future coup would be nearly impossible. Thus, it seems more likely that the Cagoule represents a convergence of various political tendencies. The group may have borrowed from earlier political models, but there can be no doubt that the Cagoule was also unique in many ways.

The Cagoule's methods are much closer to those of the Blanquists or the Carbonari. The men of the Cagoule seem to have been bound not by a particular view of what France should look like in the future but by the insurrectionary goal of changing the then current political situation. The *cagoulards,* particularly those of the inner circle, shared many of the same political views, to be sure, but more significant is their shared conception of how to operate successfully in order to subvert the legal form of governance. This was, in part, what made many of the *cagoulards* ideally suited for their later work in the Resistance.

This is not to say, however, that everyone was happy to admit that the *cagoulards* played a role in the Resistance. As one lengthy report noted,

> For all those who conspired against the Republic before the war, the advent of the État français represented a victory that they saw as having come cheaply, since it had only been possible thanks to the armistice, imposed by military events.
>
> Thus real democrats were not astonished to see all those who had conspired to establish an authoritarian regime in France in the turbulent years that preceded the cataclysm cluster around the Vichy government. The men of 6 February, the members of the CSAR, outlaws of yesterday, rejoiced and crowded around the old man whom they wanted to bring to power.
>
> It was necessary that each one thoroughly subscribed to these central ideas: General De Gaulle was a traitor, and the condemnation to death proclaimed

against him in absentia was perfectly legitimate. The dissolution of Freemasonry was necessary, its members having always been the enemies of the real interests of our country. Jews are not French, and they need to be removed from the national community. Communists have always been agents of a foreign power, and it is necessary to treat them as such. Ex-parliamentarians and the parties of the Left are responsible for our misery, and it is necessary to reduce them to impotence.[74]

Given the extremeness of the Cagoule conspiracy and the shock waves it sent through the country, it is no surprise that the "logical" assumption was that the entire organization, after years of plotting the downfall of the Third Republic, joined forces with Vichy without a moment's hesitation. Not only had the Cagoule proved its commitment to antiparliamentarism, but given its links with the Action française—which, owing to Maurras's celebration of the "divine surprise," was held responsible for much of Vichy—how could anyone believe otherwise? Adding further credence to the sense that the CSAR must have been complicit in the creation of Vichy was the long-held belief that the group had as its "spiritual leader" none other than Pétain. This (mistaken) belief was further emphasized after the war ended and the *juge d'instruction* of the Cagoule trial ordered an investigation into the group's links with Italy. The CSAR's contact in Italy had been Emanuele Santo, head of Mussolini's counterintelligence, who testified that "the *cagoulards* considered Pétain their spiritual leader and Darlan the real leader of the movement."[75] While neither of these assertions was true, they helped reinforce the idea that the Cagoule could not have resisted an opportunity to actively collaborate with Vichy.

And yet while some members of the Cagoule, most notably Joseph Darnand and Eugène Deloncle, went even further than collaboration with Vichy and joined forces with the Nazis,[76] others assumed positions that were far more ambiguous. As we will see, the range of actions taken by former *cagoulards* was vast. The police had arrested many *cagoulards* in 1937, but the instruction period of the trial took so long that it was only in 1939 that the appointed judge, Béteille, was able to sign off on the Cagoule dossier, a report of some six hundred pages.[77] The beginning of the war interrupted these proceedings, however, and the jailed *cagoulards* were liberated so that they could enlist. After the defeat, some left immediately for London to join de Gaulle. Others secured positions at Vichy and managed to help the Resistance in various ways, often by providing the very necessary papers required to travel around France or by ensuring the release of *résistants* who had been arrested. Some *cagoulards* joined networks of the interior Resistance and kept their distance from both Pétain and de Gaulle.

Because of the variety of choices available to the *cagoulards* in wartime, there is no easy way to classify their actions as a group. They were not collaborators across the board, nor did they necessarily support Pétain in his new role. Each made his own decision. Even those who chose to resist the German occupation did so in numerous ways. Therefore, we cannot even claim that these resisters were *vichysto-résistants*. Given that their participation in the Cagoule was likely one of the most integral parts of their political development in the 1930s, it seems reasonable to suggest that the term *cagoulard-résistant* suits these activists better than any other. They had worked diligently to destabilize the Third Republic in the 1930s and would go on, using lessons learned during those years, to fight to restore France's sovereignty, though this restoration did not necessarily include the revival of republican politics. As we will see in the coming pages, the routes they took toward this goal often differed (and sometimes seemed downright contradictory), but the connections these *cagoulards-résistants* had made with one another were durable and would serve them all throughout the war.

THE CORVIGNOLLES

lthough perhaps it received more press, the Cagoule was not the only group operating on the margins of legality during the 1930s. Its rival extraparliamentary groups sometimes came close to pushing those margins but were normally held back either by the restraints of police action or by the inactivity of their leaders. However, the Cagoule had some competition in the anticommunist struggle from several organizations led by Georges Loustaunau-Lacau. Born in Pau in 1894 to an established army family, Loustaunau-Lacau started his career at Saint-Cyr. After his distinguished performance in the First World War, Loustaunau-Lacau became a major at the École de guerre. As testimony to his early success in his military career, one need only look at his dossier at the Ordre de la Légion d'honneur. He was awarded the rank of *chevalier* in 1917, and by 1933 he had been promoted to the level of *officier*.[1] Interestingly, Loustaunau-Lacau moved up in the ranks at the same time as Charles de Gaulle. Both men went on to work directly with Pétain, and both became well known for their nonconformance within the French Army. In part, the reputations of both de Gaulle and Loustaunau-Lacau were based on their respective writings on military topics. However, it was ultimately Loustaunau-Lacau's furtive activities within the army that clinched his reputation.

The Corvignolles was a secret army organization of the 1930s, created by Loustaunau-Lacau to combat what he saw as the rising influence of communism in the army. Surprisingly, we know much less about the Corvignolles than we do about the Cagoule even though Loustaunau-Lacau himself has never denied his involvement in the group. In his memoirs, he writes that the Corvignolles was created by December 1936 and had a double objective, to "alert the civil and military authorities to the urgent need to adapt the military to its new strategic and tactical tasks" and "rid the army of the cells that the communist party is continuously creating with a view to fomenting indiscipline and destroying morale."[2] The idea for such a group does not, however, seem to have been uniquely Loustaunau-Lacau's. Among papers seized for the *cagoulard* trial was a copy of a eulogy delivered by a Commandant LeFrançois at the graveside of Hervé Gratien de Corvignolles, a deceased French Army captain. LeFrançois said in his eulogy that "for Corvignolles, the health of France depended essentially on how well *its army was protected against propaganda and revolutionary intrigues.* He felt that . . . social crises, economic or financial, as serious as they are, would not put a nation in mortal danger, *if the patriotism and moral courage* of its army were intact."[3] He went on to suggest the creation of a group that would protect the army and the nation against the communists and "restore the prestige and vitality of France in fighting with all available means against visible or secret forces that ruin her: international forces, Jewish forces, Freemasonry."[4] In fact, the name for Loustaunau-Lacau's group did not come from this deceased captain, but from the family name of the Marshal de Vauban, whose biography Loustaunau-Lacau was working on at Pétain's behest in the 1930s. Marshal de Vauban, originally a military engineer in the army of Louis XIV, is best known for his many fortifications in France and for revolutionizing siege warfare.

Although there seems to have been no connection between Loustaunau-Lacau and the deceased captain Corvignolles, their ideas on the importance of clearing the army of demoralizing forces were clearly similar, and Loustaunau-Lacau went on to create his own network of anticommunists in the army. Although Loustaunau-Lacau claimed that he formed the group with the approval, whether implicit or explicit, of high-ranking army men, he was ultimately relieved of his post in the German section of the Deuxième Bureau de l'État-major général[5] for these clandestine activities. His sense at the time was that the communists were steadily working to undermine the French Army and that during the late 1930s, especially after the electoral successes of the Communist

Party within the Popular Front, few people were willing to stop what were becoming very public attacks on the army.[6]

Although several historians have argued that civil-military relations in the 1930s conformed to the stereotype of the army as *la grande muette*,[7] others have argued that the interwar period saw a veritable crisis in which army officers in particular were becoming increasingly political. Paul-Marie de la Gorce argues that the political involvement of the officers' corps was, for France, the most significant military development of the 1930s.[8] He links this politicization of the military with many of the wider trends and crises affecting French society at the time. Pointing to the various scandals of the 1930s, the economic collapse felt by all the Western nations, the pacifist spirit of Geneva and Locarno, the rise of communism, the numerous ministerial crises, and a general crumbling of traditional values to explain both the civilian and the military angst of the decade, he writes that "in the thirties, a new trend took hold of the collective mind, and associated itself with the deep-seated military suspicion of traditional democracy, the republican state and international capitalism."[9]

Veterans' groups were an important conduit for the transfer of general societal dissatisfactions to the military world. The 1930s, as we have seen, were marked by an expansion of the most conservative, nationalistic, and antiparliamentary veterans' movements, such as the Croix de feu and the Union nationale des combattants (UNC). De la Gorce argues that these groups were a sort of "intermediate ground" between the military and French society and that it was from these politicized veterans that the most reactionary ideas found their way into the officers' corps.[10] Although there has been a good deal of debate about the role veterans played in the rise of the extreme Right and in laying the groundwork for the Vichy regime, recent scholarship persuasively shows that a considerable number of veterans were only conditionally loyal to the republican regime. The many violent attacks against the Third Republic by veterans in the 1930s tell us, at the very least, that the culture of some veterans' groups (particularly the UNC) did not contribute to any ongoing commitment to the parliamentary republic.[11] It is beyond question that both the veterans' groups and the officers' corps experienced a politicization in the 1930s that left many members inclined toward the extreme Right. Georges Loustaunau-

Lacau was, in some ways, typical of the officers who opted for political action in the thirties; he blamed the parliament for budgetary restrictions, the delay in the manufacture of matériel, and the weakening of French military strength.[12] More significant, however, than his public ranting against the parliament was Loustaunau-Lacau's creation of his secret group, the Corvignolles. D. L. L. Parry argues that "the adventure of the Corvignolles and the Cagoule showed just how little confidence military and civilian elites had in the parliamentary Third Republic."[13]

There is no question that Loustaunau-Lacau was convinced that the growing influence of the communists in the army was one of the most pernicious threats to French security in the 1930s. Although his reaction to this perceived threat may have been more "active" than others', Loustaunau-Lacau was not alone in worrying about the communists within the army. The French Army was indeed the target of communist activism, as propaganda was distributed at recruiting centers and the party very publicly disseminated information designed to demoralize army members. As Alistair Horne points out, "The Party line of the 1920s specified, 'It is better to shoot a French general than a foreign soldier.'"[14] Moreover, the fact that the French Army had been heavily involved in anticommunist campaigns immediately following the Russian Revolution and for several years afterwards meant that the anticommunism of its officers in the 1930s was certainly not without precedent and in fact had been officially encouraged by the High Command. As de la Gorce writes, "For them [the army], the world struggle against communism was not simply a matter of opinions, ideologies or class reactions; it had a direct connection with the exercise of their profession. It was [one] of the 'missions to be accomplished.'"[15] Viewed in the context of this official doctrine of anticommunism, Loustaunau-Lacau's sense that bolshevism posed great danger does not seem so unusual. The anticommunism of the army was "not a matter of political propaganda or the object of theoretical exposés; it was concrete and dramatic. It meant the surveillance of all those suspected of belonging to the Communist Party, disciplinary measures, transfer to special units, the exposure of regimental cells, the search for those who were distributing pamphlets."[16]

The real difference between this official military stance on communism and Loustaunau-Lacau's activities has to do with the fact that the political tide had turned and he found himself on the wrong side in 1936. With the success of the Popular Front, Loustaunau-Lacau's anticommunism was no longer officially sanctioned and given the internal difficulties that the Radical, Socialist, and Communist Parties were facing, the Popular Front government could not allow such "subversive" anticommunist behavior, behavior that was insulting to a political party that was cooperating with the government, to go unchecked. From Loustaunau-Lacau's perspective, the failures of the Popular Front also could not go unchecked. One of its major failures in his eyes was the lack of support for the military and the unwillingness to protect it from communist defeatism. Loustaunau-Lacau maintained a particular hatred for Edouard Daladier, the minister of national defense.[17] In inimitable fashion, Loustaunau-Lacau wrote of Daladier in his memoirs: "Exclaiming the ideas of the sans-culotte while toasting to the widow Clicquot, dry taste, is less original than repulsive."[18] While the electoral success of the Popular Front put Loustaunau-Lacau out of work, it probably also encouraged other anticommunists to join groups like the Corvignolles or the Cagoule.

Although the Corvignolles has often been linked to the Cagoule as the military arm of the civilian organization,[19] there is little evidence that the two groups cooperated beyond sharing information about communist activities in France. Loustaunau-Lacau was introduced to Eugène Deloncle by Franchet d'Esperey. Although he seems to have respected Deloncle and noted that he was a courageous man, Loustaunau-Lacau declined the invitation to join the Cagoule. "I realized immediately that Deloncle and I were in complete disagreement," he stated, "because in my opinion the army should not attempt to overthrow the state but rather protect it against all attacks, in particular against communism."[20] One of the main reasons why Loustaunau-Lacau was not keen on a coup was that the destabilization of France would allow the Germans, who were already threatening the security of the country, a perfect opportunity to invade. Another prominent member of the Corvignolles, Georges Groussard, was also respectful toward Deloncle but unimpressed by him, describing him as follows: "Truthfully, this man was a born adventurer. All that seemed monotonous or gentrified stifled him, and he no doubt would have been a splendid soldier if he had been given the chance to fight without stopping, to the very end."[21] Although both Groussard and Loustaunau-Lacau may have seen some positive qualities in Deloncle, neither one seemed to want such an adventure seeker in his organization.

In addition to its actual connection to the Cagoule, the Corvignolles's ultimate objective also cannot be properly established. Do we accept at face value Loustaunau-Lacau's justification for not joining the CSAR—that "a putsch, whether from the Right or the Left, would cut the country in two. It would prompt the invasion, at the first chance, of foreign politics"?[22] At present, there is no evidence that the Corvignolles, unlike the Cagoule, actually conspired to overthrow the government. As far as we know, Loustaunau-Lacau was entirely focused on ridding the army of communists. He claimed to have done so with some success, noting after the war that in eighteen months he had managed to dissolve from 150 to 200 communist cells.[23] While the goals of the group are unclear, the political inclinations of its leaders are not. Loustaunau-Lacau and Groussard were firmly on the extreme right; the former had also been involved with the Parti populaire français, and the latter with the royalist Action française.[24] Neither had many positive things to say about the Third Republic or its leaders. Loustaunau-Lacau's sense was that "the political and military leaders of 1939 had nothing to do with the later reversal of the war. They ensured that our country submitted to a total defeat, a humiliation without precedent in our history, the shame and misery of four years of occupation."[25]

Unlike other members of the activist Right in France, Loustaunau-Lacau did not have a clear sense of what kind of government would serve the country except that it needed to be more authoritarian. In the conclusion of his memoirs, Loustaunau-Lacau argues for the adoption of certain measures to reestablish the grandeur of France. One such measure was the restoration of authority. Loustaunau-Lacau notes that France had tried many forms of government—an absolute monarchy, an empire, a constitutional monarchy, an authoritarian republic, and a republic with no authority—and that none of them had worked. He writes that the threat of decadence made it clear that the country needed to change but that these kinds of government had been unable to respond to that need.[26] The solution, according to Loustaunau-Lacau was to be found in a government with increased authority, more along the lines of the American model. His admiration for the United States after the war may have been related to the American stance against the Soviet Union, however, rather than its governmental system. Before the war, he had never cited the United States as a model. Instead, Loustaunau-Lacau had focused on authority derived from the military. In her book on Marie-Madeleine Fourcade (Méric), Loustaunau-Lacau's longtime associate, Michèle Cointet notes that the Cagoule militaire (her way of referring to the Corvignolles) "didn't have the least bit of confidence in the regime of the Third Republic and wouldn't until it placed a strong man or a great military leader in charge."[27] Loustaunau-Lacau was described by the police as being a royalist, "but not of the 'Action Française' or the 'Comte de Paris' shade, all of his preferences going to the prince of Bourbon-Parma"; it is hard to know whether this was indeed the case.[28]

Loustaunau-Lacau was certainly close to Charles Maurras, which is perhaps why the police were so intent on labeling him a monarchist. His respect for Maurras was deep-seated; he particularly admired Maurras's philosophical abilities and remembered fondly their conversations about the future of France.[29] But Loustaunau-Lacau was not wedded to the idea of restoring the monarchy, partially because he did not think the public would accept such a move. He also did not have much confidence in the pretenders to the throne, noting that they all lacked the ability to save France from the communist threat. "To talk of a monarchical restoration to a nation that is sliding imperceptibly, but sliding, toward a dictatorship of the proletariat is like proposing a nice horse to someone who should be traveling to New York by plane, and it is not useful for the country to stir the ashes instead of lighting the fire that would warm it."[30] Unlike many of the Action française supporters, Loustaunau-Lacau clearly realized that the time for a monarchy had passed. This, however, did not stop the police from being suspicious of his active political stance.

Even though there is no clear evidence that Loustaunau-Lacau planned to overthrow the government, the nature of his involvement in the Corvignolles was conspiratorial, to say the least. As de la Gorce points out, the creation of the group was a definite indication of the politicization of a national organization that many people at the time would have preferred remain silently obedient. This preference for an apolitical army, uninvolved in matters that should, many felt, remain in the domain of the politicians, became quite apparent in the aftermath of de Gaulle's publication of *Vers l'armée de métier* in 1934. One central suggestion put forth by de Gaulle was that the French Army drastically increase the number of high-tech weapons and improve their use; he said that these tasks should be undertaken by professional soldiers rather than by the two-year conscripts typical of the army. This suggestion was met with a certain amount of horror on the part of republicans, as they feared that professional soldiers, as opposed to citizen soldiers, would always feel more loyalty to the army than to the nation and its citizens (i.e., the republic).[31] Given the longstanding suspicion on the part of many politicians that there continued to be an element of the officers' corps that had, at best, a dubious loyalty to republican institutions, it is no surprise that Loustaunau-Lacau's actions were seen as dangerous.

From a republican perspective, Loustaunau-Lacau was indeed a danger to the stability of both the army and the nation. Like de Gaulle, Loustaunau-Lacau seemed to advocate a rejuvenation of France via the army, a scary idea to those who felt that the only possible outcome of an actively political army was a coup. And indeed, this increasingly active army in the 1930s was leaning further to the right than was perhaps comfortable. Using the concept of the "Army-Nation," Philip Bankwitz describes how the French Army became increasingly politicized as military men came to see themselves, and the army as a whole, as the guardians of national integrity.[32] Bankwitz argues that like the extreme Right, which distinguished between the *pays légal* and the *pays réel*, military men came to see a clear distinction between the nation and the regime, and thus their sense of protecting national integrity did not necessarily mean protecting that of the republican regime.[33] Loustaunau-Lacau, disdainful of the republic and operating outside its boundaries, was clearly expanding the rift that existed between the army and the regime, although he considered his actions to be in the best interests of the nation. Thus, while he may not have planned to personally overthrow the government, Loustaunau-Lacau certainly contributed to paving the way for its downfall.

Even though the Corvignolles was, for all intents and purposes, dead after Loustaunau-Lacau was ordered into nonactivity, his anticommunist crusades were far from over. In 1938 he created and became president of the Union militaire française (UMF). Although they were two distinct organizations, the UMF and Jacques Doriot's Parti populaire français (PPF) worked closely together.[34] Loustaunau-Lacau and Doriot cooperated to some extent, as was noted by the police, who reported that "at the end of 1938, Loustaunau-Lacau went into business with Jacques Doriot, and . . . an anticommunist pact was concluded between the Parti populaire français and the Union militaire française."[35] This pact was announced in one of Loustaunau-Lacau's newspapers, where it was presented as a provisional agreement, though the announcement made clear that the pact could be renewed fairly easily. The two groups had come together because the leaders of both felt that the action of the communists in France represented "a permanent plot against society and the French nation."[36] Blaming the communists for both harming national defense, particularly with their activities in the aviation industry, and pushing the country toward a war that would only serve to satisfy Stalin's revolutionary goals, the UMF and the PPF vowed to join forces to destroy communism.[37]

It is difficult to ascertain the goal of the UMF, aside from anticommunist propaganda, but Loustaunau-Lacau certainly attempted to spread its message far and wide. In 1939 one Christian Steibel was arrested attempting to bring copies of *Barrage,* Loustaunau-Lacau's newsletter, from Switzerland to France. Steibel lived in Algiers at the time, and a report from the governor-general of Algeria to the French minister of the interior notes that he had tried to establish a chapter of the UMF there.[38] The governor-general also wrote that Loustaunau-Lacau, accompanied by Steibel, had landed in Oran in December 1938 to attend a meeting organized by the local PPF. Oran was the site of the PPF's most spectacular successes; membership there increased rapidly and quickly surpassed that of every other rightist party in the region.[39] The PPF was not nearly as successful in other Algerian *départements,* which explains why it was to Oran that Loustaunau-Lacau traveled. To an audience of about two hundred people, Loustaunau-Lacau spoke about how France could escape "disorder."

The governor-general did not include the full text of the speech in his report, but he did say that over the course of this conference, the speaker put the parliamentary regime on trial, criticized the actions of the Radical Socialist Party, and deplored the state of national defense. He then protested against the political activities of the Israelite element in the nation. On this subject he declared: "The Jews are not responsible for their birth or for their character. Thus it is inhumane to hate them. We must therefore accept them into our midst, on the condition that they prove respectful of the laws and ideas of our people. What is needed is to prevent them from being at the head of big businesses, because there are no other problems than those that they create themselves in bringing disorder to the social body that receives them by spreading their lust for wealth and their diabolical passion for hoarding."[40]

These statements are unsurprising, as they correspond to Loustaunau-Lacau's general political position quite neatly. Although much of this speech would have been well received by local party members, Loustaunau-Lacau, like local PPF leaders, did not prioritize a violent anti-Semitism, which conflicted with the desires of most settlers.[41] This disconnect eventually cost the PPF a great deal of settlers' support in Algeria. The governor-general's report ends by emphasizing that Loustaunau-Lacau's principal goal was the dissolution of the Communist Party by means of petitions addressed to judicial authorities. These petitions apparently argued that the PCF was led by a foreign power (the Comintern) that sought to destroy the laws of France and her most important base—patriotism and the family.[42]

Loustaunau-Lacau was quick to point out that the UMF was a legal entity, having deposited its statutes in conformity with the law regarding associations of 1901.[43] Members of the UMF could live in metropolitan France or in its overseas territories, though Loustaunau-Lacau wanted to limit the number of members to two thousand, a fact that highlights the elitism of these groups. It had an honorary committee made up of people who "were willing to lend their moral and spiritual support to the work pursued by the Union militaire française."[44] The list of committee members is a veritable who's who of rightist notables, including Louis Marin, Abel Bonnard, and Admiral Joubert, among others.[45] Loustaunau-Lacau's anti-parliamentarism is reflected in the fact that the group was never intended to be a political party but instead promised to intervene in politics when any interests of the "Nation" seemed threatened and to act "practically," but within the laws of France, to combat the occult forces threatening France.[46] Loustaunau-Lacau did warn potential members of the UMF, however, that the group, "because of the power of its principles, the routes it has chosen, the purity of its intentions, will attract hostility from those who profit from disorder: from those among the politicians who are concerned that this mess continues; from those among Freemasons who are bound up with the International; from internationalists of all forms and communists in particular; from those among the Jews who place France under the scalpel; hostility finally from those among the rich for whom capital has no country."[47] Such a warning gives the impression that only the most committed and bravest of men or those who relished the potential for conflict between UMF members and their enemies would feel comfortable joining the UMF.

Loustaunau-Lacau was also busy giving speeches in Paris in 1938. One police officer thought he was trying to replace the UMF with his Spiralien Movement, although the two groups operated concurrently and in cooperation. A note from the Sûreté nationale pointed out that "the Spirale is not looking to group together a large number of members, but rather to reach an elite. It is above all else anticommunist, anti-Masonic, anti-Jew, but not anti-Semitic. It does not oppose its members' being part of national groups; quite the contrary in fact."[48] Like the Corvignolles, the "Spirale" was concerned, above all, with the army and the security of the country. Its first two goals were "Protection—Protection of the police forces and the armed forces against subversive propaganda, against espionage. Maintenance of the armed forces at a desired level of preparation and the ongoing development of the war potential of the nation. 2. Cleaning up—Destruction of communism. To research and incapacitate all enemies of the national conscience, in collective or individual form, all those who wreck national interests."[49] The other goals of the group included social, economic, and political reform; "imperial harmony"; a spiritual renewal; and the diffusion of French ideas into the world.

The Mouvement Spiralien de l'Ordre National was headquartered in the 7th arrondissement in Paris, at 1, rue de Courty. It was based on three central principles: order, equity (clearly not in the true democratic sense), and progress. In their bulletin of April 15, 1939, the collaborators of the Spiralien Movement argued that France was in danger from both outside and within. As for many others on the extreme right, the catchword regarding dangers within the country was decadence, and the Spiralien Movement proposed to reconstruct France in all her glory with a new politics: "The *spiralien* conception of a specifically French political and social life rejects the current systems in the totalitarian states and condemns the customs and procedures in use in demagogic democracies. It rejects partisanship and instead substitutes THE SPIRIT OF COLLABORATION AND UNION."[50] Loustaunau-Lacau saw three ways to fix France's political and social institutions: through the parliament, with a coup d'état, or by a meeting of the Estates General.

It is no surprise that the first option, rejuvenation via the parliament, was out of the question, given Loustaunau-Lacau's distrust of that institution. Noting the many serious crises of the previous years, Loustaunau-Lacau argued that each one had been met with mediocre and provisionary solutions. He summed the situation up by saying that "the minute the parliament enters the scene, it paralyzes the action of the government."[51] He also denounced the option of a coup d'état, arguing that such a move was itself a sign of decadence. In the end, Loustaunau-Lacau and the other *spiraliens* favored a meeting of the Estates General, as it was the only body capable of managing, within the sphere of legality, a transition to the new political, economic, and social organization of the state. Making this happen, then, was one of the many goals of the *spiraliens*.

Loustaunau-Lacau proposed very specific regulations regarding membership and the structure of each individual *spirale*.[52] To become a member one had to be French, and Loustaunau-Lacau was quite clear that he did not mean foreign, naturalized French citizens. *Spiraliens* had to declare on their honor that they did not belong to any kind of occult group, especially the Freemasons, who were explicitly banned from joining the organization. Finally, they had to be in agreement with the guiding principles, the chosen methods of action, the spirit of the group, and the character of the UMF.[53] Much like Freemasons, Jews were not welcomed into the *spirales*; and women were invited to join, but only in their own specific *spirale*. Each *spirale* was meant to have one president and an executive, which comprised an organizer, in charge of recruitment, membership, and money; an observer, in charge of researching and transmitting all forms of information; a counselor, in charge of following the works of the central *spirale* and deciding the subjects of various studies; and a diffuser, in charge of distributing all publications. Other members were meant to form a large group of propagandists, working under the direction of the executive. Moreover, each *spirale* was meant to work toward the general goals of the organization, yet each also had its own specific objective (see table).

OBJECTIVES OF THE SPIRALIEN MOVEMENT, BY DIVISION

Objectives	Spirales	Remarks
No 1.—Protection of armed forces against subversive propaganda and espionage. Collection of intelligence and inventions suitable for national defense.	Department of National Protection, 1 rue de Courty, Paris. Protection branch. Invention branch.	Members of all Spirales contribute to the work of objective No. 1.
No. 2.—Combined studies of foreign politics and strategy. Influence and prestige.	Society for the Study of Foreign Politics and Strategy. Spirale of French abroad.	The conclusions of the studies undertaken by the Society are published in *L'Ordre National*.
No. 3.—Technical military preparation of youth.	Independent groupings of Air Youth Group, Radio Youth Group, and Motorized Youth Group.	
No. 4.—Destruction of communism.	Association for the Defense of the Nation, 15 rue Jean-Jacques-Rousseau, Paris.	The Association for the Defense of the Nation filed suit for the dissolution of the Communist Party. The anticommunist struggle is conducted with other groups, in particular the Parti Populaire Français.

(continued)

Objectives	Spirales	Remarks
No. 5.—Internal protection against the political, economic, and social maneuvers of foreigners, in particular against Jewish racism.	Department of National Protection, 1 rue de Courty, Paris.	Members of all Spirales contribute to the work of objective No. 5.
No. 6.—Meeting of the Estates General.	Reform Study Group, 1 rue de Courty, Paris. General Secretary: M. Hubert-Bourgin. Regional political movements of l'Ordre National. Overseas movements of l'Ordre National.	See, for example, the statutes of the Ordre National movement in the southwest region.
No. 7.—Recovery of the birth rate.	The Spiralien movement uses the work of the National Alliance against Depopulation, 217 rue du Faubourg-Saint-Honoré, Paris.	Members of all Spirales contribute to spreading the work regarding objective No.7.
No. 8.—Exaltation of moral and physical courage.	Legionnaires of the Struggle, 28 boulevard Raspail, Paris.	The Legionnaires of the Struggle are Spiraliens who willingly submit to an annual ordeal designed to exalt moral and physical courage.
No. 9.—Protection of elites and individual technical merit.	In the cadre of the regional political movements.	
No. 10.—Creation of chambers of expertise.	In the cadre of the regional political movements.	
No. 11.—Regional political movements.	See Objective No. 6.	

OBJECTIVES OF THE SPIRALIEN MOVEMENT, BY DIVISION

Objectives	Spirales	Remarks
No. 12.—Reform project.	Reform study group, 1 rue de Courty, Paris. Chambers of expertise. Regional political movements.	Studies undertaken with a view to assembling the Estates General.
No. 13.—Studies of Empire.	Society for the Study of Empire, 1 rue de Courty, Paris. Overseas movements of l'Ordre National.	

General remarks—The fortnightly review *l'Ordre National* publishes the studies of the Spiralien movement and the reports of its diverse activities. It is the duty of each member of the Spirale to subscribe to *l'Ordre National* if he has the means and to sell additional subscriptions to support the review.

Source: ANF, 3W 278, Mouvement Spiralien de l'Ordre National booklet. Translation by author.

These goals were all to be accomplished within the rubric of order, equity, and progress set out by Loustaunau-Lacau. Given his political position, it is very much worth exploring what he meant by these words, which in and of themselves could indicate a somewhat liberal outlook. Yet these three concepts were explicitly meant to replace the components of the revolutionary slogan *Liberté, égalité, fraternité*. Loustaunau-Lacau allowed for the fact that these revolutionary principles had in fact led at times to struggles against injustice, but he argued that "the crisis of 1936 proved that it was not sufficient to repeat these magic formulas for them to produce positive effects in the country where they first flourished."[54] He went on to suggest that these principles needed to be turned into ones that followed the "natural order of things," thus making room for his own guiding principles.

Loustaunau-Lacau's description of order is unsurprising in its reaction against the Revolution and the creation of unions and other leftist organizations. He pointed to workers who had lost their jobs because of political strikes of which they had not necessarily approved, small businessmen who had been taken advantage of by unscrupulous financiers, and pilots who had crashed their poorly made planes as examples of how the concept of liberty had been taken too far. In effect, Loustaunau-Lacau felt that the French had arrived at the point where the abuse of liberty had made it impossible to benefit from such a concept.[55] His examples clearly demonstrate whom he blamed for the lack of order: unions for their politicization of labor and faulty workmanship and the government for not protecting the "ordinary man." To solve this problem, Loustaunau-Lacau suggests that order will follow from the proper exercise of authority, an authority based on aptitude because of character, moral and physical valor, and technical competence. Responsibility must go hand in hand with authority, as do morality and discipline. Loustaunau-Lacau was particularly concerned with national order and thus argued that a reworking of the political system, with help from Christian churches (acting as a standard of morality), would help to achieve order in France.

Loustaunau-Lacau's conception of equity was clearly reactionary. Lest his readers confuse equity with equality, he was quick to point out that "the idea of Equality has taken a toll in raising, in simple hearts, hopes that could only be disappointed."[56] This was because, as Loustaunau-Lacau argued, there were natural inequalities in every domain, including those of intelligence, will, force, and beauty. The mandate of the *spiraliens* was not to make all citizens feel equal but to make inequality tolerable through charity and justice. Equity in this sense was meant to protect the weak from abuses of the powerful and to guarantee the distribution of wealth based on merit and acquired rights. Loustaunau-Lacau offered various "guarantees" as ways to create equity. The guarantee of assistance in times of misery, the guarantee of financial help to large families (reflecting his natalist concerns), the guarantee of work, the guarantee of property rights, the guarantee of justice through a judiciary that was not tied to the political system, the guarantee against favoritism, and the guarantee of hope for a better life were all promised by the *spiraliens*. This concept of equity was fundamentally and explicitly elitist, as Loustaunau-Lacau believed that the rebirth of the elite class was the only way to prepare for the future.[57]

This elite class was also to be at the head of Loustaunau-Lacau's plans for progress, which he hoped would occur in various domains—moral, intellectual, and physical/material. The elite in particular would be the target of intellectual improvements, though what these improvements might be remained generally undefined. As for moral progress, Loustaunau-Lacau had much more detailed comments to make. In essence, he blamed teachers who were distracted from their real mission by their political passions, clearly pointing the finger at leftist and republican teachers in general.[58] His solution was to create an impenetrable barrier between education and politics, which he argued would actually occur on its own if Christian teachers were allowed to resume the job of educating the nation's youth. Along with a more religious education, however, French youth were also desperately in need of physical and material help, according to Loustaunau-Lacau. Like many others on the extreme right, and indeed German and Italian fascists, Loustaunau-Lacau saw health, sport, and tourism as ways to improve the youth of France, saying that "the State can never make enough sacrifices for the medical protection, physical development, the outdoor life and travel of youth."[59] He also despaired of the possibilities for employment for these young people, lamenting that mechanization was eliminating job opportunities. His solution was to establish what was necessary for a minimum of well-being and ensure that every person was able to achieve that.

Loustaunau-Lacau wrote for *Le Figaro* under the pseudonym Jean Rivière from April to October 1937 and founded several journals of his own, including *Barrage* and *Notre Prestige*. His articles in *Le Figaro* reflected his ongoing concern about the French military, with titles like "L'invasion de la France par la Suisse" and "Sommes-nous capables de répondre à une attaque aérienne?"[60] These articles, and many like them, are remarkably prescient regarding the issues the French Army would face once the war began in 1939. They also add credence to Loustaunau-Lacau's claim that he had always been concerned about Germany and the threat that country posed to France. The contributors to the papers and presumably their readers shared many of these same concerns. National defense figures prominently in a good number of these articles, even in ones that do not deal explicitly with the armed forces.

In the July 1938 issue of *Notre Prestige*, which was devoted entirely to the imperial project, Loustaunau-Lacau highlighted the many ways in which the empire was fundamental to the health of France. Like other defenders of the colonial project, he believed that to take charge of the destiny of "primitive people" or a society that had fallen into decadence was a sage and legitimate decision that made economic and moral sense for the colonizing country.[61] However, Loustaunau-Lacau made an even more impassioned argument for colonialism when he put it at the forefront of national defense, arguing that it could serve as a natural barrier to attacks from other nations. He proposed a pact between Britain, France, and Italy and their respective empires, which he said would be able to put a stop to German ambitions. Germany would never be able to declare war, because she would be in such an unfavorable strategic position.[62] In the face of the German Anschluss with Austria in March 1938, the French Empire gave much comfort to the members of Loustaunau-Lacau's various groups. As one contributor to *Notre Prestige* noted, "Face to face with a Germany numbering, since the Anschluss, 70 million inhabitants, there would be much to fear for our 40 million French bodies if we weren't able to count on the empire."[63] This fear of confronting a much stronger Germany was evident in many issues of *Notre Prestige* in the summer of 1938. While many other rightists in France were still maintaining a pacifist perspective on international affairs, the members of Loustaunau-Lacau's groups offered a rather different take on the German problem.

Loustaunau-Lacau and other contributors to *Notre Prestige* clearly outlined how Germany had spent the five preceding years preparing for war. In all ways—militarily, economically, and spiritually—Nazi Germany had devoted all its energy to expansionist foreign policy and war. In August 1938, when Hitler's designs on Czechoslovakia were already well known, Loustaunau-Lacau pleaded with the governments of France and Britain to recognize the mortal danger of Germany's power, and he encouraged them to find a way to stop Hitler. Recognizing that alliances were going to be a fundamental part of any bulwark against Germany, Loustaunau-Lacau identified Belgium and Italy as the allies it was most important to cultivate.[64] He wrote that "Germany possesses the ability to extend its power in a few short weeks from Tyrol to the Bas-Danube. But the chances of maintaining this power will diminish as long as the French Army, made stronger by her allies, can realize a strategic plan that will allow for an offensive to the east."[65] Belgium, of course, was not at all interested in such a plan. In 1936 the country had returned to a policy of "independence," which was fundamentally a policy of neutrality, though Belgium was careful never to call it such. Britain and France, with whom Belgium had previously had alliances of various sorts, ultimately released Belgium from those previous obligations, but Loustaunau-Lacau was convinced that unless there were some kind of allied military presence in Belgium, Germany would never be stopped.

His position regarding the strategic position of Belgium did not go over well in all circles, evidently. In the following issue of *Notre Prestige*, Loustaunau-Lacau wrote an open letter to Georges Bonnet, the French foreign minister, who had publicly commented on the inappropriateness of the previous articles about Belgium. Bonnet was an outspoken advocate of détente with Germany, so it is no surprise that he and Loustaunau-Lacau would clash. In his letter, Loustaunau-Lacau wrote that "it is neither by speeches nor by these missions that the insane excesses of Hitler's Germany will be defeated. These excesses lead to war."[66] He said that Hitler would not respond to anything but force and that unless Belgium consented to some kind of agreement, France and Britain would be reduced to a passive defense of their own empires while waiting for the shock of a German onslaught.[67] Much of the remainder of that issue of the newspaper was an exposé about the German forces. In considerable detail, the contributors of the paper set out the personnel of the armed forces and their organization, alongside a warning about the secret deployment of the German forces.

Notre Prestige was a monthly newspaper that focused on both the foreign and domestic affairs of France and tended to link its stories to national defense in one way or another.[68] *Barrage,* on the other hand, was primarily a domestic journal focused on communism that differed little from Loustaunau-Lacau's other writings. Loustaunau-Lacau himself described the journal as

an organ of combat against all forces, hidden or apparent, that seek to destroy the French nation. Its principal enemy is communism, generator of civil war, foreign war, and social misery. BARRAGE leads a ruthless fight against communism that it will pursue until complete victory. BARRAGE also intends to rid France of the international underworld, which exploits and dishonors it. BARRAGE is on a strict national axis, an even distance away from all political parties. Because it is animated with the spirit of the Marne, BARRAGE will conquer.[69]

Barrage offered its readers a list of places in Paris used by the PCF as meeting places, along with many "documents" (the authenticity of which is questionable) that proved how destructive the communists really were. The journal itself was inflammatory and certainly advanced Loustaunau-Lacau's integral anticommunism, but it also linked the two dangers that occupied most of his energies in the late 1930s: communists and Germany. While he claimed to want a peaceful, strong, and united France, Loustaunau-Lacau's sense that Germany would be unstoppable without direct action was apparent even in *Barrage*. He suspected that the relationship between the Soviet Union and Germany had never fallen apart and that the "communists in France were the reckless agents of a Germany that was waiting for her hour of revenge."[70] Loustaunau-Lacau vowed that *Barrage* would play its modest role to lessen the risk of foreign invasion, whether it was "red, brown, black, or whatever else we might encounter."[71]

Anticommunism was the one thread that tied together all of Loustaunau-Lacau's activities in the 1930s. There is no doubt that he was sincerely worried about the influence of communism within the army, and though he took extreme measures, he was not alone in his concern about the communists. Closely linked to this concern was his never-ending passion for the French military and its safety and efficiency in a time of increasingly worrisome foreign affairs. Loustaunau-Lacau's commitment to the army never wavered, and it was this commitment, along with his anticommunism, that led him to undertake activities that at best demonstrated his disdain for parliamentary institutions and at worst were destabilizing and dangerous to the Third Republic. Like many of his colleagues on the extreme right, Loustaunau-Lacau, as we have seen, was also anti-Semitic, though certainly not as virulently as some others. During the 1930s he wrote articles with titles like "Comment conjurer le péril juif," "L'invasion juive," and "La question raciale juive" and suggested that Jews should be removed from government and that all naturalization of Jews should end.[72] Although anti-Semitism was never at the forefront of

Loustaunau-Lacau's political activities, it certainly did inform his prewar political philosophy and, with anticommunism and antirepublicanism, marked the kind of organizations he would lead.

In turn, these organizations, both the ones created by Loustaunau-Lacau and those similar to them, like the Cagoule, would mark the men and women who adhered to the groups. People like Loustaunau-Lacau, Georges Groussard, Marie-Madeleine Méric, and others shared these politics and the drive to implement them and thus found themselves in similar positions in 1939 and 1940. The war with Germany and the occupation of France presented a unique moment for the men and women of the extreme Right. All temporary pacts aside, Nazism was fundamentally opposed to communism, which was sure to please many of these activists. Vichy was created on the basis of many of their deeply held convictions, and Pétain was a known entity for many of these people because of their prewar dealings with him. And yet their paths were not predestined by these politics. Loustaunau-Lacau and Georges Groussard, the two leading figures of the Corvignolles, longtime friends, and fully committed army men, would find themselves in unexpected places as the war dragged on.

RESISTANCE AT THE HEART OF VICHY

As it did for many rightists, the beginning of the war in France provided an interesting dilemma for Georges Loustaunau-Lacau. Many of his goals soon became a reality, as the Communist Party was outlawed and many of his own political leanings were incorporated into the new regime. Loustaunau-Lacau was actually quite close to Pétain, but did not much like Laval or Darlan, and he faced many of the same concerns as the *cagoulards* regarding what course of action to choose in 1940. Loustaunau-Lacau mused about his choices in his memoirs: "To go to the Germans, is it not a clear path and the certainty of being done with global communism? But if we don't chase them out, what will they do to France?"[1] In the end, Loustaunau-Lacau and others, such as Georges Groussard and Maurice Duclos, were more concerned with the external threat that Germany represented than they were with the internal threat of communism, and each man began resisting the Occupation.

Loustaunau-Lacau began the war back in the ranks of the French Army, as he was reintegrated because of the increasing need for military men. His political activism barely slowed even early in the war. Furious because he thought the army and the government had ignored all intelligence suggesting that the Germans would not be playing by the rules of 1914, Loustaunau-Lacau publicly accused the French High Command of treason. He was arrested at the front in March 1940 but was released in early May after his friends, many of whom were prominent public figures, urged the government to free him. Upon his release, Loustaunau-Lacau returned to the front, where he was wounded. He was subsequently taken to a German-controlled military hospital in Châlons-sur-Marne, from which he escaped in July 1940. Quickly making the decision to continue fighting, Loustaunau-Lacau rendezvoused with Marie-Madeleine Méric, who had been heavily involved in his prewar political activities, in Oloron. The small group traveled to Vichy, for Loustaunau-Lacau was convinced that the only way to act effectively was to be at the center of power and information.[2]

It was in Vichy, at the Hôtel des Sports, that the *réseau* Alliance was created. "In 15 days," Loustaunau-Lacau later recalled, "we set up, at the heart of Vichy, the first stronghold of the interior resistance."[3] His first projects were to set up a "rehabilitation" center for demobilized soldiers and to become a general delegate of the Légion française des combattants. These actions, which Loustaunau-Lacau thought would be useful for establishing and expanding Alliance, were officially sanctioned by Pétain.[4] The main focus of Alliance was military intelligence, and the ability of its leader to maintain contacts with Pétain and other members of the government did indeed seem to benefit the organization.

The Alliance network, which has often been overlooked by historians of the Resistance, was numerically superior to most other networks. After the war, official recognition was awarded to 266 networks made up of 150,000 agents.[5] Alliance alone had approximately 3,000 agents, close to 500 of whom died while engaged in their resistance activities.[6] Unlike the resistance movements, the networks, including Alliance, focused less on propaganda and public actions and more on military intelligence. Alliance's 3,000 agents operated in various sectors of France, both in the North and in the South, patrolling and using any connections they could to gather information about German activities. They would then report back to the group's leaders, who sent the information along to the British, with whom they were working. In return for this information, Alliance received money, agents, and radio transmitters from Great Britain. By the fall of 1941, Alliance had six radio transmitters operating—in Pau, Marseilles, Nice, Lyons, Paris, and Normandy—which sent vital intelligence reports on a regular basis.[7]

Loustaunau-Lacau and his group worked with the British from the earliest days of the war and maintained only limited contact with the

London-based Gaullist intelligence organization, the BCRA. Originally Loustaunau-Lacau's organization, the Croisade, was hardly different from any of his prewar groups. Vehemently anticommunist, the Croisade was founded on the belief that following the eventual German defeat, the communists would take advantage of the ensuing disorganization and chaos to take power. In a tract that Navarre (Loustaunau-Lacau) asked the British to drop over France, he called for the French to fight against German "barbarism" and to remember their privileged position in the Christian world. However, he did not neglect his own political position and wrote that "France, victim of her political vices and punished as she deserved for having abandoned her secular mission, had to, at the end of only a few days of combat, put down her weapons. But her eternal voice still rings."[8] In addition to asking the BCRA to distribute the tract, Loustaunau-Lacau asked it for financial aid and for some BBC airtime each day. Demanding though Loustaunau-Lacau may have been, the BCRA agent who wrote the report on the Croisade remarked, "We have to take into account this movement, as its importance is considerable in France. Worth noting that it isn't, properly speaking, Gaullist, but if we provide some funds and give it several minutes a day on the B.B.C., it will, in some ways, become automatically attached to the F.F.L. and we will gain incontestable advantages."[9] Although this agent said that the Croisade was not "properly" Gaullist, he had remarked earlier in the report that its members were "entirely and fiercely against de Gaulle."[10] It was perhaps because of this stance against de Gaulle that the general resisted all efforts to bring Alliance within the sphere of the Free French, thus leaving the group free to deal almost exclusively with the British.

Like many other early *résistants*, Loustaunau-Lacau was, at least initially, supportive of Pétain. Furthermore, this support for the new régime did not particularly trouble the agents of the BCRA. When Lucas (Pierre Fourcaud), a BCRA agent, was in France in 1940, he made sure to establish links with what he described as two very important groups of resisters within Pétain's entourage.[11] One of these groups was Groussard's political police, and the other was the Légion française des combattants. This second group he perceived as preparing for a remobilization, with the tacit support of Pétain. Lucas stated that "at its head [was] a politician,

Xavier Vallat, to give it an innocent appearance. But in the wings [was] Commandant Loustaunau-Lacau, a.k.a. Navarre, former ordinance officer of the Marshal, the spirit of an important national movement."[12] Lucas went on, in his report, to call Loustaunau-Lacau's organization the most important one, and he made sure to check in with Loustaunau-Lacau before leaving Vichy. The fundamental Pétainism of the group seems to have bothered Lucas little; in fact, after years of research, scholars now acknowledge how widespread support for Pétain was among early resisters. Yet this does not change the fact that many army men were not considered resisters, no matter what help they might have provided to the Resistance, because they remained loyal to Pétain until 1942.[13]

From Vichy, the network managed to recruit its earliest members and begin the process of collecting intelligence for the British. The ease with which the network could operate from Vichy became increasingly limited, however. Loustaunau-Lacau was dismissed from his position in the Légion française des combattants in November 1940 by Xavier Vallat, who was at the time its secretary-general and who would, in the spring of 1941, become the head of the Commissariat général aux questions juives, the administrative body that created and enforced Vichy's anti-Semitic laws. Although the arrest of Pierre Laval in December 1940 may have seemed to be a condemnation of his collaborationist policies, his eventual successor as the vice president of the council, Admiral François Darlan, pursued an even more energetic vision of collaboration with Nazi Germany, one that included military cooperation. At the same time that Darlan was agreeing to let the Germans use air bases in French Syria, Loustaunau-Lacau was attempting to expand and strengthen Alliance in French North Africa. By the end of May 1941 Darlan had spearheaded the negotiation of the Protocols of Paris, an agreement that was supposed to result in closer collaboration by allowing Germany more use of French military resources, especially in the empire.[14] That same month, Loustaunau-Lacau and Léon Faye, Alliance's third in command, were arrested in Algeria after having tried, unsuccessfully, to find a way to wrest control from Vichy in Algiers.

After their arrest, Loustaunau-Lacau was able to escape and make his way back to France. Both were charged with an attempt against the security of the state, and thanks to interventions from other military men, Faye was released after five months in prison. Loustaunau-Lacau, after being reapprehended in France, was sentenced by a military tribunal in 1941 to two years in prison and the confiscation of his goods for his suspected resistance activities. He was convicted based on testimony like that of one Commandant de Chassey, who reported overhearing a discussion between Loustaunau-Lacau and Faye about

> a military movement in North Africa to provoke the Germans, without delay and before an attack, suspected to be imminent; different methods to ensure the cooperation of General Weygand, methods such as the ones that follow: creation of a group of forces with the serious and indispensable assistance, both in personnel and matériel, of the Anglo-Americans, with the assistance of the British fleet; preparation, through his immediate entourage, of General Weygand, to acquire his voluntary participation; and, if needed, to "free the conscience" of General Weygand, the creation of a provocative incident or even the fabrication of false orders.[15]

Further evidence was provided to make sure that Loustaunau-Lacau was punished for what was seen as a betrayal of his former ideals. In a letter addressed to "Guillaume" from "Granier," the latter expresses his dismay over Loustaunau-Lacau's apparent decision to fight alongside the Anglo-American forces:

> I am writing to you on the advice of Colonel Groussard. Here is why: I have been relieved of my position as chief of staff of the 15th military division under the following circumstances. . . . Three weeks ago an old friend, the Commandant Loustaunau-Lacau, came to see me at my office. . . . I have known Loustaunau for ten years. . . . Like Groussard, I contributed to his revolutionary action . . . but I was perfectly ignorant of his actual activity . . . and living at Vichy, being received by General Laure and the Marshal, he was the last person I would suspect of actions against the external security of the State.[16]

It is ironic that poor M. Granier was being helped by Groussard without ever knowing that the colonel was becoming just as involved in anti-German action as Loustaunau-Lacau.

In a letter to Commandant Gruillot dated June 6, 1941, Loustaunau-Lacau did his best to defend himself against these accusations, while neither confirming nor denying the full extent of his resistance activities. He made certain to note that in 1941, "excluded from the State after having fought for five years at the vanguard, I continue to serve France as best as I can, following instructions that I try to find in my passionate love for the country."[17] While he freely admits in this letter to having revolted against those who had sought to weaken France in the interwar period, Loustaunau-Lacau carefully skirts the issue of whom he was revolting against after the defeat of 1940. He admits to having maintained ties with all sorts of prewar colleagues, including Groussard, Deloncle, Darnand, Doriot, Dorgères, Jeantet, and Maurras and mentions that these friends and others represented a wide range of political positions, ranging from pro-Germanism to Gaullism. Ever vigilant, Loustaunau-Lacau does not comment on his own position vis-à-vis the Germans or de Gaulle.

Loustaunau-Lacau had already named Marie-Madeleine Méric as his successor, thus ensuring that Alliance was never without a leader. Méric worried that the agents might not take her seriously, but Loustaunau-Lacau thought that a woman would be a perfect leader, as the Germans would never suspect such a thing.[18] Méric took the helm of Alliance and was assisted by Faye after his release from prison in October 1941. By that time, working in Vichy had become increasingly challenging. It was no secret that Méric and Loustaunau-Lacau had been close. In her memoirs, she recalls the many times she was called to one office or another at Vichy by people who wanted to either warn her or threaten her with their knowledge of her resistance activities.[19] The war had expanded in the summer of 1941 as Nazi Germany invaded the Soviet Union, leading the number of resisters in occupied Europe to swell as communists joined the clandestine struggle. In France, as resistance grew, Vichy adopted even more repressive internal policies. Alliance needed to be more careful than ever, and Méric moved the headquarters of the group several times to avoid detection and arrest.

In its earliest days, Alliance had dealt with numerous intelligence organizations, but as the war dragged on and loyalties solidified, information became increasingly proprietary. Because of the conflicts and competitions among the various services, it is often difficult to properly establish the chain of communication, but it seems that by the time Méric took over from Loustaunau-Lacau, Alliance was dealing mostly with the

British Secret Intelligence Service (SIS or MI6). SIS had two separate French sections, A.4 and A.5. The division came from the earliest days after the fall of France, when SIS chiefs realized that their only real French connections were to men and women serving under the Vichy regime. However, the SIS did not want to lose out on intelligence gathered under the auspices of de Gaulle's organization, so A.4 was instructed to continue mining the connections to Vichy, while A.5 was placed under Commander Kenneth Cohen and charged with making non-Vichy connections.[20] Although Alliance had contact with other organizations throughout the war, Méric's real contacts were with SIS. Unfortunately, this relationship has made the study of Alliance rather more complicated, as SIS records, unlike those of the Special Operations Executive, are still closed to researchers. There has been one authorized history of the SIS, but since it is still a functional intelligence agency it cannot be compelled to release its documents. However, the importance of Alliance to the SIS is made clear in the authorized history, where Méric's connections to the service are frequently invoked.

One of the most difficult and controversial operations undertaken by Alliance demonstrates both how vital the group was to the British war effort and also how strained its relationship with de Gaulle was.[21] In 1942, with Loustaunau-Lacau in jail and Marie-Madeleine Méric and Léon Faye at the helm of Alliance, the British sent a surprising radio message to the group's headquarters. This message stated that General Henri Giraud had escaped from Koenigstein, where he had been imprisoned since the beginning of the war, and asked Alliance to approach him to find out if he would serve the British. Méric recalled that "it crossed my mind that Churchill wanted to set up a rival to de Gaulle" and that she wondered whether the group should become involved in such a political affair.[22] Faye, however, was thrilled with such an idea and argued that Giraud would be perfect to lead a North African landing. In November, Alliance, in conjunction with the British and the Americans, helped get Giraud out of France on the *Seraph*, a British submarine, which took him to a seaplane that transported him to Gibraltar. Once there, Giraud met with General Eisenhower, and he became, as Marie-Madeleine Méric had prophesied, a thorn in de Gaulle's side, not to mention a divisive force within the larger Resistance.

The point when Giraud was brought to Eisenhower's side was a low moment for the Gaullists in London. American and British political and military leaders had been planning for an invasion of North Africa—the operation that would come to be known as Operation Torch—and this planning was kept secret from de Gaulle. Giraud, on the other hand, was told of the plans and even engaged in negotiations with Eisenhower and other American diplomats to ensure that he would be given military control of the French forces in North Africa once the operation was under way. Operation Torch took place on November 8, 1942, but Giraud refused to leave Gibraltar immediately. It soon became clear, however, that the surprising presence of François Darlan in Algeria might serve the Americans better than Giraud's presence there.[23] Indeed, it was Darlan who managed to persuade the French forces in North Africa to stop resisting the Allies, and he assumed the mantle of High Commissioner of West and North French Africa, supported by Roosevelt. This meant that "there were now three claimants to French sovereignty: the Vichy regime in France; Darlan in North Africa; de Gaulle in London."[24] De Gaulle, along with many other resisters, was furious about the Darlan deal. It was as if North Africa were still under the auspices of the Vichy regime.

Darlan was assassinated the following month, to be replaced by Giraud. While Giraud had not been complicit in the Vichy project, as Darlan had been, he was equally as conservative and in no rush to undo the many repressive laws that had been put in place by Vichy. De Gaulle and Giraud did not see eye to eye, and neither wanted to concede much in order to establish a working relationship. Giraud's overarching concern was making it possible for French forces to rejoin the war, while de Gaulle was already thinking about the political future and trying to prove to Allied leaders—Roosevelt in particular—that he had the legitimacy to speak for the French. Because of his military-mindedness and his refusal to fully denounce Vichy,[25] Giraud attracted around him people who were loyal to Vichy but hostile to the Germans, remnants of the armistice army, enemies of de Gaulle, and many supporters from the Right. Alliance's role in helping him get to Gibraltar definitely marked the network as being anti-Gaullist and played a role in alienating its members from other resistance forces during and after the war.

Although Alliance was a prominent *réseau* and suffered massive losses between 1940 and 1944, its leaders and the group as a whole could never quite shake their shady reputations. Leading up to the *cagoulard* trial of 1948, when Loustaunau-Lacau was once again arrested, many people testified to what seemed to be his dubious resistance activities. Roger Loriat, a deportee and secretary-general of the Fédération des déportés et internés de la Résistance, told the court that he had been charged with investigating extremist groups, in particular the Cagoule. During his investigation he had found that "for some time this organization seems to have resumed a certain activity under the impetus of Commandant Loustaunau-Lacau, former *cagoulard*, founder of the Légion française des combattants, founder and departmental leader of the Alliance network."[26] Loriat noted that Alliance was in fact still recruiting, which "allows people who did absolutely nothing during the occupation or whose activity was even pro-Vichy or collaborationist to pass themselves off as resisters."[27]

In fact, the *réseau* was an object of scrutiny even before the war ended. In 1944 the Bureau d'études des services spéciaux alliés et neutres undertook a lengthy study of Alliance and its leaders. The reason for this: "the political character of ALLIANCE, the particular circumstances of its creation, certain troubling aspects of the attitude of its leaders, necessitate a detailed study of its origins."[28] The study notes that Loustaunau-Lacau had been accused more than once of being a double agent and that his relationship with Pétain and Laval was troubling. The report on his character was also fairly uncomplimentary, calling him, above all, "un homme d'argent" and criticizing his enormous spending habits, particularly to keep Marie-Madeleine Méric, whom the report identified as his mistress, happy. Although the report never goes as far as questioning the actual resistance activity of the group, the tone is one of overwhelming suspicion. Its author ends by saying that "the foundations of the organization were built by the former *cagoulard* Loustaunau-Lacau and his secretary, Marie-Madeleine. From its creation, the movement was not only led, but also staffed, by former *cagoulards*. This cadre was then rounded out by various elements representing the political tendencies of the extreme Right."[29]

It seems that the rightist nature of Loustaunau-Lacau's group was its most noteworthy aspect. Many people who commented on Alliance, both during and after the war, indicated that this political characteristic was of the utmost importance. They did so simply by their emphasis on that subject in particular. Inspector Pierre Gervais noted in 1945 that

the political line followed by Loustaunau-Lacau has always been solidly reactionary. While he founded the Légion française des combattants in the Basses-Pyrénées, he also founded, at the same time, the resistance network Alliance. But in both these organizations he only solicited the cooperation of personalities on the right, members or fellow travelers of extreme parties or organizations, such as Henri Saut (deported to Germany, where he died), whose family was Action française, and he himself was considered to have belonged to the Cagoule.[30]

Others were less circumspect in their assessment of Loustaunau-Lacau and his resistance organization. In a folder of documents taken by the police from a General Baston at Vichy, we find a note that reads, "We find, in particular, the formal proof in a document entitled 'LOUSTAUNAU-LACAU'S THESIS' that the subject of interest considered collaboration with Germany, under the guise of patriotism, to be indispensable. It also proves (see paragraph 8) that Loustaunau-Lacau was directly engaged in intelligence with the enemy."[31] Equally damning and just as suspect, given that none of these documents were handwritten or signed by Loustaunau-Lacau, was the letter about the *réseau* Navarre outlining its goals in 1941.[32] These goals included restoring France's national integrity and fighting for the success of Pétain's National Revolution. Attached to this document is a note that reads as follows:

This document demonstrates that the Navarre network, created under the occupation, served, purely and simply, to camouflage the military Cagoule, whose goal was to help Pétain's National Revolution triumph. . . . It demonstrates that the Navarre network, far from being a resistance network, cannot be considered anything but part of the secret service of propaganda and intelligence, in favor of the Pétain government and acting with the complicity of the Légion des combattants.[33]

Part of the hostility toward Alliance came ultimately in response to its stance vis-à-vis de Gaulle. Loustaunau-Lacau and Méric both preferred to keep the organization far removed from the Gaullist groups. After the war, Méric noted that "with de Gaulle, this did not work: he wanted the networks placed directly under his orders, but L.L. [Loustaunau-Lacau] did not want to work with de Gaulle, since it seemed that he [de Gaulle] didn't recognize his authority, and he certainly didn't want to work under Passy, whom he regarded as a kid."[34] Even his fellow rightist resister Maurice Duclos pointed out just how bad the relationship was between Loustaunau-Lacau and de Gaulle. He commented that Loustaunau-Lacau "couldn't stand de Gaulle, his classmate at l'Ecole de Guerre. He hated him out of jealousy. De Gaulle was brilliant, he [Loustaunau-Lacau] believed himself to be brilliant. Characteristic of a ringleader, he always wanted to plot."[35] Loustaunau-Lacau's attitude toward the leader of the Free French is not surprising given the political differences between the two men and, perhaps, Loustaunau-Lacau's very character. It is clear that few of his contemporaries thought particularly highly of him, and most had something unflattering to say about him. In 1941, during the military tribunal, he was described as "an elite officer, a remarkable organizer, prodigiously lucid, and a born leader. Unfortunately he is a slight megalomaniac (a certain prophecy of Nostradamus had much influence on him), and he is also extremely stubborn and never wants to admit when he is wrong; this explains his character."[36]

Even though he had cooperated somewhat with the Gaullist forces, Loustaunau-Lacau's anti-Gaullism continued to be a fundamental aspect of his political viewpoint, particularly after the war. Like many others on the extreme right, Loustaunau-Lacau responded very negatively to the publication of the first volume of de Gaulle's war memoirs in 1954. As Christopher Flood and Hugo Frey point out in their article about the reaction to the memoirs, most extreme rightists felt not only that de Gaulle was distorting history with his account of the war but also that he was actively creating further divisions in French society by insisting that the Resistance had been the only true manifestation of patriotism during the war years.[37] As we have seen, though, it was not only collaborators who disliked the man and the way he portrayed the war. There was a wide

range of anti-Gaullist sentiments, and although right-wing, Vichyist anti-
Gaullism was the most virulent, many resistance leaders also resented
de Gaulle's portrayal of *les années noires*. Julian Jackson writes that "it
was hardest for the non-Communist Resistance to find a satisfactory
interpretation of the past between the two monoliths of Communist and
Gaullist memory."[38] These difficulties were particularly explicit after the
Liberation, when both resisters and former Vichy supporters were trying
to establish how Pétain should be represented in the story of France's
experiences during the Occupation.

The fact that Alliance and its leaders never quite fit with the rest of the
Resistance, both interior and exterior, was a cause for concern on both sides
even before the war ended. We have already seen the skepticism with which
other resisters viewed the organization, but the concern about how they
would be judged after the war was not far from the minds of the Alliance
leaders either. Méric, in a letter to Commandant Manuel in 1944, explained the group's continued distance from de Gaulle and her demands
for autonomy:

> Considering that it was impossible and childish to deny the existence of the
> Vichy administration, accepted at the time by a majority of the French (especially
> given that three of what would become the "Big Four" recognized the Pétain
> government and established diplomatic relationships with it), Commandant
> Loustaunau-Lacau wanted to construct, inside and under the shelter of that
> institution, an anti-German war machine, attached at its head to the Gaullist
> organization.[39]

She argued that this actually allowed Alliance to succeed, for it was able to
recruit people who might otherwise not have cooperated with de Gaulle
because of their loyalty to Pétain. She went on to say, however, that because of this and because of the nature of Alliance's work, she had some
concerns about the postwar years:

> To accomplish their mission of gathering intelligence, career soldiers, reserve
> soldiers, and bureaucrats accepted orders to take or retain positions that placed
> them in personal contact with the enemy or his agents. Also, these proven patriots
> have degrading relationships with men notoriously labeled as collaborators
> with the enemy. They all assume the risk of being sentenced to banishment

or death if their good faith is not established in time. A dossier of all Alliance personnel will be held in London, to safeguard these people.[40]

And indeed this concern was warranted. Certainly, Loustaunau-Lacau was not treated particularly well after the war. Although he never regretted his wartime activities, he was bitter about the way the rightist *résistants* were treated in the postwar period. He wrote, "If you think that a man who has done his duty as a Frenchman and an officer of the Resistance, but whose anti-Marxist convictions are irreducible, has the right, upon returning from war, to express himself in writing, you are fooling yourself."[41] Even more serious than his inability to speak his mind, however, was his rearrest as the police prepared for the resumption of the *cagoulard* trial. The sense that his and others' resistance activity was spurious came through quite clearly in many of the pretrial reports and investigations. After an inquest into the wartime activity of the *cagoulards*, one investigator concluded, "In each of these lists we find men who eventually came to help the resistance movements, either because they believed that the Marshal was playing this famous double game, as so many traitors have claimed, or because they thought that after Germany was defeated they could create the kind of government they had dreamed of while plotting against the Republic."[42]

Loustaunau-Lacau himself complained about the lack of respect afforded him during the trial and wrote a lengthy declaration stating just that:

> It doesn't seem excessive to think that if Justice in this country can freely exercise its prerogatives, she owes it to the men who, in 1940, were the founders of various serious resistance networks. It is the greatest honor of my life to count myself as one of these men.
>
> Also, with much bitterness, I can state that the services I was able to render in this resistance and the suffering I endured because of my actions do not shelter me from the sort of persecution that persists, for noncriminal acts back in 1937 concerning a state that had miserably collapsed, against the founder and leader of a network that counts 420 dead and that represented, at the end of 1942, half of the military intelligence about the German Army occupying France being sent to London, while the saboteurs of the morale in the army did not even worry about it.

I must add that the costs of a criminal charge are not welcome for a man from whom the Germans took everything, who is already obliged to deal with the care necessitated by the wounds of 1940 and the stay at Mauthausen, and who needs to re-create from scratch the Société d'éditions, which would allow him to live.

Once again, if it is permitted to me, let me reaffirm on my military honor that the Corvignolles organization, which I was responsible for creating, had nothing to do with the CSAR, that I never belonged to that terrorist organization, and that its work in the army was stopped by my insurmountable opposition.

The day will come when homage will be rendered to the patriotism that always guided me on the field of battle, in the Resistance, and during the dreadful ordeal of the Hitlerian camps.

It seems impossible that in these conditions, the judges, who will understand my actions and the motives that always animated them, will maintain a charge that is odious to me.[43]

Just as he never denied his creation of the Corvignolles, Loustaunau-Lacau never denied his rightist politics. The only aspects of his political life that he ever repudiated were his alleged relationship with the Cagoule and the suggestion that he had ever intended to overthrow the Third Republic. Even though he was "considered to be very dangerous in Republican circles and he enjoy[ed], politically, a very bad reputation,"[44] Loustaunau-Lacau never admitted to any plan to replace the republic with any other form of government. However, his extraparliamentary activities were ceaseless, and his political stance never changed.

Through all these ventures and into his years in the Resistance his basic political stance remained constant. Above all, he believed that the communists must be prevented from corrupting the army and taking any power. As Loustaunau-Lacau himself admitted, however, this task was made difficult by the system of parliamentary democracy that seemed to protect the communists and malign the army. Perhaps the war and the suspension of democracy that came with it allowed a certain amount of freedom for Loustaunau-Lacau to continue his political battle. He and Marie-Madeleine Méric fundamentally disagreed on Alliance's role almost from the first days of its existence. She was suspicious about attaching the group to the Légion, and although he had many good reasons to do so initially, Méric (and her biographer, Michèle Cointet) eventually wondered whether Loustaunau-Lacau's insistence on being in Vichy masked bigger political ambitions.[45] Even his decision to go to North Africa proved to be a sticking point for the Alliance chiefs. He was convinced that it was the right time, politically and militarily, to foment rebellion in Algeria. Méric argued that intelligence and politics were incompatible. According to Cointet, Méric "came to understand that a world separated them: for her, the interior resistance, the meticulous intelligence; for him, political exploitation of large strategic movements."[46] Loustaunau-Lacau's taste for political adventure had not changed much, nor had his political viewpoints. Although he vehemently claimed never to have wanted a coup, his dislike of the Republic cannot be questioned. Loustaunau-Lacau wrote in his memoirs that "we were not a *cagoulard*, but an ardent patrol on the frontiers of an army neglected by its minister and poorly defended by its leaders. We were resisters *avant la lettre*."[47]

What, then, motivated this fervently anticommunist, antirepublican, conservative army officer to resist the German occupation from the first hour? We can certainly argue that the war accentuated patterns of behavior that had been formed in the 1930s and allowed for a certain amount of continuity after the defeat.[48] Although this explains the behavior of collaborationists, it also begins to explain why a soldier like Loustaunau-Lacau would choose to resist. He was, in effect, not acting any differently than he had during the previous decade. Loustaunau-Lacau was considered subversive by the Third Republic, and because he refused to fundamentally change his values or his behavior, he continued to be subversive in the new situation. His commitment to the French Army and its integrity was bound to be seen as a challenge to the new authority of both the Vichy regime and the occupying forces. Present too was a certain degree of obstinacy among the first resisters, who had an unusually strong conviction that they were right even in the face of more practical arguments.[49] This characteristic does seem to apply to Loustaunau-Lacau, who had single-mindedly applied himself for many years to the task of neutralizing the communists even though evidence of their "plans" to destabilize France was scarce, to say the least. Loustaunau-Lacau was not alone among military men in having been a severe critic of the parliamentary system and the political parties in the 1930s and yet maintaining a military-mindedness that fueled his resistance.[50] A sense of duty and patriotism was partial motivation for the clandestine activities that these men would undertake during the war, activities that were all directed at ridding the country of the foreign invader.

Henri Michel mistakenly argues that all the career soldiers of the Resistance shared a distrust of clandestine warfare and therefore an inaptitude for it.[51] This inaptitude for clandestine warfare does not apply to a soldier like Loustaunau-Lacau, who was quite accustomed to operating in the shadows because his self-appointed crusade was unacceptable to the majority of Third Republic politicians. There are several reasons why resisters of the first hour were a minority and why people with a particular background might make that step into disobedience more easily. Not everyone could dismiss legality very easily, and "total immersion in clandestinity, the ultimate degree of the entrance into resistance, was not done without a sense of vertigo."[52] This step into clandestinity had numerous, sometimes contradictory effects on the resister: "the intoxication of illegality, the perils, the certainty of making history marks individuals, who paradoxically experience a powerful sense of freedom, the joy of nomadism, the fears and the attractions of a life out of the ordinary."[53] As we have seen, Loustaunau-Lacau was no stranger to clandestinity and secrecy. His creation and leadership of the Corvignolles, his dealings with other shady characters of the turbulent Third Republic years, his Croisade and Spiralien movements, and his participation in Alliance all suggest that he thrived on semiconspiratorial political movements. He fits best, perhaps, with a group of *résistants*, "patriotes réactionnaires," who thrived on the clandestine nature of the Resistance. These men were undoubtedly opposed to the defeat, but they were also elitist, often anti-Semitic, and not entirely against the National Revolution.[54] More importantly, they enjoyed, both in the interwar years and during the war, "a microsociety that had its own rules [and] its own autonomous mode of operation."[55] It is likely that Loustaunau-Lacau belonged to this group of resisters.

Another consistent aspect of Loustaunau-Lacau's politics was his Germanophobia. In 1946 Marie-Alexis Mermet, a retired colonel, testified that Loustaunau-Lacau had indeed been heavily involved in right-wing politics but that "he insisted particularly on the German danger."[56] Given Loustaunau-Lacau's former position in the German section of the Deux- ième Bureau, it seems likely that he was more knowledgeable about Germany and Nazism than others. Having previous knowledge of Nazi Germany often created a hostility to it, which was deepened by the expe- rience of living among the enemy during the Occupation, as in the case of Défense de la France, another resistance organization with rightist tendencies.[57] Loustaunau-Lacau claimed that he had never doubted that the Germans planned to overturn the Treaty of Versailles and would once again take up arms: "If anyone had any illusions about the Boche, it wasn't I."[58] Loustaunau-Lacau spent many years during the 1920s and 1930s investigating the evolution of the German infantry. In his memoirs he notes that "a thousand indications proved that the Germans were trying to reestablish the framework of imperial mobilization while waiting until political circumstances became favorable for them to fill it."[59] Although his Germanophobia was not as virulent as some other rightists', Loustaunau- Lacau would never forget that he had spent the majority of his life either fighting the Germans or preparing to do so. He admonishes his readers to "never forget that it is the only country in the world that dared to use a death's head as a stamp."[60]

This anti-German sentiment was made worse by the fact that Loustaunau-Lacau had had the misfortune of being delivered to the Ge- stapo and deported to Mauthausen. Although he escaped from prison after his initial arrest in 1941, his desire to see his family led the police right to him a second time. He would spend the rest of the war in the camp, and Méric took over his network—the only woman to lead a *réseau*, making Alliance even more unique. Even though Loustaunau-Lacau headed the organization for only a short time, the *réseau* was significantly marked by his leadership and influenced by his politics. Because he had been its leader during the important phase of recruitment and because its agents were indeed recruited from some of his prewar circles, it is fair to say that the network retained some rightist characteristics all through the war. When Loustaunau-Lacau returned to France at the end of the war, by all accounts severely weakened by his time in Mauthausen, it became apparent that his political views had changed little, though postwar life did present some new opportunities for expressing those views.

In an interesting turn of affairs, Georges Loustaunau-Lacau was elected to the National Assembly in 1951. Given his history, his participation in parliamentary politics seems to indicate a change of heart vis-à-vis the republican institutions against which he had fought for so many years. However, his decision likely reflects larger changes that took place in both the practice and the philosophy of the Right after 1945. The Right had a difficult time reestablishing itself in the postwar years. Not only were there the traditional schisms within the various right-wing parties but the Right was handicapped by the double obstacle of the links, whether real or imagined, between itself and Vichy and the reluctance on the part of the French to rally to social conservatism, to say nothing of more reactionary ideologies.[61] Any hint of Pétainism was an electoral liability, and there was no question of extraparliamentary organizations achieving any level of success.

This situation began to change between 1947 and 1951, as the Right struggled to reclaim political space both within and outside the parliament. Surprisingly, the members of the truly extreme Right and the more traditional parliamentary Right came up with the same arguments to legitimize their presence in postwar politics. The central aspect of this argument was that the Vichy régime, for any flaws it might have had, was a legal product of the Third Republic, not a putsch. Alongside this argument was the one that maintained that the armistice allowed certain people the opportunity to keep fighting, which they would not have had if the Germans had immediately occupied the whole of France. For the extreme Right, which had traditionally despised the *pays légal*, this Pétain apologia changed their stance regarding legality. As Richard Vinen points out, there was increasing enthusiasm for the republic, on which legality was founded.[62] It was a way for many people, including Loustaunau-Lacau and other prominent rightist resisters, to explain their denunciation of de Gaulle and their general support for Pétain without tarnishing their resistance records or becoming further ostracized. As Loustaunau-Lacau argued at Pétain's trial, "I owe nothing to Pétain, but that doesn't stop me from being nauseated by the spectacle of those, in this room, who are trying to make an old man pay for their mistakes."[63] Even the more moderate Right was forced to rely on the legality of Vichy to try to avoid the blame for the downfall of the Third Republic. Their argument, according to Henry Rousso, was that "to condemn the Vichy regime was to condemn the Third Republic, because the first was nothing but a constitutional creation of the second."[64]

This newfound "respect" for the *pays légal*, as self-serving as it might have been, changed the face of the post-1945 Right. As Vinen argues, the new extreme Right, because of its emphasis on legality, its internationalism, and its enthusiasm for America, easily fit into the new political system.[65] As the communists came to be seen as increasingly suspect and were pushed away from the nucleus of power, there were fewer and fewer reasons for a man like Loustaunau-Lacau to stay out of parliamentary politics. At the helm of the resurgent extreme Right was Jacques Isorni, Pétain's legal counsel and defender, who led the Union des nationaux indépendants et républicains into the elections of 1951. Loustaunau-Lacau was one of the few "nostalgiques de Vichy" to be elected when he stood with the Union des français indépendants, and once he was in the Assembly he allied himself with the Groupe paysan.[66] (The absorption of the Groupe paysan into the Indépendants created the Centre national des indépendants et paysans—CNIP—to which Loustaunau-Lacau continued to belong.) Although the CNIP is generally seen as the more liberal of the then emerging rightist parties, Loustaunau-Lacau's politics seem not to have changed. His biography on the National Assembly website indicates that he was generally critical of both France's foreign policy and its military policy.[67] He fought against the rearming of Germany and the restoration of her sovereignty. He was hostile to the idea of Franco-German cooperation and thus disdainful of the European Defense Community and the European Coal and Steel Community. In short, Loustaunau-Lacau continued to distrust the Germans, continued to privilege the French military, and continued to criticize the republic.

The minutes of the National Assembly sessions from 1951 to 1955 reflect Loustaunau-Lacau's participation in all these discussions, often in the face of extreme hostility from his colleagues, particularly those on the left. His openly antagonistic relationship with communist deputies reads as the most puerile of stories, but Loustaunau-Lacau was more often than not at the receiving end of this antagonism. One deputy in particular, Fernand Grenier, led the most frequent attacks against Loustaunau-Lacau. Literally every time Loustaunau-Lacau spoke, Grenier and the bench of communist deputies would shout "fascist" and demand to know about Loustaunau-Lacau's role in the murders of the Rosselli brothers. Although these attacks quickly become repetitive, it is worth reproducing one here to illustrate the relationship between these men and their respective benches. In this particular discussion, the communist deputies originally complain of abuses in the electoral system, and Grenier asks if it is legal for Isorni to present his list of candidates, which he believes has the sole purpose of rehabilitating the men and politics of Vichy. Grenier goes on to talk about the Resistance in 1940 and how its members were persecuted by the French police.

> *M. Georges Loustaunau-Lacau.* You do not have the right to talk about a communist resistance before the 22nd of June 1941. Before that date we did not meet you in the Resistance [*protests from the extreme Left—various movements*].
> *M. Jean Pronteau.* M. Loustaunau-Lacau, the *cagoulard* and the traitor!
> *M. Le Président.* Coming back to the debate.
> *M. Georges Loustaunau-Lacau.* I do want to render homage to your resistance, Monsieur Grenier, but not before the hour when it started.
> *M. Fernand Grenier.* Monsieur Loustaunau-Lacau, in response to your interruptions, allow me to tell you that I know you as a man about whom many people spoke regarding a plot that actually existed at the moment of the Popular Front.
> *M. Georges Loustaunau-Lacau.* About the destruction of your communist cells in the army, which I denounced because they were responsible for the defeat of 1940 [*applause from various benches*].
> *Numerous voices from the extreme Left.* Cagoulard! Cagoulard!
> *M. Fernand Grenier.* We know that the Cagoule . . .
> *M. Le Président.* All this is outside the debate.
> *Grenier.* . . . was capable of blowing up the building of the French Employers on the rue de Presbourg to make it seem that the guilty parties belonged to the C.G.T.
> *L.L.* It's you the communist Cagoule, the Cagoule in the army [*lively interruptions from the extreme Left*].[68]

This exchange ends with Loustaunau-Lacau being accused by the communists of having worked for the Boche in 1940, although most of the time Grenier preferred to accuse him of being an Italian agent working for the OVRA, the Italian secret police.[69]

It was not only in the chambers of the National Assembly that Loustaunau-Lacau was under attack in the postwar years. The PCF also waged a media war against him in *L'Humanité*. Loustaunau-Lacau's comments in one Assembly meeting suggest that he took legal action against the newspaper for its campaign against him. He noted to Fernand Grenier, "I have had you condemned in the appeal court, as in the trial court, for this insult of *cagoulard*. Monsieur Grenier, you can repeat this insult because you run no risk, but you cannot write it in *L'Humanité*, because your journal has been warned by the presiding judge that there will be a fine of a million francs if it starts again."[70] This fact, however, did nothing to stop Grenier's attacks, which continued right up until Loustaunau-Lacau's death.

Loustaunau-Lacau was also accused of having participated in the so-called Plan Bleu of 1947. This plot shared many similarities with that developed by the Cagoule in the prewar years, as it was, generally speaking, a right-wing organization seeking to overthrow the government under the guise of ensuring that the communists did not take power in France. France in 1947 was suffering economically and the communists staged massive strikes across the country demanding increased wages. Contrary to this demand, the socialist prime minister, Paul Ramadier, put a freeze on wages and ousted the communists from his cabinet. While these political maneuverings were taking place within the government, some members of the extreme Right were developing the ambitious Plan Bleu. Daniele Ganser argues that this plan was part of a larger pan-European movement coordinated by NATO and the CIA that organized clandestine armies all over the continent to resist communism.[71] According to Ganser, in France the secret network of anticommunists included many members of the police and of the military secret service of the Service de documentation extérieure et de contre espionnage (SDECE), and "the Blue Plan, in other words, aimed to prevent France from turning red."[72] The plan was exposed on June 30, 1947, by the socialist minister of the interior, Edouard

Depreux, who explained, "Towards the end of 1946 we got to know of the existence of a black resistance network, made up of resistance fighters of the extreme right, Vichy collaborators and monarchists."[73]

It is true that all these groups of individuals were involved in the creation of the Plan Bleu, but Jean-Marie Augustin points out that there were only a few Vichyistes and that the majority of the conspirators were former maquisards, often from the Armée secrète, and that they fondly remembered the Resistance's climate of clandestine struggle.[74] He does not place the conspiracy in any larger context. Instead, the Plan Bleu seems to have been a uniquely French plan, with the comte de Vulpian and Roger Aurouet de Mervelce at its head, though Augustin presents the comte de Vulpian as a bit naïve and useful more for his financial support than for anything else. The plan was just as disorganized as that concocted by the Cagoule in the 1930s, and although it may have held some attraction for Loustaunau-Lacau given that its members wanted to create "a psychological element which stands opinion against the Communist Party and allows, in frightening the population, the legitimization of insurrectionary operations in presenting them as measures of self-defense,"[75] we already know that he found that kind of conspirator both somewhat childish and dangerous at the same time.

Loustaunau-Lacau's police file certainly notes his involvement in the plan, although it was never proven. As Augustin notes in his book on the Plan Bleu, the same judge (Levy) led the postwar investigations into both the Cagoule and the Plan Bleu. "In his [Levy's] mind and that of Edouard Depreux," writes Augustin, "Commandant Loustaunau-Lacau, destroyer of communists and great lover of covert action, could not be a stranger to such conspiracies."[76] Loustaunau-Lacau's implication in the plot seems to have been based solely on the sense that he could not have resisted such an opportunity. Augustin confirms this by noting that Levy's evidence of Loustaunau-Lacau's involvement rested on his one meeting with the comte de Vulpian at a banquet in 1945. This banquet, apparently organized by Loustaunau-Lacau, brought together many members of the Breton resistance, many of whom were noted for their rightist sentiments.[77] His conversation with the comte de Vulpian was no more nor less conspiratorial than the rest of the evening's conversation, which focused on ways to prevent the communists from taking control. That Loustaunau-Lacau would continue to be involved in anticommunist activity of one kind or another should come as no surprise, but it does not prove his complicity in the Plan Bleu.

One reason for the ongoing hostility between Loustaunau-Lacau and the PCF was, quite simply, their respective positions on key issues of the postwar years. The discussion in 1951 about the potential ratification of the European Coal and Steel Community illuminates these problems. Loustaunau-Lacau was the reporter for the commission of National Defense. In explaining to the National Assembly why the commission was passing along *un avis défavorable* on the ratification, he conveniently neglected to mention that the communists had voted in favor of the ratification. In fact, the bloc voting against the ratification had only won by a margin of six votes.[78] Yet Loustaunau-Lacau was unequivocal in presenting the opposition to the treaty. He noted that it was childish to assume that economic issues could be separated from military ones and that the proposed law would give the High Authority (in which France would be a minority) the right to collect information from key industries, which would make it impossible to keep national defense matters secret. Moreover, he was very concerned about the fact that the treaty would give supremacy to the Ruhr. "I shouldn't have to mention that if Germany initiates a united Europe, we should not be surprised if Europe takes on a German accent," he commented.[79] Among the many reasons why Loustaunau-Lacau was uncomfortable with establishing links with Germany was the fact of the communist influence in half of the country. While not wanting to doubt the good intentions of Western Germany, he argued that "first we have to consider that a treaty concluded with a nation that is occupied at the same time and from both ends by powers that are in a state of constant friction, cut in two by a demarcation line that is even less permeable than the one we have known, and, what is more, is unstable in its essence, in which the majority of phrases end with the word *werden,* which we know is so torn by conflicting currents, such a treaty, I say, is like a dialogue between trees and the wind."[80] It is clear from these statements that Loustaunau-Lacau had not become any less suspicious of Germany and perhaps had become even more so with the establishment of communist control over her eastern half.

This double-edged sword of Loustaunau-Lacau's traditional Germanophobia and his hatred of communism became even more vitriolic as the National Assembly discussed the idea of a European army and German rearmament in 1952. He remained opposed to both proposals until his death. The furthest Loustaunau-Lacau would go was to suggest that perhaps Germany could slowly be integrated into the United Nations, but he maintained that a common defense agenda would, in effect, dig the graves of French soldiers. Partially this was because of the communist presence, as Loustaunau-Lacau basically argued that Germans would desert the European army, particularly if the order were given to retake the Eastern borders. As he said to the Assembly, "Desert? It would not be to betray that a German would quit the European army to rejoin his comrades, the comrades of a clandestine mobilization. It would not be to betray, it would be doing one's duty. . . . Open the dictionary ("Saxon: inhabitant of Saxony. Figurative expression: the one who changed sides"). . . . You will find yourself paralyzed by your European army because you will not get Germans to fight against Germans."[81] As these statements show, Loustaunau-Lacau was worried that should the European army ever find itself in a conflict with the Eastern bloc, it would be virtually impossible to keep the Western German soldiers engaged in a battle against their fellow countrymen.

In addition to his concern about the communists, Loustaunau-Lacau had a long-standing suspicion of the Germans, particularly the German Army. He was quick to point out that although the Reichswehr had been fairly well-behaved during the war, the same could not be said of the rest of the German military machine. Noting the atrocities committed by the Germans, Loustaunau-Lacau commented that "already the general von Gille, commander of the Wiking SS division, travels around Germany setting conditions other than M. Adenauer's for Germany's rearmament and the European army. He says, 'First morally rehabilitate the SS in the eyes of the world.' Well! Let them rehabilitate themselves; they can't count on my signature, nor those of the three thousand men we left on the floor of Buchenwald and Mauthausen in April 1945."[82] Loustaunau-Lacau's refusal to forgive the Germans is not surprising. Even leaving aside his experience with the Germans in two world wars and his traditional Germanophobia, the repercussions of his years in the concentration camps were enough to make it impossible for him to forgive. From all accounts, his health was severely compromised by his experience in the camps, which ultimately led to his early death in 1955. It is no wonder, then, that he was unwilling to grant the former members of the Nazi structure any amnesty for their crimes. Moreover, it seems that Loustaunau-Lacau was not convinced that what had happened in 1939 would not happen again. A further continuity is found in his conviction that France was making many of the same mistakes in the early 1950s that it had in the 1930s but that these later mistakes would have even more fatal consequences.

In 1953 Loustaunau-Lacau explicitly told the Assembly, "We are returning exactly to where we were in 1936, when we committed two major errors, the first, from a strategic point, a military error thanks to general Gamelin and the Superior War Council; the second, a complete financial error, which was to oppose the German autarky with the means of a normal budget. We are today committing these same mistakes; we will suffer the same disadvantages."[83] With a somewhat apocalyptic view, however, Loustaunau-Lacau impressed upon his colleagues that in the changed world of warfare the first blow would be a fatal one owing to the development of atomic weapons. He passionately called for further spending for atomic research and emphasized the need to protect French citizens from what he saw as an inevitable conflict between the United States and the Soviet Union. Quoting Albert Einstein, Loustaunau-Lacau noted that "there will be no atomic war, there will only be an atomic battle." And he went on to say that "if you are not ready for the atomic battle, it is absolutely pointless to prepare for other battles."[84] In response to some of his colleagues' emphasis on nonaggression, Loustaunau-Lacau said that it was a useless stance. "Nobody has the right anymore to say that they will be the aggressor or the non-aggressor. . . . Knowing that the first blow is lethal, we must decide if one is condemned to be killed or if one is condemned to be the aggressor. Here is the philosophical point that is raised by the atom. It is not enough to state your feelings, you must take a stand: Do we accept being destroyed first."[85]

Another clear continuity from Loustaunau-Lacau's prewar attitudes was his ongoing support for the French Empire. In the 1930s a central aspect of his Spiralien Movement had been "imperial cohesion." He had seen the consolidation of the French Empire as heroic in its attempt to give authority and structure to a less-evolved people. He had been quick to note, however, that it was false to claim that France was a nation of 100 million inhabitants; it was instead a nation of 40 million inhabitants who controlled a number of ethnic groups.[86] And while he had wanted the people of France and her overseas territories to live harmoniously, he had argued that it would be a racial crime to try to integrate these ethnic groups into the national collective. While he had believed that integration could not (or should not) take place, this had not lessened the importance of the empire for Loustaunau-Lacau. These attitudes did not change after the war, as is made clear by his statement in the National Assembly that "Algeria is France. There is no difference."[87]

Loustaunau-Lacau was not alone in this sentiment: many former resisters from the right and the left were absolutely wedded to the idea of the French Empire and saw no contradiction between their resistance activities during the war and the ongoing control over the overseas territories. In one 1953 session of the National Assembly, Loustaunau-Lacau told Pierre Mendès-France:

> It would be good, I think, if you would take a definitive position, even more clear than what was in your inaugural speech, by inserting into your final answer to us a sentence that could be as follows: "True to the spirit of the Resistance, my government will defend to the end, by authoritarian means if necessary, the moral heritage, the effective and efficient presence, and, in principle, the sovereignties and protectorates that the Third Republic has bequeathed to us in North Africa and in the French Union. I will keep her commitments vis-à-vis those people who confided in her, and whom she took charge of, their physical protection and their evolution toward greater maturity, social justice, and well-being."[88]

That Loustaunau-Lacau was protective of the colonies should come as no surprise, not least because of his overwhelming concern with all things related to the army. He continued to be supportive of the army's actions, even in the face of criticism, during these troubled years in the colonies. In 1952, during a discussion about allowing the combatants from the Korean and Indochinese wars the same benefits as other veterans, the communists in the National Assembly were quick to oppose the idea. The deputy Robert Manceau stated that "we are opposed to this, and allow me to say that it would be unjust and hurtful to the combattants of 1914–18 and 1939–45 for them to be subject to the same scheme as those who fight for a cause that in our view is foreign to the interests of France."[89] Loustaunau-Lacau promptly retorted that the army in Indochina was the best army they had seen in twenty years. This was perhaps a bit of an exaggeration, but it does show the lengths to which Loustaunau-Lacau would go to support the army. After his death in 1955, *Le Monde* reported that "M. Loustaunau-Lacau intervened, in public sessions, in all the debates that concerned national defense, whether they were about its organization, its budget, the war in Indochina, or the European army. His witty eloquence, often colorful, did not shy away from puns and even bawdy stories."[90]

Right before his death, Loustaunau-Lacau seems to have made several trips to Poland to take part in a "Conférence internationale pour la solution pacifique du problème allemand." In a speech given in the National Assembly after Loustaunau-Lacau's death, Pierre Schnieter noted that

> on October 8, 1954, regarding the foreign policy of the government, he [Loustaunau-Lacau] recommended a policy of mutual understanding between East and West; it was in this spirit that he went several times to Warsaw. The impression that he left there was so great that the president of the Sejm of the People's Republic of Poland took time to send me a touching telegram of condolences, for which I thanked him. And this last visit was, indeed, the last effort of our colleague.[91]

In *Le Monde,* the author of Loustaunau-Lacau's obituary clearly felt that these trips were of some significance, reporting that "he participated on several occasions in trips to Poland. The impressions that he brought back gave rise to lively controversies: he was attacked in particular by some of his political friends."[92] Although it has been nearly impossible to discover just what these impressions were, they certainly seemed to have been

favorable toward Poland. The death of Stalin in 1953, the release of Wlady-
slaw Gomulka, former secretary-general of the Communist Party in Poland
and advocate of "humane Marxism," in 1954, and the significant easing of
party control certainly inched Poland toward a more democratic place.
A reassessment of Soviet-Polish relations, along with Gomulka's insistence that Poland's national interests be upheld, certainly meant that the
door was open for increased cooperation between Poland and the West.
Loustaunau-Lacau's biography on the National Assembly website notes
that in 1954 he "returned several times to the idea of necessary dialogue
with the Soviet Union, believing that the tendency for conciliation that
was manifesting at the moment on the Soviet side should not leave France
indifferent."[93] It is no wonder that his political friends may have attacked
him for such views, but one does wonder how exactly Loustaunau-Lacau
came to advocate for even a partial reconciliation with the communists
after so many years of violent anticommunism. It is certainly possible
that he was hoping to further open the doors to the Western world in
the hope that communism in Poland would fall naturally, though this is
pure hypothesis.

Although he had never escaped the stigma of having associated with all
sorts of adventurers and charlatans, Loustaunau-Lacau was rehabilitated,
so to speak, in the later years of his life and certainly after his death. After
he legitimized many of his political positions by integrating himself into
the parliamentary system, Loustaunau-Lacau's death brought him even
further vindication, too late, certainly, but still significant. He was post-
humously awarded the promotion to general, to date back to December
25, 1945, explicitly in reparation for the prejudice suffered by him in 1938,
when he had been forced into nonactivity. Whether or not one imagines
Loustaunau-Lacau's activities in the 1930s to have been legitimate is not
important. The reality is that he created secret networks of anticommunist
vigilantes within the structure of the army, explicitly adding to the politicization of that institution at a time when military-civilian relationships
were already strained. It would seem that his "dismissal" was a perfectly
straightforward reaction to these activities. The promotion of 1955 was
surely based in part on his activities during the war, but the fact that it
was postdated is curious. Although Loustaunau-Lacau continued to be

the object of police investigations and press denunciations, the military hierarchy seemed to have forgiven any earlier indiscretions on his part.

Perhaps this forgiveness was partially owing to the fact that Loustaunau-Lacau never recovered from his time spent in the German camps during the war. His relatively early death was directly related to the health issues arising from his captivity. Even the normally unsympathetic Paris police noted in 1951 that after being liberated by the Americans, Loustaunau-Lacau returned to France in a precarious state of health.[94] Many people commented on how much weight he had lost, though, as we have seen, this did not keep him from an ongoing and vigorous involvement in public life. But on February 11, 1955, Loustaunau-Lacau became ill at the Palais-Bourbon and was taken to his house, where he suffered a fatal heart attack. A week after his death, Pierre Schneiter, in his homage to Loustaunau-Lacau at the National Assembly, noted that he had left a void that would be hard to fill. While his speech was laudatory, Schneiter made clear that Loustaunau-Lacau had lived a life "outside the ordinary."[95] Schneiter went on to say that Loustaunau-Lacau's early career choices marked him for life.

> The greatest leaders of our army appealed to his skills. His life as a soldier then took a particular direction that would mark him for the rest of his life: he entered the intelligence services, that is to say, that category of service in which one is designated only by a number or initials and one's action must remain unknown to the general public. This kind of work is largely thankless. However, it requires a rare combination of qualities: a lively intelligence that knows no bounds, decisiveness, shrewdness, courage too, not to mention a taste for risk and adventure, because in such positions there is but one law: to succeed. It also happens that while satisfying one's superiors, one becomes vulnerable. This was the fate of Loustaunau-Lacau, who on March 2, 1938, was laid off.[96]

Like some others, Schneiter seemed inclined to chalk Loustaunau-Lacau's persecution up to something other than his involvement in conspiratorial activities.

Loustaunau-Lacau's funeral at the Invalides on February 15, 1955, also seems to suggest that he had been reintegrated into the military and political world with some success. The Paris police report of that day notes that "the coffin erected in the chancel, on a bier, was surrounded by an honor guard of former members of the 'Alliance' network and the flags and pennants of the 'Honneur-Alliance,' 'Réseaux Forces Combattantes,' 'Comité d'Action de la Résistance' associations."[97] That his former colleagues in the Resistance were in attendance to bestow honors on Loustaunau-Lacau is not surprising, but the list of other attendees might be considered more so. The minister of national defense was there, and, somewhat ironically, so was the minister of justice. Many deputies and senators were in attendance as well, along with many prominent military men. Generals Georges-Picot; de Larminat; Monclar; Henri Zeller, the military governor of Paris at the time; and Augustin Guillaume, the *résident général au Maroc,* were all part of the military contingent at the funeral. These men did not simply represent the army; many of them were celebrated Resistance heroes as well. For all that, however, Loustaunau-Lacau's Resistance credentials continue to be questioned or ignored.

FROM VICHY TO EXILE

Alliance was certainly not the only resistance organization to make its debut in Vichy only to find that as domestic circumstances changed, the heart of the regime became increasingly dangerous for resisters. Deciding whether to stay or leave was often challenging, however. One of the most complicating factors was that the Vichy regime was never a homogenous government, as we have seen. One minister might be rabidly antiresistance, another more lenient. The reality was often somewhere in between, as Vichy bureaucrats had complex perspectives on resistance activity. Memoirs written by rightist resisters are replete with examples of Vichy authorities either turning a blind eye to their resistance efforts or even warning them of upcoming investigations or roundups to give them time to take evasive action.[1] It was not necessarily support for the Resistance, writ large, that prompted such leniency, but a mixture of personal engagement and loyalty, political connections, anti-German sentiment, and other, sometimes obscure motivations. It was therefore often beneficial for resisters to maintain connections with Vichy, which was more easily done by staying, if not in Vichy, at least in France. A second challenge was that many people experienced real psychological distress at the thought of leaving the country.[2] This distress was made more concrete by the fact that leaving France without authorization could result in losing one's citizenship, as could engaging in any act outside of France that was considered traitorous by Vichy.[3] A third hardship, adding to the psychological distress, was the physical challenge of leaving France. Leaving was not a matter of simply walking across a border. Crossing the

116

Pyrénées was the most common way out of France even though it was extremely dangerous and taxing for even the fittest of resisters. It was not, as we will see, the only option, though.

As challenging as it was to leave, many resisters ultimately made that choice. In some cases it was less of a choice, as the alternative was imprisonment. This was true even for resisters on the extreme right. Their connections to the personnel at Vichy might have been useful in the early part of the war, particularly when they shared a common political perspective. However, after 1942, with the return of Pierre Laval, the increasingly repressive actions of his government, and the expansion of the German occupation to cover the entire country, resisters of all political persuasions were in ever-increasing danger. Even people loyal to the regime before 1942 were forced to deal with a changing domestic situation that made it harder and harder to continue to accept the German presence. Uriage, a Vichy school set up to train a new elite of civil servants, went in 1942 from being "a faithfully Petainist to a militantly anti-German, hence anti-Laval and anti-collaborationist, institution."[4] The men there did not, however, become anti-Pétain. Rather, they adopted a more active resistance to the regime precisely because they thought Pétain had been removed from power by Laval.[5] Given that supporters of Vichy themselves were becoming increasingly alienated from the government, it is no surprise that 1942 and 1943 saw many resisters moving further and further away from the capital, often leaving France entirely to escape the repression of the regime.

This chapter details that progression in the case of Georges Groussard, who was active in the antiparliamentary and anticommunist struggles of the 1930s and linked to both the Cagoule and the Corvignolles. Like Loustaunau-Lacau, with whom Groussard enjoyed a lifelong friendship, he made his career in the military. Born on November 21, 1891, in Saint-Martin-les-Melle, Groussard started his military career in the infantry in 1911. After fighting in the First World War, Groussard was admitted to the École de guerre in 1920 and moved quickly up the ranks until he was promoted to colonel in 1938.[6] Though he and Loustaunau-Lacau claimed the title of "watchdog, a role that we exercised long enough to know the difficulties and to taste bitterness,"[7] Groussard's career was certainly less troubled than that of his comrade in arms. After being promoted to colonel, Groussard was made second in command of Saint-Cyr that same year, no small feat for someone who had been linked to the disgraced Loustaunau-Lacau and to the *cagoulards*, most of whom were in prison or on the run. By June 1940 Groussard was in the capital, where he was posted as the chief of staff for the region of Paris[8] under the direction of General Dentz.

Unsurprisingly, Groussard always had much to say about the French military. Like Loustaunau-Lacau, he seemed to have made it his goal to protect the military at all costs. In his postwar book about the French Army, Groussard praises the army of the First World War but goes on to say that the victory of 1918 made army men lazy and that the overabundance of medals and citations from that conflict detracted from true valor. "This generalization of rewards for honor devalued true heroism," he writes.[9] He also points to the economic difficulties of the 1920s to show that the life of a soldier was quite miserable and why the spirit of sacrifice seemed to disappear in that decade. His harshest criticism, however, is saved for the military chiefs of the interwar army, who, he argues, were mostly conformists without character: "Ambitious only to the point of wanting to finish their careers as commanding officers, they were, whatever their political views, dumb and submissive."[10] On the idea that the upper echelons of the army had been seduced by fascism in the 1930s, Groussard notes that this was not exactly the case. "You have to understand that the army is not against one particular political regime," he writes. "It is, in principle, against those who, whatever their opinions, want to diminish its prestige or misunderstand its mission."[11] While he denies that the army was antidemocratic, Groussard certainly has some interesting things to say about French politics during the 1930s and 1940s.

In a police file at the Archives de la Préfecture de Police we read that "Colonel Groussard can be considered anticommunist and even profascist from the national point of view, which makes him a fierce opponent of the republic."[12] There is absolutely no doubting his anticommunist sentiments, as they are made apparent by both his actions and his writings. In 1952 Loustaunau-Lacau and Groussard wrote, in an attack against communism and the democracies that allowed it to grow, that "Bolshevik rats always nibble the cheese of a careless democracy."[13] Interestingly, Groussard's early anticommunism was not so different from that of other army men. His sense of the relationship between the army and the nation—that they should be one and the same—shows that he recognized that much of the army's anti-Bolshevism was actually in line with governmental policy for some time. He points to the military intervention in Russia after the revolution and the French attempt to help reorganize the Polish army in order to defeat the Soviets as examples of this and argues that the army's anticommunism "absolutely did not signify that the army was politicized but the contrary, that it was following, with discipline, the fundamental policy lines of the Third Republic."[14] Thus it was only when the French government began cooperating, in one way or another, with the communists that Groussard's anticommunism was out of step with the will of the civil powers.

This became increasingly the case after the Second World War. In their published warning to the men of the Fourth Republic, Groussard and Loustaunau-Lacau explored the many coups that had led to fallen governments in the past and argued that Bolshevism was putting the French government at risk of death. In discussing the situation in Prague in 1948, the two men compared it to the Trojan War, or, more accurately, the Trojan Horse. They urged their readers to

> replace in this mechanized revolution, this unionized whirlwind, the name of President Benes with that of President Auriol, that of Gottwald with that of Duclos, that of Lausman, of Fierlinger, with the two or three French socialists that you can think of, and France will join in the tomb her lively and courageous Danubian sister, after a death by suffocation identical to hers. It's the same horse that the Soviets introduced here, these are the same methods that they recommend, they pull the strings of the same puppets. Is it really necessary to warn the consuls?[15]

Not only were these two upset that the communists were playing a role in French politics but they were furious that France continued to maintain diplomatic relations with the Soviet Union. They wonder how a French mother who has lost her son in Korea or Indochina must feel when she reads about French ambassadors visiting the Soviet Union or sees the communists openly subverting the French community in their newspapers and through other forms of propaganda. Groussard's anticommunism had not changed, but the stance of the French government had, and this pushed his views toward the fringe.

It is hard to say whether Groussard was actually antirepublican. He certainly did not hesitate to criticize the Republic, though many people were similarly inclined and this did not make them antirepublican per se. His verbal attacks against the Republic, however, did tend to be fairly strong. In his discussion of the defeat of 1940 and the role of the army, he also points out that in a democracy everybody is to blame: "If we consider that in a democracy public opinion can be freely expressed and has an important influence on the morale of the nation, then each French person carries his part of the responsibility."[16] He goes on to note that the extreme Right and the extreme Left cannot truly be blamed for the defeat, since they had no real role in government and thus did not carry the responsibility of power. This is a clear condemnation of the centrist republican parties, and since Groussard would never absolve the extreme Left of blame unless he had to, it seems clear that Groussard is subtly trying to ensure that the Right is not blamed for the debacle. Like many others on the right, Groussard noted a kind of decadence that spread throughout France in the interwar period. Of the defeat, he ultimately says, "Those responsible? Well, above all it was the moral numbness, the spiritual confusion that reigned in the Western countries, who were unable to predict, unable to see clearly, and sacrificed their security to their desire for their comforts and to satisfy their sordid electoral appetites."[17]

From these writings, we can see that Groussard was not particularly fond of republican politics, nor was he very impressed with some of the consequences of living in a democratic country. It is likely that these opinions, combined with his sense that France was slipping into decadence, led Groussard to the periphery of the Cagoule and the center of the Corvignolles in the 1930s. Groussard, like many of the accused, denied ever having been a part of the Cagoule.[18] Yet, his name was so closely tied to those of the leaders of that organization that even in 1986 at least one person was actively trying to determine his level of participation. One M. Poivre opened a correspondence with the head of the Service historique de l'Armée de terre, noting that Groussard was dead and no longer able to defend himself but that his role in the Cagoule still remained unclear. General Delmas responded to Poivre, "I can't give you any precise information about the participation of Colonel Groussard in the Cagoule. People have often spoken of it without providing specific evidence, . . . What is true is that there were officers in the Cagoule."[19] Delmas went on to state with some authority that Loustaunau-Lacau had almost certainly been a *cagoulard*. The small investigation that was opened thanks to M. Poivre's letter concluded that Groussard's military dossier did not have any evidence of his participation in the Cagoule and that the notes on Groussard and his behavior while in the army did not really suggest active participation in the organization, but that further research certainly needed to be done.[20]

While Groussard may not have been an active *cagoulard*, his relationship with Loustaunau-Lacau is unquestionable, and like his colleague, Groussard likely stayed clear of Deloncle's attempts to overthrow the Republic and collaborate with the Germans. In 1941 a Captain Joseph Lécussan was interviewed regarding Loustaunau-Lacau's activities. He was asked, among other things, whether he knew if Loustaunau-Lacau or Groussard was in contact with Deloncle or other members of the Rassemblement national populaire (RNP). He answered without hesitation that "it would surprise me very much, and I even consider it impossible. It is possible that their ideas about the political situation in France after the war are the same. But they are in complete disagreement about current foreign policy."[21] Although Groussard's wartime activities were often viewed with suspicion, as we will soon see, this statement does reinforce his own claims to having remained anti-German throughout the war. Interestingly enough, however, Groussard actually defends Deloncle in his memoirs: "I can attest that at that time neither in the M.S.A.R. nor in the U.C.A.D. . . . , I can attest, I say, that there did not exist in these organizations any indication of a plot against the Republic. The real objective, proclaimed by Deloncle and by Duseigneur, was the organization of a system of self-defense against an eventual coup by extremist forces."[22] Although Groussard notes that Deloncle was not trying to overthrow the Republic (which he clearly was!), he does clearly state that they had nothing to do with each other, as they were enemies.

Groussard is happy enough to mention his connection to Loustaunau-Lacau, though, with whom "I maintained a long friendship that I am far from denying today, despite all these phantom plots that he has been accused of with an inconceivable levity after he had returned from a terrible deportation."[23] By Loustaunau-Lacau's own admission as well, he and Groussard were frequently in contact both before and during the war. Loustaunau-Lacau fully admitted that Groussard was a member of the Corvignolles, which Groussard himself never denied.[24] Groussard, while never explicitly discussing his involvement with Loustaunau-Lacau's group, certainly viewed his friend with some admiration. Of Loustaunau-Lacau he said that "he had an obsessive love for France, which he always wanted to show with action."[25] He said that

> Loustaunau breathed the taste of action, and it was enough to approach him to know that he had an iron will and that he wasn't exactly very soft. . . . Loustaunau was antibourgeois. From the time he devoted himself to rugby . . . he constantly searched for action, and more: risk. All of his life, he launched himself into battle without considering the dramatic consequences this could have for him. . . . He was the right man to ask to fight against a hundred others or to do the impossible.[26]

If their postwar coauthorship was not enough to prove their lasting friendship, these words certainly were. Groussard's admiration and respect for his friend's abilities, even if he did not take the consequences of his action into account, are apparent.

Groussard's wartime experience truly began in June 1940 in Paris, where he witnessed the exodus of people and the eventual declaration of the capital as an open city. In his memoirs he talks about the real embarrassment of being a military man and ending the war without a single gesture of defense.[27] Even more shameful for Groussard, however, was the German entry into Paris and the fraternization that he saw between the remaining population and the Nazi soldiers. He wrote that "at Belleville, as at Pigalle, at Ménilmontant as at the Champs-Élysées, German officers and troops were constantly and everywhere accosted by onlookers from all classes of society, who laughed with the enemy and offered him all kinds of services."[28] This disappointment began what for Groussard would be a five-year period of witnessing shameful behavior from people he expected better of, and he would frequently criticize those who seemed to bow down to the Germans. After a brief internment and upon hearing of the armistice, Groussard was driven to the demarcation line and made his way to Vichy. In August 1940 he asked for and was granted an armistice leave, and he put himself at the disposal of the Vichy regime.[29] In October of that same year, Groussard was named *inspecteur général des services de la Sûreté nationale*. It is hard to say why, but the two men's careers seem to have taken opposite paths. Where Loustaunau encountered obstacles, Groussard was given one prime position after another. The latter's charmed life would not last forever, though, as we will see.

Throughout this early period following the armistice, Groussard was also working to establish a secondary police force, one that would allow him access to the inner circles of the government but would also keep order in the country, allowing him to prepare for an eventual fight with the Germans.[30] He went to see Raphaël Alibert (minister of justice at the time) and Henri Lémery (minister of colonies) and explained this project to them, emphasizing, however, that he did not want anything to do with Germans and would not have his police force cooperate with them. Groussard decided to call his group the Centre d'informations et d'études (CIE), and he set up shop in the Hôtel Parmentier in Vichy. In his memoirs, he tells his readers that the CIE was divided into regions that corresponded to military regions, and each one had a regional leader. Under each regional leader were troops called the Groupes de protection (GP), a more militaristic offshoot of the CIE. The GP were put under the supervision of François Méténier, a well-known *cagoulard,* whose patriotism Groussard did not doubt, though he supposedly asked Méténier to cut all of his ties with the Cagoule.[31]

As Groussard started to recruit for these groups, he was looking for very particular attributes in his potential members. In his memoirs he notes that he sought out men who were patriots, who were physically fit, and who "had guts." Groussard found these characteristics mostly in men who had been active in prewar nationalist groups.[32] In postwar testimony, however, Groussard did admit that this caused some difficulty: "Recruitment happened rapidly, too rapidly even, because it was directed at elements described as 'national'—elements that I realized quite quickly needed to be purged, which earned me the reputation of having recruited only 'cagoulards,' 'PPF,' etc. . . . It must be said that at that moment I had no choice. However, from the moment they entered the organization, they made the formal promise not to engage in politics."[33] Although Groussard claimed to be concerned about the political past of his recruits, this seems unlikely. He was recruiting among the very people with whom he had fraternized in the prewar years, and it clearly made sense for him to do so.

Depending on whom one asked, either the CIE and the GP were created with the intention of picking up the fight against the Germans at the earliest possible moment or they were repressive forces destined to reinforce Pétain's position, to ensure that the communists could not regroup, to inform on any "antinational" activities, or all three. Groussard, of course, maintains his intention to use the groups against the occupiers.[34] Méténier testified that the real purpose of the organization was to regroup various military men whose regiments had been dissolved.[35] Gabriel Jeantet, former *cagoulard* and friend of both Groussard and Méténier, had many positive things to say about the CIE when he testified after the war. Not only did he credit Groussard with encouraging him to help young men resist the temptation to collaborate with the occupiers but he confirmed Méténier's testimony about regrouping military men to create "a real force of combatants who could one day resume the armed fight against Germany."[36] Jeantet also did not hesitate to note that the CIE and the GP were formed at the height of the tensions between Pétain and Laval and that the CIE was to serve as support for "le vieux Maréchal" in a potential conflict with his own government.

But other people adamantly insisted that the CIE and the GP were nefarious in most, if not all, respects. In a 1946 report on the CIE, we read, copied from seized documents, that

> the Centre d'informations et d'études is a body created to defend the person and the work of Maréchal Pétain, led by the chief appointed by him, Colonel Groussard, Inspector General of the National Security Services. . . . The overall mission of the C.I.E. is to assure the internal peace of the country by monitoring and repressing antinational intrigues of (1) internationalist extremists

[communists]; (2) autonomists and foreign agents; and (3) opponents of the new regime and dissolved secrets societies.[37]

The description of the CIE as a group seeking to protect Pétain and maintain order, while far more detailed than Groussard's description, is not far off. As we saw earlier, Groussard himself admitted to a plan to keep the peace while he prepared for *la revanche*. However, others' descriptions of the group are even more damning.

A former member of the CIE, Charles Boudet, also testified about the mission of the group, though why he was so open about it is hard to say. He told investigators:

> The information obtained was to determine the political position of French officials vis-à-vis the Pétain government, the research of all information concerning the leaders of all political parties, in particular republican parties and those hostile to the regime, including Freemasonry, which was considered by the CIE to be a political group.
>
> The repression was directed against nonconforming officials and against the communists. I believe I can tell you that it is likely that communists were arrested and interned on the intervention and initiative of the CIE.[38]

The fact that Boudet admitted to being a member of a repressive force that was responsible for communist arrests and internments is astounding. But the fact that the group was engaged in such activities is not surprising. Groussard was a committed anticommunist, so actions taken against them should come as no surprise. Furthermore, his dislike of republican party politics would confirm Boudet's statements that the CIE was particularly interested in researching republicans hostile to Vichy. What we do not find in any of these descriptions, however, is any sense that Groussard and the CIE were pro-German.

Another postwar testimony, from Robert Labat, suggested that much of the information the CIE was searching for had to do with who was collaborating with the Germans, how the occupying forces were using French materials and stocks, and what the German attitude was toward Alsace-Lorraine and other parts of France.[39] Of all the evidence about the CIE's mission, however, one document stands out because it shows an inexplicable tie between the group and the Germans. François Méténier had been directed by Groussard to investigate the possibilities of expanding the group into the occupied zone, and for this purpose he traveled to Paris. At the same time, Méténier sent Helmut Knochen, the senior commander of the Sicherheitspolizei and the Sicherheitsdienst in Paris, a letter that was later found and used in the French investigation of the CIE. This letter supposedly informed Knochen that

> our sought-after goals are as follows: (a) for a secret, but real, liaison to assure the rapid exploitation of information concerning the Gaullist propaganda, as it is in the interest of both Germany and France to repress it with the utmost severity; (b) to assure the interior authority of the French Government; . . . (d) for clever propaganda, to achieve the Franco-German rapprochement. . . . Having for many years affirmed my political ideas, I was imprisoned in 1937 for twenty-eight months because of it. All the personnel recruited by me, persuaded that France will only be saved by an authoritarian government, national and social, and by a loyal collaboration with Germany, are ready to fight to the end for these ideas.[40]

This letter from Méténier suggesting that the CIE was looking for a closer relationship between France and Germany and seeking to repress any ongoing resistance to the German occupation is the only piece of evidence that indicates a pro-German attitude on the part of the CIE. On balance, much more evidence shows the lack of a relationship between the group and the Nazis, even if they did share some common political ideas.

The Germans noticed the repressive activities of the group and somewhat ironically called the CIE a "French Gestapo." The German report on the GP noted that "the principal task of the G.P. is to repress any movement against the government. In addition, it is charged to fight communism, Freemasonry, Gaullists, and the Jews." But it went on to say that "a serious government . . . shouldn't hesitate to remove or even shoot MENETIER [sic]."[41] The Nazi official who wrote the report clearly was not overly impressed with the CIE, the GP, Groussard, or Méténier, even if they may have been actively repressing similar groups of people. And there is no doubt that the CIE was indeed repressive in its role as a kind of political police. Groussard himself even admits having kept records of Gaullists, but he tries to justify it by arguing that he would not have been able to gain the trust of the authorities if he had not.[42] While we might view such justification with suspicion, we do know that Vichy's own secret services were spying on all of these same groups—communists, Gaullists, the British, and the Germans—and that British agents or resisters were sometimes arrested because Vichy's agents believed that resistance movements had been infiltrated by the Germans.[43] In other words, some of Vichy's repressive activities against resisters or Allied agents were undertaken because of anti-Germanism.

Groussard certainly did have the confidence of some official circles in Vichy, as his being approached by Alibert and Marcel Peyrouton, then minister of the interior, in December 1940 shows. He was asked to participate in the plan to remove Pierre Laval from the government, and his GPs were actually charged with arresting Laval on December 13. That afternoon Pétain had called a surprise meeting of the Council of Ministers and asked each member to write a letter of resignation. He accepted only two of these letters, those of Laval and also Georges Ripert, the minister of education. Meanwhile, Laval's rooms in the Hôtel du Parc were taken over by Groussard's police forces, and Laval was arrested as he left the meeting. It was only a matter of days before the Germans retaliated for what they saw as insubordination and the German ambassador, Otto Abetz, quickly had Laval released and brought him to Paris with him.

Laval's dismissal has been at the center of much debate concerning the real intentions of men like Pétain, Alibert, Peyrouton, and others involved in the plan. On the surface, it seemed like a rejection of the policies developed at Montoire, and Groussard certainly thought that it signified a change for the better in French governmental politics.[44] But there was little or no change in actual policy. Robert Paxton notes that the Vichy efforts to cultivate a solid working relationship with Germany were in fact intensified by Laval's successors, that relations with the British became even more strained in 1941, and that the only really decisive change was in German attitudes toward France.[45] Paxton and Philippe Burrin, among others, note that Laval was widely distrusted in Vichy and that many of the men responsible for his arrest had reason to feel personally threatened by Laval's seemingly rapacious desire to amass as much power as possible.[46] Paxton even suggests that "authoritarians like Alibert" may have wanted him gone because they "may have noticed that Laval was the only Third Republic parliamentarian left after the new government of 6 September."[47]

Motivations aside, the move to get rid of Laval certainly did annoy the Germans, who promptly demanded that Groussard's CIE be shut down. After his organization was dissolved, Groussard continued to plan for a secret mission but also decided that he needed to go to London, for he wanted to persuade the British that many people in Vichy were also anti-Nazi. He also felt that the Resistance needed unity, hierarchy, and apoliticism, all of which he thought he could provide.[48] After resigning from his official post with the Sûreté in February 1941, Groussard made contact with Pierre Fourcaud (Lucas), an agent of the Free French and the fourth sent on missions to France. Fourcaud was an obvious choice, as "he was enthusiastic about Vichy, the Vichy of his companions from the extreme right who believed in revenge," and he was well known to Groussard and Loustaunau-Lacau.[49] Even though Fourcaud counted these men as companions and positive additions to the resistance effort, he also had some reservations about them. In a report from one of his first missions back to France, Fourcaud had written that

> even within the entourage of the Marshal, resistance against Germany is organizing with his tacit consent. . . . The political police, a sort of French Gestapo, have for a mission: to identify all action against the government (communism); to constitute well-armed units with proven morals under the name of protection groups; to create an active anti-German Gestapo. . . . The leader of this organization was chosen by the Marshal from his entourage. It is Colonel Groussard who received the title of inspector general of police.
>
> He surrounded himself almost exclusively with former *cagoulards*, who devised a system that would be useful even if the organization fell victim to German pressure.
>
> The minister of the interior and Laval started by believing they could absolutely count on them, but they are wrong. This organization is dangerous. It is, however, undeniably 100 percent national.
>
> The presence on our side of Maurice Duclos, who is respected in that community, on the other hand, allows us to always obtain help and protection.[50]

While Fourcaud was enthusiastic, yet wary, about his connections to these rightist army men, other Free French agents were far more suspicious. When Fourcaud met with Groussard, he was accompanied by Gilbert Renault (Rémy), who later noted concerning both Groussard's and Loustaunau-Lacau's claims to have large networks that "in assuming that this was not premature, I asked myself *in petto* how it was possible to raise a small army of ten thousand men without Vichy or the Germans knowing."[51] Renault, like many others, was suspicious of such claims. In any event, these agents helped Groussard make it to Spain, Lisbon, and eventually Bristol in June 1941.

While in England, Groussard met with André Dewavrin (Passy), the head of the Gaullist intelligence services in London, and Churchill, among others, but he was unable to meet with de Gaulle, who was in Syria at the time. By all accounts, these meetings were amicable and Groussard certainly tried to persuade the British that people like Charles Huntzinger, Maxime Weygand, Admiral Leahy, and even Pétain were all interested in a secret alliance with Britain.[52] Nothing concrete came of these meetings, and there is no way of knowing what would have taken place had Groussard not been arrested almost immediately upon his return to France in July 1941. On the orders of François Darlan and Pierre Pucheu, Groussard was interned in Vals-les-Bains along with Georges Mandel and Paul Reynaud. While there, he certainly had plenty of time to think about his new networks, which he had baptized "Gilbert" because the fake passport he had used to get to England had identified him as Georges Gilbert, a French Canadian. Groussard was eventually given conditional liberty by Pierre Pucheu, who Groussard thought would resist the Germans in time.[53] After being liberated, Groussard continued to focus on his *réseaux* Gilbert, and he cut his ties with Vichy by moving to Cannes in the winter of 1941/42.

Shortly after this move, Groussard's armistice leave came to an end and he was offered the choice of returning to active military service in the armistice army or retiring from the military altogether. Noting that he was saddened by the inactivity of his colleagues in the army, Groussard chose retirement.[54] This choice obviously also provided more time to focus on his resistance activities, the nature of which was somewhat unclear at the time. His networks seemed to include many of the same people who had been a part of the CIE, but what they were accomplishing is hard to say. Certainly later on, as we will see, these networks were quite significant, but there are no records of activity in early 1942. This may be owing in part to the fact that Groussard was under near constant surveillance, and shortly after Laval returned to power in April 1942, Groussard was arrested yet again. Taken to Vals-les-Bains once more, Groussard responded with what was becoming his signature move, a hunger strike.[55] This prompted his captors to put him in a psychiatric hospital, where he continued to refuse to eat but was secretly given tidbits of food by one of the nurses, who supported his cause. Eventually he was liberated for "humanitarian" reasons, though he was still under house arrest.

At this point, Groussard clearly recognized the need to leave France. He had been arrested three times since the beginning of the war, and it must have seemed that it was only a matter of time before one of those arrests became permanent. In his memoirs he describes sending an agent to Switzerland to make contact with the Secret Intelligence Service (SIS) and also sending a telegram to London, but he never got a response from the BCRA, which he suspected was because the Gaullists were not fond of him.[56] In reality de Gaulle's men were keeping tabs on Groussard, and his name figures prominently in a note dated September 1942 from France Combattante to André Philip about getting certain people, such as Robert Lacoste, Pierre-Henri Teitgen, and François de Menthon, transport out of France. The notation about Groussard reads, "Clandestine activity in liaison with BCRA, closely watched."[57] However, possibly because they were hesitant to actively collaborate with those on the extreme right in France, the BCRA was unable to establish a meaningful relationship with Groussard. Much like Loustaunau-Lacau, who had also received little help from the Gaullist camp, Groussard had to turn elsewhere for support.

Groussard managed to escape his house arrest and left for Switzerland in November 1942. Like many others resisters, he used a route through Annemasse and set up shop in Geneva. The former *cagoulard* and noted *résistant* in the resistance group Combat, Guillain de Bénouville, also traveled to Geneva quite a bit in 1941 and 1942.[58] He made a point of seeing Groussard and later wrote that

> Groussart [*sic*] had begun by being interned at Vals. There he had gone on a hunger strike, which had cut short his internment and allowed him to go to Cannes on a sort of supervised liberty. When the Germans overran all France,

he had been able to shake off his shadows and escape to Switzerland. In the old days, when he was Commandant of the Saint-Cyr Military Academy, his monocle and his close haircut had earned him the nickname of "Eric." At that time he did bear a striking resemblance to Eric von Stroheim, the actor. But nobody would have called him "Eric" had they seen him with me in Geneva. He was growing a big postman's mustache, he wore no monocle, and his scalp was no longer close-clipped; it was vulgarly bald. And when he left his modest apartment, his gun-metal eyes were hidden beneath the lowered brim of a faded felt hat which gave him the appearance of a travelling salesman. As a matter of fact, Colonel Groussart was in full labor. With the aid of the British, he was bringing forth in Geneva an important intelligence center. From his neutral refuge, his fierce will and his astounding self-effacement were soon to spark a network of more than a thousand secret agents working in France, with whom he was in constant contact.[59]

In addition to providing information to the Secret Intelligence Service, Groussard also seems to have helped people cross the border into and out of Switzerland on a fairly regular basis. Some people, like Jeantet, Méténier, and de Bénouville, were not surprised by this resistance activity. Others most certainly were. In a postwar report on the CIE, the author, after grudgingly admitting that it was possible that Groussard wanted to fight the Germans (though the tone of this comment is certainly skeptical), writes that "we also note with interest that the network created later on by Groussard operated in Switzerland. One can easily guess which matters of conscience were put to Colonel Groussard before he started to work in liaison with services opposed to Marshal Pétain, who, moreover, had him interned at Vals-les-Bains for a certain period of time."[60] Similar comments are found in Groussard's police files, as it seemed to shock certain people that he had made the move into full-fledged resistance. In the same report that called Groussard an anticommunist, a committed enemy of the republic, and a profascist, the author was forced to admit that "during his stay in Switzerland he had displayed violently Germanophobic feelings."[61]

Indeed, it would have been difficult for Groussard to make the decision to act against Pétain. Even after the war, Groussard maintained that Pétain had many good reasons for behaving as he had. In his memoirs, he reminds his readers that if Pétain had not been in power, somebody like Jean Luchaire or Marcel Déat would have been.[62] Like many others on the far right of the Resistance, Groussard certainly had a difficult time believing that Pétain was not acting in the interests of France. Loustaunau-Lacau and Groussard wrote in 1952 about Pétain's fate:

> The prosecutor Mornet will believe for a moment that it is his duty to ascribe the role of apprentice dictator to an eighty-four-year-old marshal who for a long time had been sick of men and bored by things, when this aged leader simply accepted, at the hour when everyone was begging him, to serve as a buoy in a terrible storm. Preoccupied with his personal future, eaten away by ambition, certain of his forces, Marshal Pétain certainly would not have made the mistakes that we are imagining he did; rather, like so many others, in due course he would have opted to join the more profitable and comfortable camp of the victors.[63]

Groussard's defense of Pétain, like Loustaunau-Lacau's, centered on the idea that an old man should not be blamed for the many mistakes his entourage had made. Although Pétain might not have been entirely blameless in Groussard's mind, he was seen as being responsible for the armistice, which Groussard continued to laud well after the war for having allowed a resistance to grow and for improving the Allies' chance for victory.[64]

However, we already know that Groussard was not fond of other members of the Vichy government and may also have struggled to accept some of its policies, particularly the anti-Semitic laws, which became increasingly stringent as time went on. Though Groussard himself was a Protestant, his first wife, Vera (née Bernstein), was of Jewish origin. When Groussard sought permission to marry in 1913, the army report on his choice of wife noted that she lived with her family in Kiev, that her mother was deceased, that her father was an engineer ("very honorably known"), and that Vera herself "is blessed with perfect conduct and a good education."[65] The two were married in January 1914,[66] and this relationship may have influenced Groussard's later views on Vichy's anti-Semitism. This is not to say that Groussard was a crusader against these laws in any way, but he did note, for example, that although he and Xavier Vallat saw eye to eye on many things, he could not work with the man, because he was too anti-Semitic for his tastes.[67] Vichy's increasing anti-Semitism may have prompted Groussard to move further away from governmental circles and closer to a real form of resistance.

His decision to work with the British directly, as previously discussed, was partially owing to the fact that he was not getting the response he desired from de Gaulle's forces. But Groussard was also quite critical of the internal resistance, which likely influenced this decision as well. He was, as might be expected, critical of the political nature of much resistance and noted that recruits should have been gathered under the umbrella of patriotism, not politics, and that many resistance leaders were unconcerned with the actual fight and simply wanted to gain power.[68] He wrote of the civil resistance groups that "instead of uniting under the banner of the fight against the occupant, instead of making this fight the clear and sole goal, almost all of these groups had, from the start, the look of electoral committees searching for a party clientele, and they directed the puerile remainder of their efforts far more against the government of Vichy than against the foreign enemy."[69] This theme of irresponsible recruitment and leadership is found in all of Groussard's postwar writings. It seems that he never forgave much of the internal resistance for focusing on Vichy rather than on the Germans. Groussard hated the fact that early resistance organizations recruited among the "victims" of the National Revolution, who were already politicized and recruited other politicized people.[70] It is clear that Groussard would have preferred a widespread recruitment from within the army, which he notes was generally ignored by resistance organizations.

While it is true that the army was underrepresented in the interior resistance, officers actually made up a large proportion of *résistants* outside France.[71] Groussard's decision not to work with the exterior resistance is somewhat puzzling. We know that he was in contact with BCRA agents but that he felt that the French in London did not like him. Unlike Loustaunau-Lacau, however, Groussard did not seem to have any serious problems with de Gaulle during the war. In his *L'Armée et ses drames,* Groussard notes of de Gaulle, "I knew immediately . . . the great advantage that the presence of one of ours in London could bring to the preparations for revenge. Knowing de Gaulle, his dignity of manner and his ability, I felt he could help us greatly, through his personal influence and with his direct links to the official British services."[72] This flattering description of de Gaulle would suggest that Groussard would not have had any difficulties working with him, so perhaps it really was just the lack of response he got from de Gaulle's forces that made him turn directly to the British for support.

Ultimately, Groussard was probably very happy that he had not tied his considerable network to de Gaulle. While the two men may have been on decent terms during the war, that certainly changed in the postwar period. Groussard, in fact, begins his 1964 book *Service secret* by underlining how his opinion of de Gaulle had changed since 1948. "I thought I knew him; this was presumption on my part. I don't know him at all."[73] The reason for this change becomes manifestly clear toward the end of the book. Like many other rightist resisters (and those on the left, for that matter, but for vastly different reasons), Groussard was disgusted by the way in which de Gaulle handled the Algerian crisis. He wonders, "Is it acceptable, in a world we call civilized, after the terrible ordeal we have just suffered, that the transplanting of a million men from Algeria and elsewhere, men forced to abandon all they live for, can be tolerated?"[74] Although the topic has not been widely explored, many former resisters linked their fight against Nazism with keeping Algeria French. They saw no contradiction in fighting for "civilization" against the barbarous Nazis and maintaining absolute rule over the colonies.

Of all the responses of rightist resisters to the loss of Algeria, Groussard's is one of the most powerful. He writes that "since the existence of France, that is to say, since the Merovingians, twice, and only twice, has a French government uprooted masses of French: 500,000 in 1685, after the revocation of the Edict of Nantes. It was the shame of the reign of Louis XIV. A million two centuries later, in 1962. . . . History will not forget this new shame."[75] His disapproval of the expulsion of the *pieds-noirs* goes beyond these words, however. Groussard actually testified at the military trial of Raoul Salan, one of the generals responsible for the Algiers putsch and cofounder of the Organisation de l'armée secrète (OAS) in May 1962. It is noted in Groussard's police file that he "in particular declared that he was not surprised that this general officer kept his word, and he added that he might have done so in his place."[76] His testimony at Salan's trial seemed to mark the end of Groussard's involvement in political or military affairs. He had already quit the army. He had turned down a promotion in the Légion d'honneur that he had been offered, along with many others, immediately after the capitulation of Dien Bien Phu in 1954. In refusing the promotion, Groussard purportedly wrote to the grand chancellor of the Légion and told him that he "refused to belong to an order that had neither the valor nor the prestige that had been desired by its founder."[77] He ended whatever relationship he had once enjoyed with de Gaulle and took up the cause of the Algerian generals.

As we have seen, Groussard's resistance record is somewhat tarnished by the original ambiguity of his CIE and its stated mission of working against foreign agents, including British ones. Although there is little doubt that Groussard fully believed in Pétain's desire to prepare *la revanche* against the Germans and that he was contributing to that effort through his activities, his actions at that point were not those of a resister per se. Robert Belot points out that there was no real anti-German activity within the CIE at that time and says that the fact that Groussard was investigating the same people as the Germans makes it difficult to see how exactly he was resisting in those early years.[78] But Groussard's time in Switzerland placed him firmly, I would argue, within the pro-British resistance. The British certainly placed their trust in Groussard, as is evidenced by the scheme developed by the SIS, the vice-consul of the British Embassy in Switzerland, and Groussard. When persons of French nationality presented themselves to the embassy, they were directed to Groussard, who would try to persuade them to work for his network.[79] Although his ties to the British were definitely stronger, Groussard did eventually reconnect with de Gaulle's forces through Jean Moulin, who certainly approved of Groussard.

Sadly, it was also Jean Moulin, or rather his death, that shed further unflattering light on Groussard and his network. Like Guillain de Bénouville, with whom he had quite a bit of contact during the war, Groussard also played a role in the now infamous Caluire affair. As de Bénouville was making his cardinal mistake by preparing to send René Hardy to the meeting, Groussard was in the process of encouraging one of his own agents,

Edmée Delétraz, to play the dangerous role of a double agent. Delétraz was the liaison agent in charge of the drop boxes in Lyon and Grenoble; she was responsible for ensuring that the contents of those boxes were delivered to Annemasse. She was arrested by the Gestapo but liberated on the condition that she check in with Klaus Barbie each time she traveled through Lyon. In her role as a double agent Delétraz was not only forced into the witch hunt for Berty Albrecht, Henri Frenay's companion, but also forced by Barbie to follow René Hardy and report to the Gestapo the location of his meeting. While the whole episode remains shrouded in mystery, it seems that Delétraz did inform Groussard of what had happened and of following Hardy. There is even a suggestion that she warned several resisters, including Groussard, before the day of the meeting.[80]

Delétraz and by extension Groussard were almost as much on trial as Hardy when the case was brought before the judge in 1947 and again in 1950. Originally, Hardy swore that he had not been arrested by the Gestapo before the meeting. Delétraz gave evidence that Hardy had actively participated in the roundup by creating an intricate plan with her and Barbie to lead them to the meeting.[81] Unsurprisingly, Hardy's lawyer took this opportunity to turn the accusations of working for the Germans right back onto Delétraz. When she testified to having received her orders from Groussard, Hardy's lawyer, Maurice Garçon, took that as an opening to revisit Groussard's less than salubrious dealings with Vichy and his role in surveiling Gaullist agents early in the war. Painted as a traitor, and with few people coming to his defense, Groussard was left to defend his own actions and those of Delétraz.[82] It seems that this whole episode was the nail in the coffin, so to speak, for Groussard. As Bénédicte Vergez-Chaignon writes, "This Groussard affair, at the heart of the Hardy affair, demonstrates above all that between the purges, the punishment of traitors, and the settling of political accounts, this resistance, which claimed to take shape independently of Vichy, could no longer make itself understood."[83]

Groussard's involvement in the Hardy trials, his early participation in the official bureaucracy of Vichy, his decision to work with the British rather than de Gaulle, his unchanging political views, his support for Algérie française, and perhaps even his general intransigence all overshadowed his contributions to the Resistance. Like Loustaunau-Lacau's, Groussard's politics provoke a certain level of discomfort. It is often hard to believe that a man so committed to the anticommunist, nationalist, militaristic, and sometimes antidemocratic cause would be a valuable addition to the Resistance against the Germans. But while he may have been all of those things, he was also anti-German, patriotic, and certainly hopeful of reestablishing the liberty of his country and, more importantly, the sovereignty of its army.

RIGHTIST GAULLISM

Like Georges Groussard, many rightist resisters found that their initial impetus to remain attached in some way to Vichy, or to the venerable persona of Pétain, was misguided. Some found a way to flee France, often using their Vichy connections, while others chose to remain in the country but adopted a much more stringent anti-Vichy tone. The decision to leave or stay was often influenced by the connections a resister had made. Groussard, for instance, left but went not to London, because of strained relations with the Gaullist forces, but to Switzerland, where he could work with the British and Americans directly. Other resisters starting from the same position of neutrality vis-à-vis the Vichy regime or admiration for Pétain also moved more firmly into resistance against both the Germans and Vichy but did not necessarily leave the country. Some of these resisters ended up grudgingly supporting de Gaulle; others supported him more wholeheartedly after it became clear that he was indeed successfully uniting the Resistance.

In some ways, it was natural for people of the extreme Right to rally to de Gaulle. Not because he had been particularly active in those circles in the interwar years (although nor was he entirely distant) but because he was, in the early days of the war, largely silent about politics. He did not talk about the restoration of republican politics, which might have led people to imagine that he would be open to other, perhaps more authoritarian kinds of regimes once the war had been won. In response to charges that he was too authoritarian, de Gaulle was forced to publicly commit to democracy. In these statements, like one in the *New York Times*, he reiterated his position that the Free French Forces were nonpolitical, that the French did not want a dictatorship, and that "if they cheer my name, it is because I have been associated with resistance to the Germans and as such am a symbol of the France that fights on."[1] However, these pledges did not come until 1942 and 1943; until then there was plenty of cause to believe that de Gaulle was not necessarily wedded to the idea of a fourth republic. His own autocratic style may have been appealing to men and women of the Right, who similarly wished to see a government with more authoritarian leanings.

Part and parcel of these tendencies was de Gaulle's insistence on a strict hierarchy within the Free French.[2] This hierarchy, with its military emphasis, would have been familiar and comfortable for many of the men from the extreme Right. Also in de Gaulle's favor from the perspective of some rightists was the fact that he criticized Vichy for collaborating with the Germans but avoided condemning Pétain too harshly at first. For this reason, people like Geneviève Duclos-Rostand, Maurice Duclos's sister, could sincerely believe that Pétain and de Gaulle had some kind of tacit agreement to work together, even if they seemed to be at odds on the surface. Many of de Gaulle's public pronunciations were constrained by his initial reliance on the Allies for transmission of his messages.[3] The British Broadcasting Corporation gave him airtime but censored his messages quite heavily. In turn, the BBC was guided by the Foreign Office on its treatment of Pétain and the Vichy government in radio broadcasts. The BBC was instructed to make the British displeasure of Vichy known, but "personal attacks on Pétain or Weygand should be avoided; they command the loyalty of a large number of friendly Frenchmen in France and the Empire, and it is harmful to class them with the crooks and traitors."[4] It suited the British, as it did de Gaulle, to be somewhat ambiguous vis-à-vis Pétain, to whom many French people rallied. This ambiguity meant that in the early days of de Gaulle's resistance from London, people who were not entirely unsympathetic to Pétain could believe that in joining the Free French they were resisting the Germans so that political changes could be made in France without foreign interference.

There are two important points to bear in mind about the Gaullism of members of the Cagoule and the Corvignolles. First, it was conditional. By and large, de Gaulle had the support of these men and women only insofar as he was practicing a kind of politics that appealed to them. As we will see, that support diminished substantially the moment de Gaulle made decisions that were out of step with the goals of these rightists. Second, those rightists who lent their support to de Gaulle had a considerably easier time reintegrating into French political culture after the war and having their resistance activities recognized than did those who kept their distance from the Gaullist forces. Because de Gaulle was able to so effectively link the legitimacy of the Resistance to his leadership, rightists who stayed clear of de Gaulle found it much harder to have their role in the Resistance acknowledged after 1944.

Pierre de Bénouville, also known as Pierre Guillain de Bénouville, was one *cagoulard* who made his way to the Gaullists, even though he was politically quite sympathetic to Vichy's National Revolution. De Bénouville was born on August 8, 1914, in Amsterdam, but lived most of his life in France. In the 1930s he was a well-known Action française militant, a member, in fact, of Jean Filliol's 17th cell of the Camelots du roi. Along with his very good friend Jacques Renouvin (whom he would later meet again in the Resistance), de Bénouville left the AF after the failure of the street demonstrations in 1934. Like many other men from Filliol's group, de Bénouville found his way into the Cagoule. Together with other *cagoulards*, he participated in the mêlée at the funeral for Jacques Bainville in 1936. There, on the Boulevard Saint-Germain, the group blocked Léon Blum's car from passing and attacked him. De Bénouville was never punished for his participation in the group, so it is very possible that he was one of the less active members, though it seems unlikely given that he left the AF because of its preference for words over action.

It may come as a surprise, then, that de Bénouville was—even at that time—a journalist and author, having taken a degree in literature from the Sorbonne. He wrote literary criticism for newspapers like *Paris-Soir* and authored several books on other French figures, such as Baudelaire, Chateaubriand, Stendhal, and Pascal. At the beginning of the war, he was mobilized in the infantry, and he was on the Alsatian front when the German attack came on May 10, 1940. De Bénouville fought and was taken prisoner by the Germans when his unit collapsed. He managed to escape and made his way to the unoccupied zone, ending up in Nice. In his memoirs, de Bénouville makes much of the fact that it was quite difficult to do much of anything immediately after the defeat, as his financial situation was less than promising. To make ends meet, he took up journalism again, working for *L'Alerte*, the weekly newspaper of the National Revolution, which one source describes as an "anti-communist, anti-Gaullist, antisemitic newspaper."[5] De Bénouville's writing in *L'Alerte* was "far from simple literary activism, he animated an editorial line resolutely anti-Semitic, anti-Gaullist, antirepublican, and anticommunist. Written in an inflammatory tone, his articles underlined a profound hatred for the Third Republic and proclaimed his commitment to the National Revolution, coupled with boundless admiration for Pétain."[6]

De Bénouville does not comment on the nature of the paper in his memoirs, but it was while working there that he heard that some people were planning to leave for the colonies and carry on fighting from there. He decided to make contact with some of these people and left for a short trip to Paris but noted that "it was still a Paris full of danger for us, for we had learned that little groups of our comrades who had belonged to the same political organizations before the war had gone over to the enemy."[7] He explained that "the treason of some of these old-time nationalists, although it was just beginning, increased the risk of capture for true patriots. Our former comrades were not only bitter about our refusal to bow to defeat. They were resentful of the old internal political quarrels which had caused some of us to resign from the *Action Française* before the war, and which neither the heat of the conflict nor its tragic outcome could make them forget."[8] Although he never specifically identifies the men who caused him concern, there were certainly many former militants of the AF in Paris seeking to establish closer ties to the Germans. Of further concern would have been Eugene Deloncle, whose newfound alliance with Jacques Doriot and Marcel Déat made him a danger to his former colleagues who had chosen to resist.[9]

Late in 1940 de Bénouville decided to make his way to Algiers, hoping to end up eventually in London. Upon arrival in Algiers, he was arrested for suspected resistance activities, given his freedom, arrested again, and sent back to France. Imprisoned in Toulon until August 7, 1941, de

Bénouville came to understand the unity forced upon all who opposed Pétain's armistice. He writes that the prisoners anxiously awaited each morning, when they could walk side by side, "the priest with the free-thinking engineer, the barrister with the laborer, the Communist teacher with the devout army officer."[10] Unsurprisingly, given the simplicity of this narrative, de Bénouville's memoirs have been called "un livre à la guimauve" by at least one resister.[11] It is true that he focuses on the idea of unity and apoliticism, to the exclusion of any analysis about the many conflicts within the Resistance, in some of which he played a central role. He writes that "men who sought action left their political parties and came over to the Resistance, where there was truly no question of politics. I don't mean by that that we abandoned our own private ideologies, but we did abandon the pusillanimous political chiefs who had been our leaders until now. Men of all parties became men of good will with a single aim: Liberty."[12]

After his acquittal and his release from prison in the summer of 1941, de Bénouville joined the Carte network, also known as Radio-Patrie, which was led by André Girard and was operating mainly for the benefit of the British Special Operations Executive. Girard and the *réseau* Carte have also been neglected in many histories of the Resistance, and the title of Thomas Rabino's book tells us why. Entitled *Le réseau Carte: Histoire d'un réseau de la Résistance antiallemand, antigaulliste, anticommuniste et anticollaborationniste,* the book rehabilitates this network, which was resolutely against the perceived unifying factors of the Resistance, Gaullism and communism. Rabino's book exposes de Bénouville's clearly reactionary editorial practices but also details the later conflicts between the journalist and Girard. One notable conflict between the two men was the date when de Bénouville joined the Resistance, as he claimed it had been in September 1941 and Girard maintained that it had been in November 1942, a difference of fourteen months.[13] Girard was actually so incensed with de Bénouville's book *Le sacrifice du matin,* which he thought overlooked much of the truth about the first resistances, that he responded with his own entitled *Peut-on dire la vérité sur la Résistance?*

De Bénouville was, in any event, not a member of Carte for long, as he encountered his old Action française comrade Jacques Renouvin in

1942 and was easily persuaded to join Henri Frenay's group, Combat. He became an important figure within the group, so important, in fact, that he replaced Frenay for a time, after the group merged with other networks to become the Mouvements unis de la Résistance and Frenay was required to travel to London and Algiers.[14] Although his time with Combat and the MUR allowed de Bénouville to claim a solid resistance heritage, it was not unmarked by scandal. In early 1943 Frenay asked de Bénouville to use his contacts in Switzerland to investigate the possibility of acquiring more funds and a more reliable radio liaison with London. Through Allen Dulles, de Bénouville was offered money and the use of the American Embassy radio to establish contact with de Gaulle in return for military intelligence. This arrangement caused an immediate and bitter fight between Frenay and Jean Moulin, who was convinced that the American offer was a way to strengthen the position of their chosen leader for the Free French, Henri Giraud. This "affaire Suisse" was seen as a betrayal of de Gaulle and resulted in de Bénouville being recalled to France.[15]

There is no evidence that this was an attempt on the part of Combat or de Bénouville to usurp de Gaulle's leadership, especially given that de Bénouville was at this point and for many years to come a confirmed Gaullist. Even his postwar description of what the term *resistance* meant supports his pro-Gaullism:

> The term "Resistance" is used here to designate the eight movements which were to unite and form the basis for the National Council of the Resistance in 1943—that is, the official groups recognized by London and in contact with General de Gaulle. I do not include in this category the fly-by-night groups or those which were to fuse with the eight official movements—such as the Carte organization—or the intelligence networks. The agents of the latter led much the same sort of life as any secret agent on enemy territory, whereas the life of a fighter in the Resistance—a phenomenon new to history—was entirely different, and, if I may say so, infinitely more dangerous.[16]

He may, however, have been rather upset with Jean Moulin for canceling the deal with the Americans, and it was in dealing with Moulin that de Bénouville found himself in the midst of another scandal, one far more serious than the first. It was none other than de Bénouville who decided to send René Hardy to the fateful Caluire meeting in June 1943 that resulted in the arrest, torture, and eventual death of Moulin. The Caluire affair is a complicated and murky subject about which there is no need to go into great detail here. De Bénouville's exact role remains somewhat unclear, but as Laurent Douzou and Dominique Veillon point out, "Despite conflicting evidence, it seems that his responsibility was being morally involved in the arrest of Jean Moulin," because he did break very well established security protocols by sending Hardy even though he had been picked up and interrogated by the Gestapo only several weeks before the meeting.[17] Like many others, including Georges Groussard, who was also implicated in the Caluire affair, de Bénouville defended Hardy both times he was brought to trial after the war. As Robert Belot notes, though, the trial "casts a tragic shadow on the past action of Groussard. He did not recover. Smarter, Bénouville fared much better."[18]

The Caluire affair notwithstanding, de Bénouville did very well for himself. In May 1944 he went to Algeria and both asked for and received permission to join the fight on the Italian front. One month later he was ordered back to Algeria, where he, along with Maurice Chevance-Bertin, headed the French Forces of the Interior (FFI) office within the Commissariat à la guerre. De Bénouville finished the war in France after being promoted to the rank of brigadier general. He was a member of the Gaullist Rassemblement du peuple français (RPF), in charge of foreign affairs and national defense issues, and he was a Gaullist deputy in the National Assembly from 1951 to 1955 and again from 1958 to 1962 as a member of the Union pour la nouvelle République (UNR). Although de Bénouville was a Gaullist deputy, his stance on many issues was not so very different from that of his fellow rightist deputies, for example, Loustaunau-Lacau. De Bénouville was against the European Defense Community project and very much wedded to maintaining French colonies. It was his desire to protect French Algeria that ended his relationship with de Gaulle and with the UNR in 1962. From 1970 until 1993 he was again in the National Assembly as the deputy of the 8th district of Paris, and he was also the mayor of La Richardais in Brittany from 1953 to 1965.

De Bénouville demonstrates how easily one could go from being a committed member of the extreme Right to an ardent supporter of de Gaulle to a position of firm anti-Gaullism without ever fundamentally changing political perspectives. His participation in republican politics after the war certainly indicates that he had given up on clandestine political clashes, but as we have seen, the political situation in France after the war made it much easier for a man of the Right to become involved. De Bénouville died in 2001, and his burial in the Passy cemetery, next to his old friends Jehan de Castellane and Michel de Camaret from the 17th cell of the Camelots du Roi, is ultimate proof of his long-standing ties to French royalists.

Based on his own writings and postwar trajectory, one would hesitate before calling de Bénouville a *vichysto-résistant*. But as Vergez-Chaignon points out, he illustrates the necessity felt by many resisters in the postwar period to simplify their narratives to fit within the Resistance schema so neatly laid out by de Gaulle—that capitulation was a crime, that Vichy was illegal and illegitimate, that there were a handful of collaborators, while the vast majority of the French supported, in the abstract if not in action, a unified Resistance.[19] She also rightly argues that de Bénouville "erased the contents of his relationship with Colonel Groussard at Vichy in 1940; the tone of his articles in the very Pétainist journal *L'Alerte*, for which he wrote until March 1943; his passage into the British network Carte, led by André Girard—everything but Gaullist; his brutal confrontation, after his entry into Combat at the end of 1942, with Jean Moulin, who wanted to impose the influence of de Gaulle on the movements."[20] All these observations are spot on. Although it seems that de Bénouville had a straightforward Resistance record, the reality is that it was anything but. His participation was complicated, and his motivations complex. Yet his postwar experience was generally untarnished. He was not punished for his involvement with the Cagoule; his authorship of articles supporting Vichy has mostly been forgotten; and the Caluire affair was simply so complicated that it was difficult to truly assign blame. Although some controversy still surrounds his memory, particularly in the context of his friendship with François Mitterrand—no stranger to controversy himself—de Bénouville largely escaped any consequences of his questionable past.

In this respect he was very much like his old Cagoule colleague Maurice Duclos, who, however, dissociated himself from Vichy much earlier and left for London early in 1940. Duclos is perhaps the most celebrated of the former *cagoulards/résistants,* as his position of authority in the BCRA and his successes in setting up various networks in France were both highly publicized after the war. His biography on the Ordre de la Libération website[21] only recently mentioned his prewar activities with the Cagoule, obscuring the fact, for many years, that Duclos was an unrepentant right-winger who spent many years attempting to demolish the Third Republic. Furthermore, because he moved to Argentina immediately after the war and only returned to France once between 1945 and his death in 1981, the memory of Duclos as an *homme de la Résistance,* rather than an explosive-wielding terrorist, is secure.

Maurice Duclos was born in 1906 in Neuilly-sur-Seine. He studied at the Sainte-Croix college before signing up for a two-year stint with the colonial artillery and serving in Madagascar. In 1928 he was released from duty and put on reserve status. He then joined his father's business at 8, place Vendôme, Paris. At the time of the *cagoulard* trial in 1948, Duclos's occupation was given as broker.[22] On an information sheet for the Chancellerie de l'Ordre de la Libération in 1963, Duclos described himself as a managing partner in an unspecified industrial setting. He had been married and divorced, and the marriage had been annulled by Rome. He had one child, Richard Frederique Maurice, who had been born in Vienna in 1951.[23] Duclos remarried after moving to Argentina; the ambassador of Uruguay described her as "a good little Argentinian woman—with swarthy skin and grey hair—whom he calls 'Pucho' and who is surely very devoted to him (his former marriage having been annulled in Rome. Saint Jacques has principles!!)."[24] Not much more is known about this woman, but she did follow Duclos's wishes and send his archives back to France after his death. Shortly thereafter, however, a letter was sent to the then president of the Association des Français libres noting that the woman they all knew as Duclos's wife in Argentina was not legally his wife, because divorce was not yet accepted in that country. The letter writer, Philippe Ditisheim, went on to say that "the person who legally remained Mrs. Duclos is Austrian, was married right after the war, I believe, had a son, and abandoned Duclos shortly after the birth of this son. The son of Maurice Duclos never knew his father and only came to Buenos Aires for estate matters."[25]

Although other *cagoulards* received much more press than Duclos, he was just as central to the organization as the other leaders but perhaps more cautious. In one police report, the investigator notes that

> Mr. DUCLOS, importer-exporter, Place Vendôme à Paris, is none other than Maurice François DUCLOS, born August 23 in Neuilly-sur-Seine and living at 108, rue Charles Laffitte. A search was undertaken at his house on November 14, 1937, by the Sûreté nationale. He was part of the general staff of CSAR and was suspected of hiding practice weapons and of distributing guns to members of CSAR. DUCLOS, who is an expert in commodities, has offices at 4, rue Mondoir in Paris and 25 bis, rue de la Ferme in Neuilly sur Seine. A second search was undertaken by the judicial police, but like the first, it was unsuccessful, and so far no specific charge can be made against him.[26]

It is quite possible, though pure hypothesis, that the fact that Duclos was significantly more wealthy than the other *cagoulards* allowed him to avoid the legal consequences of his actions for a longer period.[27] He certainly owned enough properties to be able to more successfully hide evidence of his involvement with the organization. His finances were mentioned several times in police reports, and some people even wondered whether he was a major financial contributor to the group.[28]

Wealth and secrecy aside, Duclos was eventually arrested and imprisoned for his *cagoulard* crimes along with his colleagues. He was, however, released and mobilized at the start of the war and rejoined the tenth regiment of the colonial artillery. While engaging in action in Norway in the early summer of 1940, Duclos was detached from his unit to serve as a liaison officer with the thirteenth *demi-brigade* of the French Foreign Legion. After hostilities were suspended, Duclos left for London. There, upon meeting de Gaulle for the first time Duclos was entirely honest about his background. He introduced himself as "Lt. Duclos, presumed *cagoulard*, 3.5 months in the Santé" and said, "I have come to respond to your appeal."[29] De Gaulle asked him to stay in England but also asked, "Now, about your little friends the *cagoulards*, where are they? Hey?"[30] According to the woman who interviewed Duclos after the war, he found this comment particularly injurious and responded, "I am certain that those whom I know will fight for France against the Germans."[31]

As Duclos would later discover, this loyalty to his former colleagues was somewhat misplaced. His meeting with Eugène Deloncle and Gabriel Jeantet in August 1940, as he was undertaking his first mission in France, is described in detail by every historian of the Cagoule. Philippe Bourdrel notes that Jeantet chose to work with Vichy, while Deloncle notoriously formed the Mouvement social révolutionnaire (later to become the Rassemblement national populaire, with Deloncle and Deat at its helm).[32] Bourdrel writes that we can find the *cagoulards* "wherever events are happening, wherever history is being written, until our time. In war, plots, prisons. In Vichy, London, Paris, they will be the stars. For the 'National Revolution,' armed resistance and integral collaboration. . . . Among the earliest companions of de Gaulle, but also ministers of Maréchal Pétain, founders of the Légion française antibolchevique, and leaders of the Milice!"[33]

Yet in 1949, when Duclos gave his testimony to the Comité d'histoire de la deuxième guerre mondiale, he still focused on the integrity of his friends, whom he had told that "I am with de Gaulle, that's why I wanted to see you; given the organization of the Cagoule, you can help the clandestine networks."[34] Even after the war, Duclos maintained that Eugène Deloncle had been playing a double game with the Germans (although he does note that Deloncle was never much help during the war) and that Jeantet had not wanted to "dirty" his hands with the Germans, so he had secured a posting in Vichy.[35]

Duclos himself worked tirelessly for the BCRA throughout the war. Shortly after arriving in London, he was sent back to France to organize resistance groups. His fellow resister Lucien Feltesse admiringly remembered Duclos:

Maurice DUCLOS, who would, a little while later in London, become the capitain SAINT-JACQUES. He was a reserve officer; thus he mobilized, was a volunteer for Narvik, was part of the Norwegian campaign, returned to England, then to France, where he took part in the campaign of May–June. He was able to depart with the last boat of British troops leaving Brittany and was thus . . . the 6th officer to join de GAULLE. Since July de GAULLE had been thinking about organizing intelligence networks in France to be in contact with him. He thought of SAINT-JACQUES, who, after a brief initiation to the mysteries of intelligence, was sent to France on the night of August 2/3 in a speedboat that left him offshore at Courseulles. He reached the shore in a rubber dinghy; he knew the region well because he had a property in Langrune.[36]

By all accounts, this voyage was exceptionally dangerous.[37] The German military was patrolling the cliffs below which Duclos and his colleague had landed, but luckily the two men managed to avoid the patrols and find help from an old family friend in Langrune-sur-Mer. After collecting some information about the German presence in the area and sending it back to London, Duclos made his way to Paris, where he started to establish the base of what would be the *réseau* Saint-Jacques. On August 12 Duclos stopped in at the family business, Les Fils et Petits-Fils de Maurice Duclos (his grandfather), and recruited the very first members of the network, his cousin André Visseaux and Lucien Feltesse.

Feltesse would go on to create one of the three *sous-réseaux* and was in charge of the Somme, Pas-de-Calais, and Belgium. It was also on this trip that Duclos made contact with two men who would also assume leadership roles within the network. Charles Duguy, a commercial engineer, would become Duclos's right-hand man and lead the Paris section of the network. Jean Vérines, who commanded the third infantry battalion in the Republican Guard, headed the third subnetwork, which also covered some of Paris and Normandy. By the end of August 1940 the base of the network was solidly established and was functioning well enough that Duclos was able to consider returning to London.[38] This return was no easy feat, and Duclos contacted his friends in Vichy and in Paris for help to leave the country. In October, Duclos was finally given a visa for Portugal; the visa was given, it should be noted, by the minister of foreign affairs, Paul Baudouin, who was well aware that Duclos was working for de Gaulle. Duclos returned to London on Christmas Day 1940.

Although his first trip was fairly dangerous, one of Duclos's later trips proved to be even more so. On February 14, 1941, he undertook a blind parachute drop into France. His mission was to extend his existing networks within the Caen-Paris-Dunkirk triangle, but the pilot mistakenly dropped him on a particularly unforgiving patch of land. To make matters worse, Duclos's parachute did not open properly. Passy's narrative of this dramatic moment suggests that "with pieces of wood, he [Duclos] made splints for his injured legs and attached them with cord from his parachute; then he crawled nearly two kilometers until he arrived at a small farm, in front of which he fainted."[39] Duclos was woken by a farmer, who had called a doctor, who denounced him to the local police. Although he was arrested, Duclos concocted a story about how he had gone to England as a member of the Deuxième Bureau of Vichy and infiltrated the Secret Intelligence Service there and then been sent back to France to spy for the SIS. According to both Passy and Rémy (Gilbert Renault), two other BCRA agents, Duclos managed to convince the police of the truth of this story and was let go shortly thereafter.[40] Bénédicte Vergez-Chaignon suggests that Duclos was helped by his *cagoulard* colleague Gabriel Jeantet, who at that time was working at Vichy as the head of the Amicale de France.[41]

Although Jeantet might have been able to free Duclos from the police, it was up to Duclos to find a way out of France. In May 1941 Duclos was still stuck in France and only beginning to learn more about the circumstances surrounding his arrest. He had not been alone when he parachuted into the country, and his companion, a radio operator named John Mullemen,[42] had gone missing after the disastrous drop. Over the course of the next seven months the *réseau* Saint-Jacques was decimated by arrests. On June 15 Duclos received a telegram from the BCRA agent Luke that read:

> PRIMO Received a cable from RAYMOND. Took contact with your friend DEGUY, whom we will call DASH (DASH, I say).
>
> SECUNDO Your operator MULLEMAN freed by boches has returned to PARIS with a radio set in working order. Story seems very suspect. DASH will monitor him. Do not use ATHOS. Make use of the set brought by GUY.
>
> TERTIO We will try to send another operator with a set. Can you indicate a parachute drop point.[43]

Although Luke had been in contact with Deguy in June, by the beginning of August Deguy had been arrested and was in prison at Fresnes. He was shot at Mont-Valérien the following July along with Roger Pironneau, the network's liaison between Paris and Saumur.[44] Lucien Feltesse had been arrested the same day and also taken to Fresnes but was liberated after a German military tribunal found insufficient evidence against him. Duclos's oldest sister, Marie-Anne Lefèvre-Duclos, and his niece Monique were both arrested on August 8th and sent to the Prison du Cherche-Midi and the Santé until April 27, 1942, when they were deported as *Nacht und Nebel*.[45] Until they were liberated in 1945, the two women were transferred from camp to camp in Germany.[46] At some point it became clear that Duclos and the *réseau* had been denounced by the radio operator. Postwar reports indicated, in fact, that Mulleman had not been tortured by the Germans but that the threat of torture had been enough to get him to agree to work for them. Mulleman continued to work for the Germans as an interpreter until he was inexplicably deported. In 1945 he was repatriated to France, whereupon he unwisely presented himself at the ministry of the navy looking for work, which prompted a closer look into his background and led to his arrest and a death sentence. He was shot at the fort of Montrouge in Paris in 1946.[47]

After a brief reprieve, the *réseau* became the target of new investigations in October 1941 because of a second betrayal and real German commitment to shutting down the *réseau*. Roger Derry, a priest at the Saint-François-Xavier parish in Paris, and three of his companions were arrested on October 9. They had been working with Jean Vérines, who was himself arrested the following day. Interrogated by the Gestapo, transferred to Fresnes, then incarcerated in Rheinbach, Dusseldorf, and finally Cologne, Vérines was condemned to death and shot. Many of the men who had been arrested with him were decapitated, also in Cologne. The man responsible was André Folmer, an agent working for the Abwehr who had managed to infiltrate Duclos's group. Folmer was later apprehended by the American army in Germany and handed over to the Belgian authorities. He tried to persuade them to treat him like a POW (since he had managed to acquire German citizenship) and "repatriate" him back to Germany, but this request was continuously denied.[48] While these arrests put an end to the original *réseau*, by and large it did continue, albeit with different leaders. Lieutenant Daroussin reorganized the subnetwork of Vérines and later reported that it had more than four thousand agents supporting other resistance networks and British agents.

The subnetwork ran a printing press, distributed fake papers, published press bulletins, collected military intelligence, and engaged in sabotage, particularly toward the end of the war.[49]

Duclos was advised in October 1941 to "try to reach SPAIN present yourself under name JACK JACKSON nationality French Canadian. . . . We know reaching SPAIN difficult and are ready to do anything possible to mount an extraction operation by boat COTE D'AZUR at a later date."[50] This proved even more difficult than expected, and after several failed attempts to retrieve him, Duclos was forced to lie low until March 1, 1942, when he was retrieved by air and then able to make his way back to England and the BCRA.

The history of the BCRA as it is set out in the *livre blanc*[51] mentions Duclos's return to London and notes that the chief of the BCRA asked Saint-Jacques, "who had just finished two extremely dangerous missions in France, to direct the service that took the name Section d'action, études, et coordination."[52] The history of the BCRA, however, is anything but straightforward. In July 1940 de Gaulle created the Deuxième Bureau de l'État-major géneral in London. Mainly an information-gathering organization headed by Passy, it took the name Service de renseignements (SR) on April 15, 1941. Several months later it was split into four sections—Renseignements, Action, Évasion, and Chiffre—and a fifth section, Contre-espionnage, was added later in the year. In January 1942 the SR was given official status and renamed the Bureau central de renseignements et d'action militaire (BCRAM). Its sections now included Renseignements (R); Action Militaire (AM); Contre-Espionnage (CE); Technique, Chiffre, Finance (TCF); and in March 1942, Action, Etudes, et Coordination (AEC), which was created from within the AM and led by Duclos. In September 1942 the organization's name was shortened to BCRA.[53]

Duclos certainly had no shortage of work as the head of the AEC. This section was responsible for keeping incoming documentation (from couriers, mainly) up to date, interrogating volunteers and keeping that information current and in order, giving directions to people on missions in France, maintaining liaisons with de Gaulle's people and ensuring that interested British organizations had access to gathered information, and transmitting any demands for information to the appropriate section,

usually Renseignements or Action Militiare.[54] Duclos was also charged
with several important missions during the war, notably Armada and
Armada II, both of which were focused on sabotage of key industrial sites
in France. In addition, he played a central role in planning for the Allied
landings and was a noteworthy participant in the creation of several plans
for that eventuality—Plan Violet, Plan Tortue, and Plan Vert. Plan Vert
called for the neutralization of transportations during the Allied landings,
while Plan Violet focused on enemy telecommunications. Plan Tortue was
less technical in the sense that it was focused on fighting enemy divisions.

In August 1944 Duclos was detached to S.F.3 Det. (Special Forces 3rd
Detachment) as part of the staff of the 21st British Army Group. He actively participated in the campaigns in Normandy, Belgium, Holland, and
Germany. While in Germany, he created and led a French commando unit,
A220, which was involved in sabotage and information gathering behind
enemy lines. For this work, Duclos was commended by the American
army. Commanding officer Paul W. Baade, of the Thirty-fifth Infantry
Division, US Army, wrote to Duclos on April 29, 1945, noting that "your
skill, audacity and resourcefulness enabled you to operate for 72 hours
behind the enemy lines in the city of Herne without any casualties. . . .
While working as a patrol, you inflicted 34 enemy casualties, took and
held 85 prisoners, and caused great confusion among the enemy."[55]

That Duclos was a former *cagoulard* was no secret among BCRA
agents. In his memoirs, Colonel Passy described Duclos as "the giant
cagoulard, friendly and jovial, big eater, big drinker, womanizer, courageous like a lion, and thus we will never understand what pushed him one
day to conspire, because he was born for trade and detested politics."[56]
Although Passy was, to all intents and purposes, his boss, Passy's knowledge of Duclos's past seemed to trouble him little. He apparently did worry
about the rumors that the BCRA was "a den of unrepentant *cagoulards*,
plotting together against the Republic, of which I was supposedly the
soul,"[57] but that did not stop him from sending former *cagoulards* on
missions to France, because he was confident in their national and anti-
German feelings. Another BCRA agent, P. L. Thyraud de Vosjoli, wrote
in his memoirs that the Cagoule was an offspring of the Synarchy, which
itself was an offspring of early Freemasonry. According to de Vosjoli, some

of his colleagues, notably Duclos, were former *cagoulards*, but they were devoted patriots during the war.[58] Duclos's colleague Colonel Rémy talks at length about the *cagoulard* in his memoirs, giving the impression that they were good friends, and he does not even mention Duclos's previous political affiliations.

These political tendencies were still proudly detailed a full forty years after the war ended in the memoirs of one of Duclos's sisters. The whole immediate family had been involved to one degree or another in his resistance activities. Geneviève Duclos-Rostand, because she had three young children, was dissuaded by her brother from full participation in the network, though she did maintain a radio transmitter in her home, which itself was very dangerous. Her 1995 memoirs express a political perspective that is similar to Duclos's and provide us with an interesting insight into the political leanings of the family even well after the war. Duclos-Rostand writes unashamedly about her brother's role in the Cagoule conspiracy, noting that the electoral victory of Léon Blum in the 1930s had made France "easy prey" for the communists and that the *cagoulards* were preparing themselves to resist a possible communist coup.[59] She notes that her brother turned himself in when his friends in the group were arrested, but she writes of these arrests as if they were episodes of harassment and nothing more. She is quick to point out that the government of 1939 was happy to release all these accomplished army men to lead regiments that lacked morale and discipline after four years of the Popular Front and communism.[60]

The remainder of Duclos-Rostand's memoirs describe the movement of her family throughout the war and the happy times when her brother was able to rejoin them in France. The book is hagiographic in some ways, but she is sometimes remarkably frank about the politics of the Duclos family. She is not at all shy about admitting that she thought there was a tacit agreement between Pétain and de Gaulle, though she eventually came to understand that there was not.[61] Even with this knowledge and in the context of 1995, when the reality of the Vichy regime was well understood, Duclos-Rostand still writes that Pétain was "excessively courageous"[62] and that even when he made decisions that shocked the Duclos family, it was because he was surrounded by less honorable men and poorly counseled by them.[63] She does not say much about de Gaulle in her memoirs but devotes most of her attention to her brother's many adventures and his bravery during the war.

When Duclos left France after the war and moved to Buenos Aires, where he lived until his death in 1981, he left with a plethora of decorations, including the Compagnon de la Libération, four citations for the Croix de guerre, the Military Cross (UK), the OBE (Officer in the Most Excellent Order of the British Empire), and the Krieg Korset (Norwegian), and he was an officer in the Légion d'honneur.[64] Awards aside, Duclos was still considered to be a criminal on the run when the court started assembling the necessary material to resume the *cagoulard* trial in 1945.[65] Several years later, when the trial had actually started, Duclos did return to Paris and was arrested. At that time, few could ignore the long list of his accomplishments during the war. In a demand for provisional liberty, his lawyer, before asking for leniency, reminded the court that

> Maurice Duclos gave himself up October 10, 1948; That he returned from overseas in deference to a court order and to appear before the jury of the Seine to answer for his actions; That in the course of the 1939–1944 war his brilliant conduct earned him the following distinctions: Officer of the Légion d'Honneur, Croix de guerre (several citations), Croix de guerre from Norway, Military Cross and l'Ordre de la Libération; That he gained the ranks of Captain, Major, and Lieutenant-Colonel.[66]

There is no record indicating whether this request for freedom was granted, but Duclos was found not guilty on November 26, 1948, and as quickly as he had come to Paris, he returned once more to Argentina.

Although Duclos was not present to experience it, France was not done celebrating him. In 1947 the Amicale Réseau Saint-Jacques was headquartered in Neuilly-sur-Seine with Lucien Feltesse as its president. Given the number of *amicales* that operated immediately after the war, it is perhaps only to be expected that Saint-Jacques would have one too. What is perhaps more surprising is the commemoration of 8, place Vendôme, Duclos's former workplace and the Saint-Jacques headquarters, in 1986. At the official inauguration of the commemorative plaque, witnesses would have only heard about the most laudatory aspects of Duclos's history.

Michel Caldagues, a senator and mayor of the 1st arrondissement, praised the former *cagoulard* as follows:

> Saint Jacques was the nom de guerre of Maurice Duclos, who worked in the building before which we are today reunited. He was one of three Free French who, after August 4, 1940, performed a first mission of intelligence on the Channel coast. But his goal was even more ambitious, since, at the behest of General de Gaulle, it involved setting up a vast network in Paris that was born right here, at the headquarters of the Duclos company, where his cousin M. André Visseaux, as well as M. Lucien Feltesse, worked.[67]

He went on to give credit to the *réseau* Saint-Jacques for establishing the first clandestine radio contact between London and Paris. In the next speech, General Jean Simon acknowledged Duclos's move to Argentina but noted only that "when General de Gaulle paid an official visit to that country in 1964, he overturned protocol in saluting Colonel Saint-Jacques before all the government authorities."[68] Clearly de Gaulle had gotten over his initial suspicion of former *cagoulards*.

Even in 1990 the Saint-Jacques network continued to be central in the commemoration of the Resistance. For the commemoration of June 18 that year, flames were to be lit in each arrondissement. Three of them were to honor the *réseau* Saint-Jacques, which "was the earliest of the Networks of Free France."[69] Of course, one flame was placed at 8, place Vendôme. One was at Le Bon Conseil de l'Abbé Roger Derry, 6, rue Albert de Lapparent, from where seven people had been deported to die in Germany and where two young people had died during the liberation of Paris. The third flame was at the Vérines barracks of the Republican Guard, where eight members of the FFI had been tortured and killed during the Liberation.[70] Three years later, in 1993, on the fiftieth anniversary of the death of Jean Vérines, a celebratory postcard was issued featuring a heroic photo of Maurice Duclos. Although as a distinct *réseau* Saint-Jacques was not operational for very long, it was clearly significant, particularly in the early days of the war, and it retained a key position in memorialization of the Resistance.

Of what real significance was this memorialization, however? Such celebration subtly indicates that the relationship between Duclos and his country of birth was straightforward. Yet it is clear that this relationship was, to say the least, strained in the 1930s. After the war it was no less complicated though characterized by far less violence than in the prewar period. Duclos's move to Argentina does suggest, upon first glance, that he was perhaps seeking a political milieu that was more hospitable to his rightist tendencies than the communist-dominated scene in France immediately after the war. Although his rightist background may have inspired the decision, Duclos was actually sent to Argentina by the Direction générale des études et recherches (DGER).[71] As one might expect, the details of this mission are shrouded in some mystery, but Duclos was there to set up a commercial society in South America. Thus, he had not broken off all connection with France after his move.

Perhaps the most surprising aspect of Duclos's postwar life was his ongoing relationship with de Gaulle. Although there was no obvious hostility between the two men during the war, Duclos had been much further to the right than de Gaulle, and one might suppose that this political divide could have been a source of tension. Yet all evidence indicates that the two men were quite close, at least in the 1950s. Upon de Gaulle's reelection in 1958, Duclos sent him a personal radiogram that suggests true happiness at the turn of political affairs: "Congratulating France, which, for the second time and for her greatest destiny, has made the right choice of our respected leader. I wish you, as well as your charming 'présidente,' and your family, which is also ours, a very merry Christmas, truly French at last, and my wishes for a prosperous and good presidency. Your loyal companion, Duclos Saint Jacques."[72] This message is not simply a professional congratulations, nor is it simply a message from one veteran to another. The entire tone of the message is one of intimacy, and it suggests that Duclos and de Gaulle were fairly close. Duclos's private archives are full of invitations from de Gaulle for events and receptions, both at the embassy in Argentina and at the Palais de l'Élysée in Paris. Obviously he did not attend those in Paris, since we know that he only returned to France once, but he likely attended those in Argentina, either as an individual or in his capacity as president of the Union française des anciens combattants d'Argentine.

In 1961, in the midst of the generals' putsch in Algeria, Duclos sent de Gaulle another message. This one was less personal, signed by several people in Argentina in addition to Duclos in his capacity as the president of the Association des Français libres. The telegram read: "In the face of serious events that confront the country wish to renew the expression of our attachment to republican institutions and legality stop Are persuaded you will find a definitive solution to crisis created by elements whose irresponsible action endangers unity and future of the nation stop We trust President de Gaulle to assure once again the health of France."[73] This telegram reads much more ambiguously than the previous one from Duclos. It is neither laudatory nor overtly critical. It is possible that the senders were interested in simply showing their support for de Gaulle, but one might detect a subtle warning between the lines. Clearly the senders were not supporting Challe and the other rebellious generals in their attempt to overthrow the government, but they might also have been trying to pressure de Gaulle into resolving the crisis, though by what means remains unsaid. Though the senders reaffirm their attachment to republican institutions and legality, one might wonder why they felt the need to do so. The wording of the telegram makes one wonder if this attachment to the republic was conditional upon de Gaulle finding a "definitive solution." It seems unlikely that these men thought autonomy for Algeria would be such a solution. Unfortunately, there are no further telegrams after 1961, and it is impossible to know what Duclos made of de Gaulle's decisions and Algeria's ultimate independence. As we know, many prewar rightists who made the decision to support de Gaulle both during the war and after felt that his actions in Algeria were the ultimate betrayal and quickly became his most passionate opponents.

Though Duclos seems to have retained a certain measure of respect for de Gaulle, we cannot take this to mean that he had changed his political outlook. Although his role as president of the Anciens combattants in Argentina was seen as providing equilibrium among "the other members of the office, former Vichystes or O.A.S.,"[74] Duclos's politics were never uncomplicated, nor was he simply a loyal Gaullist. In 1945 Duclos wrote a letter to the prefect of Paris on behalf of a friend's father-in-law, who was under investigation. He asked that the court speed up its investigation because the troubles it was causing this man, who "passed before the purge commission. He answered the different questions that were put to him. . . . Monsieur FRANCOIS is very affected by being equated with 'Collaborators,' he who did not even see the Germans. From the material point of view, he has not touched anything and his retirement is suspended . . . and a bureaucrat who raised four children cannot have a big income."[75] Although Duclos does not ask that the case be dropped, his willingness to intercede on behalf of someone who was in danger of being purged for collaboration is itself noteworthy. It may have been that he fully trusted that this man had not been involved with the Germans or that he was skeptical of the purging process, but either way, his decision to become involved indicates that he was not as keen on *l'épuration* as some of his fellow combatants.

This attitude is further illustrated by a letter sent to him in 1966 by one Jean-Marie Pruvost, whom Duclos had never met.

> I only heard talk of you in 1947–48 in Buenos Aires by people who had to abandon France because of ideas contrary to those of "The Purge," who found in you an intelligence free from partisanship and help for which they are still grateful. As a French officer who fought in both wars, I cannot be a partisan. I always placed myself—and remained there—on the exclusively national political plane. Not without grave consequences for myself: I also had to, in extremis, take the path of exile.[76]

Pruvost's letter suggests that Duclos was well known in certain circles that, while they may not have been inclined toward collaboration during the war, were certainly opposed to the events in France during the Liberation and beyond. It is reasonable to assume that Pruvost expected a certain amount of sympathy from Duclos after hearing his story of being forced into exile because of his "nationalist" attitudes. Whether Duclos responded with sympathy or even to address the questions Pruvost asked him about Gabriel Jeantet's book *Année 40* is unknown. But the letter does suggest a rather more complicated relationship between Duclos and the larger Resistance than one might otherwise imagine.

The other members of the BCRA were definitely targets of Duclos's criticism, his admiration for de Gaulle notwithstanding. In his postwar testimony Duclos confirmed that Passy had definitely not been a *cagoulard* and suggested instead that he had been seduced by politics with the creation of the Commissariat à l'intérieur and had been too heavily influenced by the SFIO. This influence, according to Duclos, had been nefarious, in part because the socialists would not accept that France would be liberated by force alone rather than by the resumption of politics, and Passy had begun to agree with them. Duclos told his interviewer that Passy "found himself caught in the clutches of those fellows there, who managed to persuade him that we should not count on the liberation of France by force, that we should cling to a political party to transition softly. All politics is guided by these socialists towards a 'smooth return'; they did not believe that France would liberate herself by force."[77] Although Duclos had tried to persuade them otherwise, he had generally been ignored.

In this conversation about the socialist influence, Duclos named all of the men he thought had been too concerned with politics—Passy, Vallon, Manuel, Brossolette, Boris, Bingen, Brilhac, Bloch. Most of these men, however, escaped Duclos's harsher criticism. This he reserved for people like Manuel, whom he called an "unrepentant socialist and a disgusting type."[78] Pierre Brossolette, brought to the BCRA by Rémy, had been, in Duclos's words, "a little nothing man who, when he no longer had his loudspeaker, was obliged to sell pencils in front of the school"[79] and did not contribute one single useful piece of information to the BCRA during the war. Of Emmanuel d'Astier de la Vigerie, Duclos noted that he had been "un mal fou" and was already a communist, though he did not admit it.[80] Duclos juxtaposed the concern these men had for their mistresses to the concern they showed for valuable agents in the field. Instead of helping agents return to England, these men had flown their wives and mistresses in, their pockets full of gold, dripping with jewelry, and laden with furs. Clearly, the respect Duclos had for de Gaulle did not extend to many of the agents he worked with during the war, demonstrating, it seems, that he did remain true to his rightist political outlook.

POSTWAR MEMORIES

One thing that most rightist resisters had in common was an inability to fit comfortably into any narrative of wartime activity. Whether they broke entirely with Vichy to move on to resistance activities or maintained an official position at Vichy while secretly engaging in the Resistance, these engagements were never entirely straightforward. As other scholars have noted, the very term *vichysto-résistant* rests on a paradox: those loyal to Vichy and those loyal to the Resistance had different ideas about what was legitimate between 1940 and 1944 and what was not.[1] However, these same scholars have also noted that it is perfectly imaginable that contradictory ideas and attitudes might reside within the same individual.[2] This tension, according to Johanna Barasz, causes discomfort in the individual, who feels the need to resolve these contradictions. In some cases, however, the individual's discomfort is not what is immediately apparent. Rather, it is the discomfort their seemingly contradictory loyalties cause in others that is clear. Gabriel Jeantet, who was both celebrated for his participation in the Resistance and punished for his connections to Vichy, provides us with an even more striking example of how complicated the stories of *vichysto-résistants* are. Jeantet also illustrates a second common feature of all the rightist resisters investigated in these pages: their links to one another. No matter what form their resistance took, whether it began at Vichy or in London or slowly moved from one locale to another, all these men and women continued to make use of old social networks. Gabriel Jeantet, who never stopped believing in the value of the armistice or the righteousness of Pétain's cause, saw Loustaunau-Lacau, Groussard,

Duclos, and others at different moments in the war. Because of his official position at Vichy, often he was able to give them assistance when they needed it most.

Born in 1906, Jeantet was a young member of the Action française who with his brother Claude collaborated on the student journal of that royalist organization. An early and enthusiastic adherent of the Cagoule, Jeantet was one of the lucky members who escaped the police in 1937 by fleeing to Spain and then Italy. Jeantet later claimed that upon returning to France after the declaration of war and presenting himself to the military bureau in Annemasse, he was asked to return to Italy to investigate the possibilities of recruiting antifascists hostile to the Axis for a potential military operation in Piedmont.[3] After his return from this "mission," Jeantet's luck ran out: he was arrested and imprisoned in the Santé for two months. Though we need to approach Jeantet's testimony with caution, a letter from the ministry of national defense in support of Jeantet does give the impression that he had indeed been engaged in something important. The author of this letter, from the Cinquième Bureau, notes that Jeantet had a relationship with the division and wonders whether a certain amount of benevolence might be shown in view of the services Jeantet had already provided and those he was likely to provide in the future. The Cinquième Bureau was a central intelligence service and was largely responsible for counterintelligence, so it is possible that Jeantet was telling at least a partially true story.[4] Like the other *cagoulards,* he was given provisional liberty to rejoin his military unit, which he did until he was demobilized in July 1940. Jeantet then made his way to Vichy, where he quickly became the head of the newly founded Amicale de France, a Pétainist propaganda organization.

Although the Amicale was not operational for long, as it was dissolved on Darlan's orders in 1941, Jeantet nevertheless stayed in Vichy and remained an ardent supporter of Pétain throughout the war and after. When asked to explain the dissolution of the Amicale, Jeantet noted that "the anti-German and moderating action of the Amicale de France was well known in informed circles in the southern zone, as in the northern zone. After the dismissal of Laval on December 13, 1940, it became the object of lively criticisms in the Franco-German circles of Paris, and the embassy

authorities indicated that they wanted it suppressed."⁵ Jeantet never criticized Pétain for having been the one to sign the dissolution papers but
instead blamed Darlan and other pro-German elements at Vichy. After
the dissolution of the group, Jeantet and some of his colleagues from the
Amicale decided to continue publishing their journal *France* but also created the Société d'éditions de l'État Nouveau, a publishing house, which
would finance their future activities.

Although Jeantet was a well-known figure at Vichy, a supporter of the
National Revolution, and a Pétainist through and through, he was also
an early supporter of the Resistance. It would be dangerous to say that
he was a resister per se in 1940 and 1941, but he was already sustaining
resistance activity. Paul Dungler, also a member of the AF, organized the
first resistance network in Alsace in August 1940. Originally called the 7e
colonne d'Alsace, it later came to be known as the Martial network. Dungler also displayed a certain amount of ambiguity in his political choices.
His ongoing connection to Vichy and Pétain seemed suspect, but his
Alsatian resistance network certainly placed him firmly within the non-
Gaullist resistance. After the war, he spoke freely of his relationship with
Jeantet: "Afterwards and throughout the whole war I saw him regularly.
He provided me with precious information about Vichyite politics and
on the Germans, which I transmitted to London to the B.C.R.A. . . . I can
assure you that throughout the war Jeantet was on very bad terms with
the old leaders of the Cagoule; he even confided that it was necessary to
be wary of Deloncle."⁶ Like Jeantet and the other *cagoulards* in the Resistance, Dungler suffered for his hostility to de Gaulle and the political and
ideological views he shared with Vichy,⁷ but these shared views certainly
helped him renew his relationships with people like Jeantet, who could
be of help to the resistance network.⁸

Jeantet also made contact with Colonel Gaillard (code name Triangle),
a regional chief of the FFI, and other members of the BCRA, to whom he
provided political intelligence, since he was "particularly well placed to
do it."⁹ Along with Dungler, Jeantet also claimed to have made contact
with anti-Nazi Germans. When asked by the police after the war about
his contact with certain groups of Germans, Jeantet replied that a former
officer of the Deuxième Bureau had made contact with him in Vichy and

"told me that contacts had been had in Nice with elements of the German fifth column. They were German soldiers who planned the overthrow of Nazism and the eviction of Hitler from power."[10] Jeantet agreed to help this group of military men as much as he could. Without much proof of this whole episode, it is difficult to say what is true and what is not. We certainly know that there were German officers who were keen to remove Hitler from power, but whether Jeantet was truly involved is difficult to say. As Bénédicte Vergez-Chaignon points out, "The only thing that is evident is that Jeantet wanted to believe that Pétain could serve as an intermediary between the Americans and the anti-Nazi Germans and rivals of Hitler."[11]

Jeantet clearly believed that Pétain was acting in the best interests of France. In his postwar testimony, Jeantet repeated many times that Pétain had known about the Resistance, had recognized its utility, and had done his best to support it clandestinely. Jeantet also related that he had told Pétain that the time for double speak with the Germans was over, that it was time to let them in on Vichy's true stance, that Germany would lose the war eventually, and that the Germans' increasingly repressive behavior in France would not do them any favors at the war's end. According to Jeantet, Pétain had very much approved of this plan.[12] Even in June 1944 Jeantet still very much supported Pétain's behavior. A note from the police pointed out that

> we are signaling that a new political group called "Groupe d'Action et de Révolution" is being created.
>
> Constituted as a secret association, [its] president will be M. Gabriel Jeantet, director of the magazine "France" at Vichy, and [it] will include various personalities loyal to the Marshal or compromised in the eyes of the Allies.
>
> The goal of this association will be to retain, after the end of the hostilities, the benefits of the work done by the Head of State since 1940, that is to say, the measures that were instituted by the National Revolution. Anticollaborationist, all the while counseling prudence, the group is equally opposed to the action of the Milice, which it judges to be harmful, and to the C.F.L.N., as well as any government of Algiers that is likely to take power in France after the war.[13]

Whether Jeantet would have followed through with this new group, destined to support the goals of the National Revolution against those who would oppose it, is impossible to say, as he was arrested one month after this police report was filed. It is clear that Jeantet maintained a strong attachment to the values of the Vichy regime even as he was assisting various resisters. His assistance, as useful as it was for his friends, did not cause him to reconsider his ideological attachment to Vichy. Even reminiscing about his first wartime reunion with Maurice Duclos, Jeantet wrote that "they understood that their antagonism came, not from their goals, but from the actions they were taking to accomplish them. The Londonian and the Vichyssois noticed that they were equally vigorous in their hopes for a restored France and a defeated Germany."[14]

Jeantet blamed his July 27 arrest entirely on Joseph Darnand, head of the Milice. Interestingly enough, their former *cagoulard* connection had no positive effect on the relationship between these two men. Both had been active participants in the group and fairly close until, according to Jeantet, Darnand changed his political views in the midst of the war; from that point on, instead of seeking to fight against the Germans he had done his absolute best to serve them.[15] Jeantet claims to have tried to steer people away from the Milice, and this hostility to the group made Darnand look for any way to arrest his former colleague. After his arrest, Jeantet was handed over to the Germans and transferred to Eisenberg in Germany. As the Russians continued to push into Germany toward the end of the war, the prisoners in Eisenberg were set free to fend for themselves. Jeantet and his party managed to find American troops in Karlsbad and were repatriated to France in May 1945.

Not long after his return, however, Jeantet was arrested yet again. Not only was his participation in the Cagoule problematic, to say the least, but he was under heavy suspicion for his wartime activities because of his closeness to Pétain and other Vichy notables. Ironically, and illustrative of the difficulty inherent in attempting to classify people like Jeantet and other *cagoulards*, he was both awarded the Croix du combattant volontaire de la Résistance and stripped of many of his rights of citizenship as part of his punishment of twenty-five years of national indignity. The Croix was awarded to people who had served at least ninety days with a (recognized) resistance organization or had been wounded or killed in resistance action. The punishment of national indignity sprang from various laws developed in 1944 to facilitate the process of *l'épuration* (purge). It stripped individuals of many citizenship rights (e.g., the right to vote) and excluded them from further participation in many public functions and professions.

After four long years of occupation, France was finally liberated in stages throughout 1944. De Gaulle had managed to persuade the Anglo-Americans that an Allied military occupation of France was unnecessary, saving the country from further humiliation after what had been an ignominious four years. For all that, however, de Gaulle still had to find a way, as head of the provisional government, to lead a country that had been engaged in a fratricidal war, one that had peaked as the Liberation was taking place, with intense violence directed at those who had collaborated (or who were suspected of having collaborated) with the occupying forces. At least ten thousand people were summarily executed in what has been described as an "anarchic settling of differences" by members of the Resistance and other French people with a score to settle.[16] While this kind of violence was ideal if one was planning to bring the country to the brink of revolution, de Gaulle and his closest resisters had no desire to encourage such insurrectionary goals. To bring the spontaneous vengeance to an end, de Gaulle needed to reestablish the normal channels of justice as quickly as possible. To do this, he created special courts to deal with collaborators and thus institutionalized *l'épuration*. Yet those people who were participating in the revolutionary justice and who were hoping to rebuild France along rather more leftist lines had also been active members of the Resistance. How could de Gaulle reconcile their version of events with his own, which tended to minimize divisions, in hopes of normalizing the situation in France?

The process whereby de Gaulle managed to assert his legitimacy started early in the war, but was solidified in 1944, as he established what Henry Rousso calls the "founding myth of the post-Vichy period": that France had been liberated thanks to her own efforts, that all of France except a few traitors had "resisted," and that the French Republic had never ceased to exist, making Vichy merely a parenthesis in an unbroken history of France.[17] The ramifications of this myth were far-reaching, as detailed by Henry Rousso, and though it mostly affected how the French viewed the

events from 1940 to 1944 in a general way, it also had specific ramifications for how the Resistance was viewed. If, as in de Gaulle's vision, all
French resisted, it was not to a politically active, not to mention politically
diverse, resistance that they rallied. De Gaulle's unifying vision outlined
a Resistance without politics, without divergences of opinion, without
individuality—a Resistance without resisters, ultimately. De Gaulle's
vision did not withstand the test of time; it did not take long for cracks
to appear in this "resistancialist" myth.[18] However, resisters of the Right,
and particularly the extreme Right, had their own battles to fight in this
post-Vichy world.

As we have seen, the postwar years brought new challenges for some
of these men and new opportunities for others. How did they fit into the
postwar political culture after so many years of underground plotting?
Although these men were losing in the battle to create a narrative of
resistance and thus did not fit comfortably into the postwar culture,
they mostly found themselves in line with postwar politics. This was
particularly true as the dynamics of the Cold War began to make a real
impact on the French political scene. After 1947 and the expulsion of the
communists from the government, men like Georges Loustaunau-Lacau,
Georges Groussard, Guillain de Bénouville, and others had little difficulty
justifying their lifelong anticommunist missions. Very little changed in
their attitudes toward the party of 75,000 *fusillés,* except that they perhaps
grudgingly admitted that the PCF had indeed contributed to the resistance
effort, though even that admission was tempered by frequent commentary
on the party's late entry into the struggle and its leader's desertion from
the army.[19] As we have seen, Loustaunau-Lacau did not hesitate to bring
these issues to light in the National Assembly, and Maurice Duclos, for
all his usual caution, was so incensed by the communists that his dislike
formed a major part of his postwar testimony. These men had not changed
their perspective on communism, but because the government itself
continued to push the PCF to the margins of the political realm, their
attitudes once again became acceptable. Moreover, these attitudes found
favor in the political circles that were drawing ever closer to the United
States, which was certainly hostile to communism and was also seen by
many rightists as being anti-Gaullist.

Another striking continuity between the pre- and postwar political attitudes of these men was their anti-Semitism. As we have seen, none of these men were prone to espousing the virulent, racial anti-Semitism of the Nazis, but we cannot discount the fact that most of them shared the cultural anti-Semitism of the Action française and did not hesitate to point to the supposed inability of the French Jewish population to assimilate as one of the major causes of France's downfall. Simon Epstein's examination of *antisémites-résistants* is one of the first scholarly works to acknowledge that the Resistance counted among its members many anti-Semites—of varying degrees, certainly—and that they came from both the Left and the Right. Epstein argues that only a minority maintained their anti-Semitism after the war and that most renounced these attitudes and many became friends of both the Jewish people and the state of Israel.[20] He notes that Loustaunau-Lacau, though vocally anti-Semitic before the war, was changed by his experience in the concentration camps; that Marie-Madeleine Fourcade spoke against anti-Jewish aggression at a meeting of the Ligue internationale contre l'antisémitisme (LICA) in 1960; that de Bénouville became the president of the parliamentary Groupe d'amitié France-Israël in 1973. Though Epstein's research is beyond reproach, his optimistic perception of these "former" anti-Semites is perhaps misguided.

It is no secret that the French reaction to the events of the Second World War focused far less on what had happened to the European Jewish community than on what had happened to French political deportees or resisters, for example. Not surprisingly, immediately after the war the influence of resisters was great in the press and government agencies, and the privileging of resistance victims of Nazi oppression over Jewish victims comes as no shock. The relatively obscured story of what had happened during the Holocaust meant that few people in France were forced to reexamine their own attitudes toward the Jewish community. This silence would not last forever, but in the immediate aftermath of the war rightist resisters were not forced to comment one way or another on the issue of Jewish persecution. This does not mean, however, that they had fundamentally changed their perspective, even if they seemed more sympathetic to the plight of the Jews. Even through the lens of the Holocaust, French anti-Semites could always argue that their anti-Semitism had never been like that of the Nazis, and they could also point to the fact that as resisters they had helped many Jewish families during the war.

Though Simon Epstein is right to point out that many of these men and women drew closer to Israel, this does not mean they were necessarily less anti-Semitic. As Richard Vinen argues, anti-Semitism and Zionism were not mutually exclusive; the creation of a Jewish state was often seen as a way to rid Europe of Jews.[21] Vinen's article successfully shows that contrary to most assumptions, anti-Semitism did continue in France in the postwar period but was unimportant in politics. Vinen notes Pierre Mendès-France's investiture as *président du conseil* in 1954 and the Suez Crisis of 1956 to show the double edge of rightist political anti-Semitism (directed against Mendès-France) but also how little that mattered when Israel could be a useful ally.[22] He goes on to argue that

> the single experience that did most to change the attitude of the French right to both Israel and the Jews was the Algerian war, and especially France's withdrawal from Algeria under the leadership of de Gaulle between 1958 and 1962. Most of the right supported the Organisation de l'Armée Secrète (OAS) of army officers and settlers that sought to defend Algerie Française. The OAS viewed Israel, which provided an example of European settlers defeating Arab resistance, with growing admiration.[23]

Except in the case of Marie-Madeleine Fourcade, who remained a Gaullist supporter after the war, there is no reason to believe that someone like Guillain de Bénouville did not use his rapprochement with Israel as a way to more fully express his dislike of de Gaulle after 1962. As Vinen notes, de Gaulle turned away from Israel and toward Arab countries in an attempt to mend fences after the Algerian War. By 1967 "few leaders of the extreme right approved of attacks on Israel, and most of them would have cut their tongues out before saying anything that might be interpreted as an expression of support for de Gaulle."[24] Given that many rightist resisters felt betrayed by the loss of Algeria and de Gaulle's role in that, it is very possible that their pro-Israel sentiments were part of an expression of that betrayal.

Although the Right—with its anticommunism, its political anti-Semitism, its increasing enthusiasm for the United States, and its expanding internationalism—had found a place in French politics, the real test of its integration came with the Algerian War. The loss of Indochina had already led some rightist resisters to make clear their position regarding the French colonies. Loustaunau-Lacau, as we have seen, repeatedly defended the French Army and its mission in Indochina. Georges Groussard had quit the army and refused promotion in the Legion of Honor because of the embarrassment of Dien Bien Phu. Both men were quick to point out the Fourth Republic's failure to maintain the colonies or support the army. The Algerian War would elicit even stronger reactions from former resisters, test the postwar spirit of cooperation, and reopen unhealed wounds of the Second World War. The Algerian War, much like the interwar period in France, clearly represented another example of an ongoing *guerre franco-française,* a virtual civil war between French citizens. Former resisters were not at all unified in their response to the prospect of Algerian independence; many were understandably outraged by the blatant violations of human rights that were occurring in Algeria, and their memories of Nazi crimes led them to offer their support to the independence movements. But other former resisters who shared the same memories and experiences of the Second World War were headed down much different paths, supporting Henry Rousso's point that "the resistance heritage was not the sole possession of those who opposed the war in Algeria."[25] Just as few people wanted to admit that the Right had participated in the Resistance, the fact that some former resisters were wedded to keeping Algeria French has also been underplayed. In part, this is because of the enduring popular myth that all resisters were staunch defenders of human rights, so that the fight of some resisters to keep a depressing colonial legacy alive has presented itself as a contradiction. It also reflects a popular tendency to emphasize discontinuity and painful ruptures with the past, during both the Second World War and the Algerian War.

The creation of the Organisation de l'armée secrète, a secret military organization, in 1961, in response to de Gaulle's referendum on Algeria's self-determination, offers a perfect example of the kind of continuity that can sometimes be overlooked. This highly illegal initiative was supported not only by current army officers but also by former resisters in both France and Algeria. While the OAS was clearly overstepping its authority by encouraging sections of the army to sabotage the process of granting independence to Algeria, it could point to recent examples of this kind of insubordination to prove its legitimacy, if not its legality. The most notable example was the fact that de Gaulle himself had appealed to the French military to continue fighting against the armistice in 1940, arguing that it had been signed by an illegitimate government, and continued to encourage the Resistance to engage in subversive acts against that same government all through the war. Although historians like Edgar Furniss have argued that there is a difference between calls for action against an occupying external enemy and similar calls for action against the president of France,[26] I would suggest that in the eyes of the former resisters who supported French Algeria, that difference did not really exist. In 1962 many former resisters saw little difference between the way de Gaulle was betraying France and the French Army and the way Philippe Pétain had done the same by bowing to the Germans in 1940. Georges Groussard wrote that it was quite a coincidence that Pétain had asked for an armistice while the army was still willing to fight and that de Gaulle, who had been quite close to Pétain in the 1930s, did the same thing. Groussard compared the two betrayals by noting that "another head of state, between 1958 and 1962, having assured our soldiers (and with what conviction) that it was necessary to defeat the *fellagha* to preserve Algeria for France, has, as these soldiers fought and died for this goal, addressed message after message to the French to show them that it was necessary to withdraw from Algeria."[27]

Groussard later testified in support of Raoul Salan, one of the generals who attempted to lead a coup against de Gaulle's government in April 1961. Groussard, as we have seen, could never have been called a supporter of de Gaulle, even if he did grudgingly admit de Gaulle's usefulness in the Resistance. Therefore, Groussard's opposition to de Gaulle during the Algerian War is unsurprising. However, some of his fellow rightist resisters, most notably Guillain de Bénouville, had wholeheartedly turned to Gaullism after the war. He, like many other Gaullists, seemed to imagine that de Gaulle would follow the loosely constructed policy of "integration" for Algeria and did not hesitate to support de Gaulle's return to power in

1958.[28] Like most supporters of Algérie française, de Bénouville was sadly misinformed about de Gaulle's plans. After years as a Gaullist deputy, he was forced to leave the Gaullist Union pour la nouvelle République in 1962. This break would mean the end of de Bénouville's support for de Gaulle and a return to his rightist roots.

Other rightist resisters, such as Gabriel Jeantet, had never even tried to reconcile their political positions with Gaullism but still found the Algerian War a perfect moment to revisit their memories of the war. Jeantet had continued to be fairly active in political life for some time after 1945, first as a member of the extreme Right group Occident and then as an adherent of the Parti des forces nouvelles, an offshoot of the Front National. He also worked for the publishing company Éditions de la Table Ronde until the 1970s, focusing particularly on their contemporary history collection. It was in this collection that Jeantet published, in collaboration with Jacques Laurent, a book entitled *Année 40: Londres—de Gaulle—Vichy* in 1965. The book is part narrative, part collection of various "documents" that are meant to serve as proof for the main argument of the book, namely, that de Gaulle did not present the first case of resistance and that the myth of him as a solitary leader of a national resistance was created deliberately by de Gaulle, who wanted, more than the resumption of the fight against the Germans, to single-handedly lead a new French government.[29] Laurent and Jeantet argue that even though de Gaulle knew that Pétain was supporting resistance efforts, he deliberately waged war on the Vichy leader because he needed to discredit Vichy so that he could prove his own legitimacy. Replicating the myth of Pétain's double game, these two rightists argued that de Gaulle was even harsher in his treatment of Pétain than he was in his treatment of Hitler or Mussolini.[30] They used their own memories of the war and early resistance at Vichy to assert a rightist opposition to de Gaulle in 1965. There is no doubt that the moment of publication, a few short years after the end of the Algerian War, was determined in some way by contemporary affairs. Laurent and Jeantet make much of the Gaullist "abuses" of the empire in the book, devoting more than fifty pages of documents to that subject.[31]

That the French Right would support the maintenance of the colonies comes as no surprise. The battles that were being waged in Algeria were seen by many in France as a showdown between the forces of democracy and those of communism. There was a widespread sense that the nationalist forces in Algeria were being unduly influenced (and supplied) by Gamal Abdel Nasser in Egypt and thus also, by extension, by the Soviet Union. This sense that France and the Western world more generally were being threatened by communist forces was aptly summed up by Jacques Soustelle, himself a Resistance hero, who noted that "if the tricolor is lowered in Algeria the red flag will soon fly in Paris."[32] Soustelle had been de Gaulle's right-hand man during the war, working with the Free French, and in the immediate postwar period he became the minister of information and then the minister of colonies. Soustelle was the governor-general of Algeria in the mid-1950s and lent his considerable support to returning de Gaulle to power in 1958. However, like de Bénouville, he did not support de Gaulle's decision to promote Algerian independence, and his decision to join the OAS led him to live in exile from 1961 to 1968.

This sense that the Algerian War was a major strategic point of the Cold War and that its outcome could mean a setback for global communism was sure to attract the extreme Right in France. Had these men not spent much of their lives fighting communism at home? It was only natural that men like Groussard, de Bénouville, Duclos, Jeantet, et al., would support any measure that would stop the red tide. In addition to the fundamental anticommunism of this effort to keep Algeria French, the nationalist aspect would have also appealed to these rightist resisters. The embarrassment of Indochina only intensified the desire to maintain France's position as a world power, and the loss of Algeria was set to ruin any such plans. The situation in Algeria was so complex, however, that it was not only rightist resisters who heard this siren song of rebellion against the republic. Many former *résistants*, of various political stripes, also saw the fight for Algeria as something more than an issue of colonialism. Soustelle certainly was not a rightist, nor was his colleague Georges Bidault, both of whom ended up in exile because of their "resistance" to Algerian independence.

The Algerian War was a pivotal moment for members of the Resistance. The rightist resistance had managed to slide fairly comfortably into the postwar political scene at a time when politics was truly dominated by the Resistance as a whole. Although the extreme Right could not fully assimilate with its former comrades of the Resistance, it did have enough tenacity to weather the storms of the European Coal and Steel Community debate, the European Defense Community discussions, and the war in Indochina. Men like Loustaunau-Lacau, de Bénouville, and Groussard could all publicly use their pasts as resisters to justify their positions on these issues. But the Algerian War changed that. The Resistance, as a concept that was supposed to mean something, was used by all sides of the conflict. Georges Bidault, a prominent resister, formed the Conseil national de la Résistance in 1962 to prevent the abandonment of Algeria. He could not have picked a more explicit reference when he chose to name his new organization after the one he headed in 1943 to fight the German occupation. Others similarly drew this connection and argued, in order to head off any attempt to link the Algerian nationalists with the Resistance, that the French Army should be seen as the logical continuation of the Resistance.[33] This argument was unsuccessful, however, as the opponents of the war claimed this heritage for themselves and made direct links between the army and the Gestapo. Claude Bourdet published a now infamous article with the title "Votre Gestapo d'Algérie," and he and other anticolonial activists used these comparisons between the Nazi regime and supporters of Algérie française to identify the "real" resisters in the struggle. The legacy of the Resistance was up for grabs again.

Vergez-Chaignon writes that

> a moment of rupture in the republican consensus, this war destroyed, at the same time as the institutional and partisan equilibrium, the links and the solidarities born of the Resistance or redrew them. There was a resurgence of fronts of opposition, which presented the opportunity to settle old political scores. By reviving the debates on legality and legitimacy, the nature of patriotism, and the hierarchy of national and democratic values, the Algerian War revived the issues that prevailed between 1940 and 1944.[34]

Vergez-Chaignon also notes that the revival of the political divides of the Second World War had a particular impact on those people who had opposed the Occupation, all the while believing that they were following Pétain's wishes. It was those people—people who had links with Vichy, real or suspected—who lost not only the battle for Algeria but also the battle for use of the Resistance legacy. The tide had turned again for rightist resisters. Loustaunau-Lacau was deceased by 1962, but it is easy to see the impact of this war on the surviving men. Groussard retreated from public life and continued to distance himself from the army until his death in 1980. Duclos never returned to France, and there is no evidence that his relationship with de Gaulle continued after 1962. After a break from politics, Jeantet returned to the fold of the extreme Right through his membership in the group Ordre nouveau and its later manifestation, the Parti des forces nouvelles, until his death in 1978. Of these rightists, only de Bénouville maintained his public position in politics alongside his businesses in the private sector, though his death in 2001 sparked further controversy over his resistance record.

The wounds opened by the Algerian War and the renewed connection between the Right and forces of repression made it even more difficult for these men to explain their trajectories from antigovernment conspiracy in the 1930s, to working for the Resistance during the war, to finding their niche in politics in the late 1940s and early 1950s, to advocating full-on rebellion against the Republic during the conflict in Algeria. The reality, I would argue, is not so much a matter of their trajectories being inexplicable as it is a matter of the changing context in which they lived. Most of these men demonstrated a striking continuity in both thought and behavior over the years. When their ideologies were in line with more general trends in France, they were acceptable members of society. When the cultural or political atmosphere shifted, they were seen as rogues. One only has to look at the anticommunism of the Right to see this. Sanctioned by the government in the 1920s, active anticommunism was forced into the shadows during the Popular Front era. When the PCF was banned at the outset of the war and the communists were linked with the Nazis, it was again acceptable to demonstrate disdain for the party. Not so, however, once the PCF started resisting the German occupation in 1941 or immediately after the war. However, by 1947 anticommunism was not only accepted but welcomed, as the Cold War continued to "heat up." During the Algerian War, the struggle against communism could have gone either way. Perhaps with the American support they sought, the supporters of Algérie française could have made a case for keeping Algeria as a bulwark against global communism. But they misunderstood the situation, and their anticommunism was not enough to justify their actions in Algeria. These rightist resisters did not change, but the context did, and being unable, or unwilling, to adapt to the changing nature of French society contributed to their erasure from the Resistance legacy.

CONCLUSION

The men of the Cagoule and the Corvignolles are unlikely to command much sympathy for their active attempts to destabilize the Third Republic in the 1930s, but the fact that their stories of resistance have been neglected should cause concern. Although in many ways they were ordinary men, their actions during the war were extraordinary, in the most literal sense of the word. They were part of a minority who devoted themselves, at major risk to both life and liberty, to freeing France from the German occupants. At the risk of glorifying these rightist *résistants*, the unique nature of their endeavors and the risk associated with those actions needs to be emphasized. Although these men often seemed fearless, particularly in their vocal criticisms of French politics, they, like most resisters, had much to lose. Many of these men had families, and families were easy targets for German and French police in their hunt for "terrorists." Georges Loustaunau-Lacau, as we have seen, was arrested the final time before his deportation because he could not bear to go any longer without seeing his wife and children. While his family remained mostly safe from German reprisals, those troubled years affected them all in many ways. Marie-Madeleine Méric, taking a lesson from Loustaunau-Lacau's fate, first sent her children to her mother, and when that became too dangerous, she paid someone to accompany them to Switzerland. The guide abandoned them along the way, however, and her twelve-year-old son and ten-year-old daughter were forced to make their own way to find help.[1] Maurice Duclos was faced with the arrest and deportation of his sister and his niece. Georges Groussard's twenty-two-year-old son, Serge, now a well-known French journalist and author, was arrested by the Gestapo in 1943 and deported to Germany. Contrary to the perception of the resistance fighter as a dashing young man with few responsibilities and fewer connections, living in a surreal world of shadowy struggle, these men exemplify just how "normal" most resisters were. And yet they were extraordinary, because all of these things—families, jobs, social networks—were put at risk because of their decision to keep fighting.

This decision was even more exceptional given the past activities of these men. Maurice Duclos, Gabriel Jeantet, François Méténier, and Guillain de Bénouville all had been active members of the Cagoule in the 1930s. The organization was antirepublican, anticommunist, anti-Semitic, and an active element of the French extreme Right. These men had used guile, threats, bombs, sabotage, and murder in their attempt to destabilize the Third Republic to the point of collapse. The fact that the CSAR failed in its insurrectionary goals should not diminish its importance, its seriousness, or its lasting influence. Of the six reasons that Joel Blatt offers for the failure of the conspiracy, only one was the fault of the group itself. He argues that the group's members made some key mistakes, that it was weakened by having to battle for turf with other organizations of the Right, that it had no support from traditional conservatives, that it had no important military backing, that the timing did not work for their plans, and that the strength of the Third Republic was great enough to prevent a successful coup.[2] Certainly the members of the Cagoule made some fatal mistakes that led to their arrests, but ultimately the Third Republic was strong enough to resist such a threat. When the Republic did fall, however, these men were faced with a unique opportunity.

By all early indications, the Vichy government was set to embody the very political and moral principles these men held so dear. It was an authoritarian government, led not by any ordinary man but by the "victor of Verdun," with whom most of the leading *cagoulards* had had some contact. The Vichy regime had an immediate and vehement policy of anticommunism, it would develop an increasingly anti-Semitic one, and like the members of the Cagoule, its leaders had no problem blaming the Third Republic for any of the country's ills. It would have been very easy for the newly liberated *cagoulards* to slip into the political circles at

Vichy and remain there for the duration of the war. And yet it is hard to imagine that these men would choose such an uncomplicated path, and in the end they did not. Even someone like Gabriel Jeantet, who did take up an official position at Vichy and supported Pétain throughout the war and beyond, helped the Resistance in manifold ways. Maurice Duclos did not hesitate to distance himself entirely from Vichy, and Guillain de Bénouville combined early Pétainism with immersion into the world of resistance.

Alongside these men were the men from the Corvignolles. That organization too was led by men who sought a more authoritarian form of government—one that could cure France of *la décadence*—and a total destruction of communism within and outside France. Georges Loustaunau-Lacau and Georges Groussard were committed to creating an army and a government cleansed of the (perceived) pernicious influence of communism, and while they may have disagreed with many of its aspects, the Nazi regime was doing just that. Yet they also chose options other than collaboration, and as the war and occupation dragged on, both men moved further and further away from the Vichy government. They did so, however, without abandoning their politics. Their increasing distance from Vichy did not bring them any closer to the Left, nor did the eventual participation of the communists in the Resistance do anything to ease their deep-seated hatred of communism. Neither man was particularly reticent about expressing these thoughts, and both remained committed activists in the postwar years.

The participation, to varying degrees, of all these men in the Resistance suggests several things. First and foremost, as this work has shown, there was simply no way to determine in advance what course of action men and women would take in a time of great crisis. The question who would or would not join the Resistance is one that can only be answered in retrospect and, moreover, cannot be answered with simple generalizations. Sociological studies of *résistants* can tell us, for instance, that young people were more inclined to join the clandestine interior resistance, while the exterior resistance was staffed by older men and women; or that most resisters were fairly well educated and came from a republican elite.[3] But these studies will never be able to tell us that action during the war was *determined* by these factors. Passing the *bac* may have made it more likely that a person would choose to resist the German occupation, but there were also many well-educated people at Vichy. In all likelihood, a scholar who maintains a deterministic link between, say, where in France one was born and that person's decision to join the Resistance would be challenged on several fronts. And yet, when it comes to political affiliation, some people have hesitated to challenge the entrenched idea that the Left was largely responsible for the Resistance and the Right for Vichy. It has been more than twenty years since Rémy Handourtzel and Cyril Buffet wrote *La collaboration à gauche aussi* in order to "break the taboo by remembering that authentic men of the left, among the most sincere and engaged in the prewar years, joined the partisans of a direct collaboration with Nazi Germany or on their own initiative became participants in the National Revolution."[4] William Irvine has also shown how members of the Ligue des droits de l'homme ended up on the "wrong" side during the war, and Simon Epstein has definitively explored the topic of anti-Semites in the Resistance and antiracists in collaborationist circles.[5] For all this scholarship, however, many people are unwilling to admit that prewar affiliations did not determine wartime activity. A person could be the most violently antirepublican, anticommunist, anti-Semitic, murderous, and corrupt individual and still have fought against the Nazis and against Vichy. The fact that we may have little respect for that person and his politics does not mean we can simply ignore his accomplishments during the war.

Though the Cagoule and the Corvignolles may seem to have advocated values that matched those of Vichy or even those of the Nazis, this did not mean that all of their members were Pétainists or collaborators once the war began. The wartime activity of these men was not determined by their prewar political activity. They were faced with many options, and each member chose his own path, which leads us to a second conclusion. Upon superficial examination, one might expect that these men would choose Vichy over resistance. Not only had many of them known and respected Pétain in the prewar years but they had shared many of his goals and the goals of the National Revolution. In choosing to resist, however, these men were not necessarily abandoning the principles of the National Revolution or other goals they had for the government of France. Their story further emphasizes that the Resistance was not the embodiment of everything opposite of Vichy. Both Vichy and the Resistance were made up of individuals, some good, some bad, some courageous, some cowardly. It is a mistake to see the choice to resist as one that *necessarily* meant opposition to everything that Vichy stood for. In many instances, as we have seen, if the changes that happened under Vichy had occurred without the strain of the German occupation, many French citizens would have been quite content.

Georges Loustaunau-Lacau, for example, would have been thrilled to find the PCF banned permanently if France had not had to pay for that with her sovereignty. The men of the Cagoule, determined adversaries of republican politics as they were, could easily have supported an authoritarian government, especially if they could have played significant roles in the new regime, but they did not admire Hitler and were even less enthusiastic about the prospect of playing host to his soldiers. None of these men exemplified the kind of concern for human rights and dignity or the passionate defense of republican freedoms that we normally associate with resisters. This should cause us to question why the Resistance has been defined in such a way and encourage us to continue to explore the many contradictions within it. By imagining the French war experience as a spectrum, with the Resistance at one end, Vichy in the middle, and outright collaboration with the Nazis at the other end, we neglect to account for the permeability of these lines. One could venerate Pétain, be ideologically close to the Nazis, and still resist the German occupation. One could also despise Pétain, recognize the dangers that the Nazis presented for France, and still collaborate with them. One could do nothing at all and just wait the whole thing out.

In thinking about the nuances of thought and behavior during the war, we need to account for multiple factors. One possible way of doing so is to think about the intersections between action, conviction, and official positions during the war. These categories can be further refined by thinking about their range of intensity and chronology.[6] Points of intersection among these categories can help us understand the range of choices people had during the war. For example, Georges Groussard started the war with an official position at Vichy, and a fairly prominent one at that. He maintained a political perspective (conviction) that was similar to the one being espoused by the regime, but he also shared values with the Resistance, notably a refusal of defeat and the desire to resume the fight against the Germans. His actions during the war intersected with both Vichy and the Resistance in that he consciously served both sides at different points. Gabriel Jeantet, on the other hand, maintained his position at Vichy for the duration of the war and was an outspoken supporter of Pétain and the National Revolution (conviction), but he acted in ways that assisted the Resistance, particularly in helping resisters avoid apprehension and escape France. The options, in fact, were endless, and the complexity of the occupation and of human behavior during *les années sombres* should continue to be acknowledged.

Studying the extreme Right in the Resistance also forces us to challenge the very way we understand the concept of resistance. Though the word *resistance* has been saturated with revolutionary meaning, of the 1789 kind, scholars have generally failed to take into account the fact that the heritage of the French Revolution no longer belonged exclusively to the Left. As was set out in the introduction, the more relevant tradition born of the 1789 revolution was one of insurrection, a goal-oriented cooperation between people of diverse political beliefs with a view to challenging the legally constituted government. As Jacques Semelin argues, resistance as seen through the lens of 1789 is a rather simplified vision. He notes that it was only during the Second World War that the word *resistance* rediscovered a revolutionary tone, and he is careful to remind us that it had earlier been used to describe the conservative Orleanist opposition to the July Monarchy.[7] Understanding that the Right also had some claim to a revolutionary tradition (if not a Revolutionary one) allows us to redefine resistance in a way that no longer privileges the Left over the Right, that allows for a more diverse explanation of motivations, that recognizes continuity of thought and behavior in rightist resisters, and that more fully explains the participation and cooperation of politically opposed people in the Resistance.

By examining the participation of the extreme Right in the Resistance, this book attempts to shed light on the actual experience of the *résistants* but also on the legacy of the Resistance. Although we may agree with

Henry Rousso that the late 1960s started a process whereby a generation repudiated a particular vision of their national past, leading to a "broken mirror," the memory of the Resistance is anything but clear many years after the fact. Historians can certainly point to various events in more recent French history that have caused a reconsideration of the war years. The Algerian War, which was as much a battle for control over territory as it was a battle for control over the legacy of the Resistance, certainly was a pivotal moment for reexamining the past. In the end, though, the victory of the anticolonial Left, generally speaking, meant that the image of resisters as champions of the oppressed remained fairly secure. Later events, such as the release of *The Sorrow and the Pity* (1971), the publication of Robert Paxton's *Vichy France* (1973), the release of *Lacombe, Lucien* (1974), the indictment of Maurice Papon and Klaus Barbie for crimes against humanity (both in 1983) and their respective trials, caused historians both within and outside France to revisit previous assumptions about the war experience. While this process of reconsideration has been of the utmost significance, it did not impact the memory of resistance as much as it clarified the extent to which the French had been involved in collaboration. To be sure, nobody could argue any longer that, à la de Gaulle, the nation had been united behind a large and cohesive Resistance movement from 1940 to 1944. It was these movies, that research, those trials that allowed us to acknowledge that many French people had collaborated and that even more French citizens had done nothing at all during those years.

And so we learned that de Gaulle was wilfully optimistic when constructing an image of France during the dark years, that most people were not involved in the Resistance, and that the nation was nowhere near as unified as he might have liked to have people believe. If anything, however, this strengthened the mythological status of people who did resist. Few in numbers, yes, but that made them seem all the more courageous. What this revisiting of the past failed to do was force anybody to change the way the Resistance was conceptualized at the most basic level. Some historians and many members of the public still tend to see the Resistance and resisters as guardians of freedom, human rights, and republican values. This unchanging perspective is all the more ironic when one considers that the legal status of a *résistant*—what legally defines a resister—has changed several times over the years.[8] This irony is also highlighted by the case of Gabriel Jeantet, who, as we have seen, was decorated as a resister and punished with national indignity *simultaneously*.

Although I argue that not all resisters were motivated by republican sentiment or concern for human rights, I do not mean to denigrate the Resistance. Men like Loustaunau-Lacau, Groussard, de Bénouville, Duclos, Jeantet, Méténier, and others may not command our respect, politically speaking, but they did help accomplish a return to republican democracy, a restoration of basic rights, the end of the Nazi regime, the liberation of France, and the end of the Second World War. We do not have to ignore their politics to respect these accomplishments. They may not have been happy with the outcome of their struggles as postwar France was rebuilt on a model that was not necessarily to their liking, and their fortunes may have risen and fallen depending on the political context, but these men demonstrated a seemingly unshakeable continuity in thought and behavior. Their stories help us further nuance our understanding of what it meant to resist during the Second World War and the ways in which that resistance has been remembered, both popularly and academically.

NOTES

INTRODUCTION

1. Henry Rousso's now very well known book *The Vichy Syndrome* offers an excellent introduction to these changes. For a more recent publication that deals with many of the official, or political, negotiations, see Olivier Wieviorka's *Divided Memory*. For an analysis of the elaboration of resistance history by actors and historians (i.e., the historiographical construction of resistance memory), see Laurent Douzou's *La Résistance française* or his edited collection *Faire l'histoire de la Résistance*.

2. Veillon, "Vichy Regime," 174. Veillon goes on to encourage scholars to "identify a range of responses and behaviors, and ultimately, to sketch a typology of resistance groups and the political positions they adopted early in the struggle to free France" (174).

3. Both men and women chose such unique paths. This study focuses mostly on the men and does not attempt to tackle any of the very interesting gender analysis that could inform our understanding of both the extreme Right and the Resistance. For some additional work on the gender dynamics at play, see Deacon, "Fitting in to the French Resistance."

4. In suggesting that we take seriously the role of the extreme Right in the Resistance and how that role was acknowledged or forgotten in the postwar years, I do not mean to throw the baby out with the bathwater. That I do not discuss the considerably larger communist resistance in this book should not be taken as a "problem of perspective." It is simply a different history.

5. This is true too for the communists, though the Parti communiste français had only been banned since 1939. While the PCF certainly had some experience operating illegally, the *cagoulards* had had much more time to learn the lessons of secrecy.

6. The Action française was a monarchist and integral nationalist organization controlled for most of its existence by Charles Maurras, perhaps the Right's most influential philosopher in the 1920s and 1930s.

7. A debate has been raging for decades about the true character of these leagues, particularly whether they represented a form of French fascism. Since it is not the goal of

this work to add to that particular debate, I suggest as further reading the following: Soucy, *French Fascism: The First Wave* and *French Fascism: The Second Wave*; Rémond, *Right Wing in France*; Plumyène and Lasierra, *Les fascismes français*; and Machefer, *Ligues et fascismes en France*, among many others.

8. Pellissier, *6 février 1934*, 320.

9. Colton, "Formation of the French Popular Front," 12.

10. Jenkins, "*Six Fevrier 1934*," 339.

11. See Millington, "February 6, 1934."

12. Simmel, "Sociology of Secrecy," 497.

13. See, e.g., Young, *France and the Origins of the Second World War*; and Young, "Preparations for Defeat."

14. Jackson, *France: The Dark Years*, 113.

15. French communists had been put in an awkward position when the Soviet Union signed the Non-Aggression Pact with Germany. Though they still maintained an antiwar/national-defense line for some time, the official guidance from the Soviet Union was to advocate for an end to the war. The PCF was officially dissolved by decree on 26 September 1939.

16. Two excellent, rather different studies of pacifism in France are Ingram, *Politics of Dissent*; and Siegel, *Moral Disarmament of France*.

17. Irvine, "Domestic Politics and the Fall of France," 91.

18. An excellent study of the exodus is Diamond, *Fleeing Hitler*.

19. Jackson, *Fall of France*, 101.

20. Sartre, *Iron in the Soul*, 22–23.

21. This has been shown by a number of studies, the most recent of which is Lee, *Pétain's Jewish Children*, which highlights the various ambiguities in the Vichy regime in 1940–42 and the possibilities for coexistence between the regime and Jewish youth during that period. See Baruch, *Servir l'état français*, for a through study of the bureaucrats at Vichy and the ruptures and continuities therein.

22. Jackson, *France: The Dark Years*, 390.

23. The best discussion of how difficult this process was is found in Belot, *La Résistance sans de Gaulle*.

24. While some people deliberately left France, many others, particularly military men, found themselves in England only because of having been rescued from the shores of Dunkirk along with their British allies when they were forced to retreat.

25. Marcot, Leroux, and Levisse-Touzé, *Dictionnaire historique de la Résistance*, 248.

26. For more on the career of Jean Moulin, see Cordier's three-volume *Jean Moulin*; and Péan, *Vies et morts de Jean Moulin*, among others.

27. Aglan, "Décision individuelle et discipline collective," 339.

28. Dominique Veillon and Jacqueline Sainclivier remind us that agents who worked with these organizations were also classified according to a military hierarchy, usually using a three-class system: a P0 was an occasional agent; a P1 was an agent who maintained his

or her professional duties while regularly serving the network; a P3 was an agent who had abandoned professional life to devote all his or her time to the network, committing to the network until the end of hostilities. Veillon and Sainclivier, "Quelles différences sociales entre réseaux, mouvements et maquis?," 46.

29. For more on Operation Torch and Anglo-American planning, see Walker, "OSS and Operation Torch"; Funk, "American Contacts with the Resistance in France"; and Rossi, "United States Military Authorities and Free France."

30. See Azéma, "La Milice"; and J.-P. Cointet, *La légion française des combattants*.

31. Burrin, *France under the Germans*, 440.

32. See Burrin, *France under the Germans*.

33. Kedward, *Resistance in Vichy France*, 79.

34. Wieviorka, "Structurations, modes d'intervention," 60.

35. See Diamond, *Women and the Second World War in France*; Weitz, *Sisters in the Resistance*; Schwartz, "Partisanes and Gender Politics in Vichy France"; and Andrieu, "Les résistantes, perspectives de recherché," among others, for a sense of how women, in particular, benefited (or did not benefit) from prewar affiliations.

36. D'Astier argued that resisters were generally found on the margins of society; that is, they were generally outcasts.

37. King, "Emmanuel d'Astier," 32.

38. Marcot, "Réflexions sur les valeurs de la Résistance," 81.

39. Douzou, "L'entrée en résistance," 10.

40. Blanc, *Au commencement de la Résistance*, 259. While this is an important point to bear in mind, this argument does not accurately capture the diversity and nuances in the decision making of resisters.

41. Kedward, *Resistance in Vichy France*, 78.

42. Wieviorka, "Pour une lecture critique," 91.

43. Bédarida, "Sur le concept de résistance," 46.

44. Ibid., 48–49.

45. Jankowski, "In Defense of Fiction," 461.

46. Ibid., 478.

47. Fournier, "Contestations collectives, résistances et Résistance," 57.

48. Tombs, "From Revolution to Resistance," 52.

49. Kedward, *La Vie en Bleu*, 282.

50. By *Revolutionary* with a capital *R*, I mean a tradition born in 1789 that is essentially left-wing; *revolutionary* with a lowercase *r* refers more to means than to ends and, as such, can be applied to right-wing groups as well. This distinction was suggested to me by Robert Alexander, who uses it in his book on the Revolutionary tradition, *Re-Writing the French Revolutionary Tradition*.

51. Hutton, *Cult of the Revolutionary Tradition*, 171.

52. Spitzer, *Old Hatreds and Young Hopes*, 279.

53. Ibid., 212.

54. In this way, the French Carbonari were very similar to their counterparts in Italy, who similarly shared some ideology but focused essentially on a particular goal. R. John Rath points out that almost every Italian lodge had its own idea of what kind of government was desirable, but they were more concerned with ridding the country of foreign invaders. Rath, "Carbonari," 367.

55. Robert Alexander writes that "in doctrinal terms the Carbonari shared the ambiguous mix of republicanism, Bonapartism and liberalism typical of the Opposition." He goes on to point out that the Liberal Opposition was forced to appeal to a diverse range of interests and thus "searched for broad, common values and avoided potentially divisive clarity." *Re-Writing the French Revolutionary Tradition*, 184–85.

56. Hutton, *Cult of the Revolutionary Tradition*, 35.

57. Spitzer, *Revolutionary Theories of Louis Auguste Blanqui*, 121–22.

58. Bernstein, *Auguste Blanqui and the Art of Insurrection*, 9.

59. Ansart-Dourlen, *Le choix de la morale en politique*, 10.

60. Laborie, "L'idée de Résistance," 26.

61. Archives Nationales de France (hereafter ANF), F^{1a} 3729, B.C.R.A., 1942–1944, Questions militaires et paramilitaires, "Rapport politique sur les mouvements de Résistance, 3.10.43."

62. See, e.g., Andrieu, *Le programme commun de la Résistance*.

63. See ANF, F^{1a} 3730, B.C.R.A., 1942–1944, Questions politiques, and F^{1a} 3756, Réponses aux questionnaires politiques du B.C.R.A., among others. Philip Nord's book on the postwar institutional landscape, *France's New Deal*, clearly outlines how the transfer of ideas and personnel between Vichy and the Resistance created a third-way kind of statism, which was "neither socialist nor Vichyite. It was in part an amalgam of the two: consultative and expansionist, but still guided from the top by managers and civil servants bandying the technocratic catchphrases of the nonconformist thirties—the importance of leadership, the social role of elites, the value of team play" (91). Come the Liberation, there were numerous plans for social and economic renewal. Some were certainly of the Left, but alongside them were ones that clearly owed a fair amount to the discredited Vichy regime. Nord calls this diverse group the "not-so-Left."

64. ANF, F^{1a} 3730, B.C.R.A., 1942–1944, Questions politiques, "Note sur les perspectives politiques," n.d.

65. Ibid.

66. ANF, F^{1a} 3756, Réponses aux questionnaires politiques du B.C.R.A., "La situation politique 15.10.43."

67. See Belot, *Aux frontières de la liberté* .

68. Passmore, *Right in France*, 12.

69. It is also worth noting that Pétain was not necessarily seen as a committed member of the Right before the Second World War. Although his ambassadorship to Franco's Spain may suggest that he was seen as someone who could easily operate in a rightist environment, Jacques Szaluta suggests that "his prestige as a soldier, his Catholicism, and his past relations

with Spain in the Riff rebellion in Morocco" made Pétain ideally suited for the post. Moreover, Szaluta, like many others, emphasizes Pétain's characteristic of remaining fairly aloof from political intrigues. Szaluta, "Marshal Petain's Ambassadorship to Spain." If any army officer was seen as being intimately connected with the right wing and intransigent vis-à-vis the republic in the interwar period, it was Maxime Weygand. As chief of staff and vice president of the Supreme War Council, Weygand worried republicans far more than Pétain did. See, e.g., Adamthwaite, *France and the Coming of the Second World War;* Bankwitz, "Maxime Weygand and the Fall of France"; and Horne, *French Army and Politics.* Weygand's replacement by Maurice Gamelin in 1935 was celebrated by most moderate politicians, as Gamelin was a far better practitioner of military *mutisme.*

HISTORIOGRAPHY AND TERMS

1. Rousso, *Vichy Syndrome,* 264.

2. Sweets, "Les historiens anglo-américains," 217–18. Sweets notes that the *American Historical Review* did not publish a single article on the Resistance between 1945 and 2001.

3. Judt, *Past Imperfect,* 46.

4. Hessel, *Time for Outrage!,* 24. This popular pamphlet is indeed inspirational, and Hessel's admonition to young people to look around their world and be outraged is a worthy message, but it does not represent the nuances of the resistance experience.

5. Michel, *Les courants de pensée de la Résistance,* 6.

6. Ibid., 13.

7. Novick, *Resistance versus Vichy,* 16.

8. Blanc, *Au commencement de la Résistance,* 17–19.

9. Guillaume Piketty, "L'histoire de la Résistance," 39. This sense among resisters that only they could fully understand the Resistance made it hard to create a thoroughly rigorous body of scholarship. For an excellent discussion of this process and the problems that arise when actors are also historians, see Douzou, *La Résistance française.*

10. Douzou, Frank, Peschanski, and Veillon, preface to *La Résistance et les Français,* 8.

11. Andrieu, "L'histoire de la Résistance en question."

12. Wieviorka, *Une certaine idée de la Résistance,* 33.

13. Ibid., 45.

14. Ibid., 50.

15. In addition, there were many sites of commemoration and other *lieux de mémoire.* For examples of these, see Becker, "Les Britanniques dans la Grande Guerre."

16. Wieviorka, *Une certaine idée de la Résistance,* 144–47.

17. Since the publication of Vinen's very interesting *Bourgeois Politics in France,* we have a much better sense of just how pervasive the remnants of Vichy were in the postwar years. Jérôme Cotillon has written about the quick reintegration of the Right after the war and suggests that many Pétainists and their ideas survived with much more vigor than might previously have been imagined. Cotillon's work clearly fits into a larger trend of seeing

continuities, rather than ruptures, in these major transitions. Cotillon, *Ce qu'il reste de Vichy*. An even more recent book by Cécile Desprairies, *L'héritage de Vichy*, also outlines the major continuities between Vichy and the Fourth Republic, including various modernization plans and the elaboration of a modern welfare state.

18. Vinen, *Bourgeois Politics in France*, 116.

19. ANF, 72 AJ/42, Résistance intérieure: mouvements, réseaux, partis politiques, "Témoignage de M. Marin."

20. ANF, 72 AJ/42, Résistance intérieure: mouvements, réseaux, partis politiques, "Témoignage de Mme Madeleine Regnault."

21. ANF, 72 AJ/42, Résistance intérieure: mouvements, réseaux, partis politiques, "Notice sur André Mutter—Renseignements tirés de sa brochure 'Face à la Gestapo.'"

22. Vinen, *Bourgeois Politics in France*, 129.

23. Ibid., 131.

24. Ibid., 105.

25. Douzou and Peschanski, "Les premiers résistants face à l'hypothèque Vichy," 428.

26. Ibid., 431.

27. See, e.g., Laborie, *L'opinion française sous Vichy*.

28. ANF, 171 Mi 23, "Rapport Rémy, no. 29," 10 October 1940.

29. ANF, F^{1a} 3756, Réponses aux questionnaires politiques du B.C.R.A., "Une opinion sur ce que veut ou ne veut pas la France, 1.2.44."

30. Jackson, *France: The Dark Years*, 507.

31. Ibid., 511.

32. Albertelli and Barasz, "Un résistant atypique."

33. Barasz, "Un vichyste en Résistance."

34. Belot, *La Résistance sans de Gaulle*, 11.

35. Belot reminds us among the challenges de Gaulle faced early on were that many were skeptical of de Gaulle's attempt to form a government because he was a military man; that few people actually knew of de Gaulle in 1940; that exile was not viewed positively; and that people worried about the divisive nature of de Gaulle's actions. Perhaps most interestingly, Belot notes that the first obstacle may have been what he calls "penser la France comme une absence" (conceiving France as an absence).The idea of "roots" in one's native land and *terroir* were initially linked to Vichy, making adherence to Gaullism even more difficult. Ibid., 91.

36. Ibid., 121.

37. Ibid., 175.

38. Vergez-Chaignon, *Les vichysto-résistants*, 543.

39. Ibid., 574.

40. Ibid., 726.

41. Kitson, "Arresting Nazi Spies in Vichy France," 80. Kitson published a full-length study on this topic, *The Hunt for Nazi Spies*, the same year that Vergez-Chaignon published her book about the *vichysto-résistants*.

42. Kitson, "Arresting Nazi Spies in Vichy France," 85.

43. Belot, *La Résistance sans de Gaulle*, 221–310.

44. Dreyfus, *Histoire de la Résistance, 1940–1945*.

45. Barasz, "Les vichysto-résistants," 37.

46. Sternhell, *Neither Right nor Left*.

47. Irvine, "Beyond Left and Right," 229.

48. Read, *Republic of Men*. For discourses about foreignness common to Vichy and the Resistance, see Adler, "Demography at Liberation."

49. Labrosse, "La Dérive Bergery / The Bergery Drift."

50. Ibid., 67.

51. Kalman, *French Colonial Fascism*, 12. Kalman uses *fascism* and *extreme right* interchangeably but notes that this is only possible in the colonial setting. The differences in metropolitan France were too significant and the divisions in those leagues too great.

THE CAGOULE

1. Monier, *Le complot dans la république*, 290.

2. Brunelle and Finley-Croswhite, *Murder in the Métro*, 4.

3. Monier, *Le complot dans la république*, 301.

4. Interestingly, Kevin Passmore has argued that if the Croix de feu was fascist, the PSF was a party of the nonfascist radical right. Passmore, "French Third Republic," 421.

5. Adereth, *French Communist Party*, 82.

6. Monier, *Le complot dans la république*, 299.

7. Bourdrel, *La Cagoule*, 179.

8. Brunelle and Finley-Croswhite, *Murder in the Métro*.

9. Pugliese, "Death in Exile," 317.

10. Ibid., 313.

11. Brunelle and Finley-Croswhite, *Murder in the Métro*, 95.

12. Monier, *Le complot dans la république*, 301.

13. Bourdrel, *La Cagoule*, 185.

14. Weber, *Action Française*, 340.

15. ANF, F7 14815, Partis et mouvements politiques, police interview with Michel Bernollin, 10 November 1937.

16. Monier, *Le complot dans la république*, 277.

17. Bourdrel, *La Cagoule*, 59–60.

18. Jean-Claude Valla suggests that the initial nucleus was composed of the following men (whose pseudonyms are given in parentheses): Eugène Deloncle (Marie), Aristide Corre (Dagore), Jean Filiol (Philippe or Fifi), Jacques Corrèze (La Bûche), Henri Deloncle (Grasset), Gabriel Jeantet (Gabès), François Méténier, and Dr. Martin (le Bib). Valla, *La Cagoule, 1936–1937*, 35.

19. It is important to note that not all the members were involved to the same degree. The leaders and those I call "active members" regularly took part in the Cagoule's notorious

activities. However, there were also men who could not fully participate, because of age or other reasons; these men, I call "adherents." Frédéric Monier finds an interesting correlation between level of involvement and class position among the CSAR. He argues that the leaders and active members came mainly from the bourgeoisie and the less involved adherents came from the petite bourgeoisie. Monier, *Le complot dans la république,* 295.

20. Tournoux, *L'histoire secrète,* 48–49.

21. ANF, F7 14815, Partis et mouvements politiques, police interview with Gaston Jeanniot, 13 November 1937.

22. ANF, F7 14815, Partis et mouvements politiques, police interview with Charles Nicod, 4 March 1938.

23. Bourdrel, *La Cagoule,* 62.

24. After police infiltrated the group in 1937, the members who were not quick enough to flee the country were arrested and imprisoned. Their trial was interrupted by the outbreak of the war in 1939; it was resumed in 1948.

25. Monier, *Le complot dans la république,* 289.

26. For instance, it has been estimated that the Croix de feu had a million members at its height in the 1930s. Robert Paxton, *Europe in the Twentieth Century,* 344. There were important doctrinal and structural differences between the Croix de feu and the Cagoule, many of which are explored in Kennedy, *Reconciling France against Democracy.* Kennedy rightly notes the influence these groups had on French political culture, even if they were never able to achieve their goals.

27. Corre broke all the organization's rules about keeping records, as he wrote frequently and candidly in his diary, which he managed to keep out of the hands of the police in 1937. Before he was shot by the Germans in 1942, Corre entrusted his writings to a fellow *cagoulard,* Father Joseph Fily. In the late 1960s Fily was approached by Christian Bernadac, who was doing a story about clandestine religious life in German concentration camps. Fily had been incarcerated in Dachau and ended up giving Bernadac more than the story he had been looking for. Fily decided that it was time to give the diaries to someone who could publish them, as Corre had asked for them to be made public after a certain amount of time had passed. Thus, Bernadac took the massive collection of papers and published the volumes written between April 1937 and February 1940.

28. Bernadac, *Dagore,* 445.

29. Ibid., 377.

30. Ibid., 464.

31. Ibid., 229.

32. Ibid., 90.

33. This suspicion was voiced particularly after the war, when Pétain was basically blamed for every disaster that befell the Republic. The reality, however, is that in the 1930s Pétain was almost certainly aware of the Cagoule and also of the antirepublican activities of the military men who served beneath him. But Pétain, while certainly ambitious, was also a prudent man

and quite comfortable with the republican regime, which, we must remember, served him well over the years.

34. Bernadac, *Dagore*, 444.

35. Ibid., 452.

36. Ibid. In an article about French conspiracy theories, D. L. L. Parry notes that "the existence of an evil conspiracy also necessitated and justified the creation of a virtuous counter-conspiracy." He tells how prevalent conspiracy theories were in the Third Republic, coming from many different political angles, and sees Deloncle's conspiracy theory and counterconspiracy as one of the most extreme. Parry, "Articulating the Third Republic," 181.

37. Bernadac, *Dagore*, 325.

38. ANF, F7 14815, Partis et mouvements politiques, police interview with Jean Doquin de Saint Preux, 28 October 1938.

39. ANF, F7 14815, Partis et mouvements politiques, police interview with Elie Doquin de Saint Preux, 19 December 1938.

40. ANF, F7 14815, Partis et mouvements politiques, letter from the governor-general of Algeria to the minister of the interior, 29 March 1938.

41. Kalman, *French Colonial Fascism*, 31.

42. ANF, F7 14815, Partis et mouvements politiques, letter from the governor-general of Algeria to the minister of the interior, 29 March 1938.

43. It is very important to note that while the *cagoulards* may have been anti-Semitic, there is no indication of any racial policy. In fact, native Algerians were invited to join the Cagoule and had their own cell, the Algérie française, led by Mohoumed El Maadi. There is even less information about this cell than about the group as a whole, making it almost impossible to explain its existence.

44. Bernadac, *Dagore*, 79.

45. All this information about the membership comes from the Archives de Paris (hereafter ADP), 30W 0006, Cour d'Assises de la Seine, 16 January to 31 December 1948. It is difficult to say whether the group did not recruit among the working classes or was unsuccessful in doing so. Nonetheless, the social composition of the membership presumably would have lent a certain flavor to the organization.

46. For an excellent discussion of this neighborhood and its significance for the Cagoule, see Brunelle and Finley-Croswhite, *Murder in the Métro*.

47. ANF, F7 14815, Partis et mouvements politiques, police interview with Gerard Georges Luc Le Roy, 8 January 1938.

48. ANF, F7 14815, Partis et mouvements politiques, police interview with André Revol, 8 January 1938.

49. Tournoux, *L'histoire secrète*, 101.

50. Monier, *Le complot dans la république*, 316.

51. Bernadac, *Dagore*, 194.

52. Ibid., 411.

53. Néaumet, *Les grandes enquêtes du commissaire Chenevier*, 123.

54. Some key members of the organization managed to flee to San Remo or San Sebastien before they could be arrested, but others were not so lucky.

55. P. L. Darner, "Encore des armes fascistes et ce n'est pas fini!," *L'Humanité*, 19 November 1937, 2.

56. Jean-Maurice Herrman, "Armements de guerre civile," *Le Populaire*, 5 October 1937, 1.

57. O. Rosenfeld, "Le filet de la Sûreté nationale se resserre autour des conjurés," ibid., 21 November 1937, 1.

58. "Qui dirigeait qui payait qui armait les 'Milices Secrètes'?," *L'Œuvre*, 19 November 1937, 5.

59. "L'affaire des 'cagoulards,'" *Journal des Débats Politiques et Littéraires*, 3 December 1937, 4.

60. "Complots," *Le Temps*, 25 November 1937, 1.

61. See esp. *L'Écho de Paris* for excellent examples of conviction of communist plotting: "La Sûreté nationale est-elle à bout de souffle dans l'affaire des 'Cagoulards'?," 23 November 1937, 1; "Du ridicule a l'arbitraire dans l'affaire des 'Cagoulards,'" 27 November 1937, 1; "Vacances de la légalité," 28 November 1937, 1; Martin-Mamy, "Du poteau de torture au poteau indicateur," 19 November 1937, 1.

62. *La maison mère* was what Corre called his former organization, the Action française.

63. Charles Maurras, quoted in Magraw, *France, 1815–1914*, 263.

64. Weber, *Action Française*, 24.

65. Bernadac, *Dagore*, 307.

66. Ibid., 326.

67. Ibid., 301.

68. Ibid., 117.

69. Ibid., 449–50.

70. Ibid., 458.

71. Ibid.

72. John Sweets, "Hold That Pendulum!," 731–32. See, for examples of this debate, Milza, *Les fascismes*; Machefer, *Ligues et fascismes en France*; Plumyène and Lasierra, *Les fascismes français*; Rémond, *Right Wing in France*; Sternhell, *Neither Right nor Left*; Soucy, *French Fascism: The First Wave*; and Soucy, *French Fascism: The Second Wave*.

73. Joel Blatt calls this strategy of agent provocateurism audacious but flimsy. Blatt, "Cagoule Plot, 1936–1937," 94. It seems to me that it was more successful than Blatt allows for.

74. ADP, PEROTIN 212-79-3-48, "Liste des membres de la 'cagoule' et de ses filiales," n.d. (postwar).

75. ADP, PEROTIN 212-79-3-50, Report from the Commissaire de Police Judiciaire Georges Richier to Monsieur le Directeur des services de Police Judiciaire à Paris, Rome, 6 June 1945.

76. Darnand would eventually head the dreaded Milice and helped organize French volunteers to don the Nazi uniform and fight on the Eastern Front. Deloncle was for a time

very involved in the Parisian collaboration scene, though he ultimately found disfavor among the Germans and was killed by them.

77. This mention of the instruction period may cause some confusion in readers unfamiliar with French criminal law. In the case of serious crimes, the powers of investigation are sometimes given to a judge—the *juge d'instruction*—who has been delegated to investigate the crime. It is this judge who decides whether the case will be referred to the public prosecutor after the instruction, or investigative, period is over.

THE CORVIGNOLLES

1. ANF, Ordre de la Légion d'honneur, 19800035/27/3426. Loustaunau-Lacau's father was also a *chevalier* in the L'Ordre de la Légion d'honneur. ANF, Ordre de la Légion d'honneur, 19800035/553/63124. Both dossiers are available online via the Archives Nationales de France website.

2. Loustaunau-Lacau, *Mémoires d'un Français rebelle*, 110–11.

3. ADP, PEROTIN 212-79-3-19, papers seized from the desk of Henri Deloncle, 78 rue de Provence, Paris.

4. Ibid.

5. The Second Bureau of the General Staff. This was France's external military intelligence agency.

6. ADP, PEROTIN 212-79-3-49, "Aide-mémoire du Commandant Loustaunau-Lacau pour sa déposition devant la haute cour de justice, mai 1945."

7. This view is advanced most notably by John Steward Ambler and Henry Dutailly. See Ambler, *French Army in Politics;* Dutailly, *Les problèmes de l'Armée de terre française.*

8. De la Gorce, *French Army,* 252.

9. Ibid., 220.

10. Ibid., 230.

11. See Millington, *From Victory to Vichy.*

12. De la Gorce, *French Army,* 242–43. Loustaunau-Lacau was actually kicked out of the army in 1938 by Daladier but reintegrated upon the declaration of war in 1939.

13. Parry, "Articulating the Third Republic," 177.

14. Horne, *French Army and Politics,* 51.

15. De la Gorce, *French Army,* 209.

16. Ibid.

17. Loustaunau-Lacau, *Mémoires d'un Français rebelle*, 101.

18. Ibid.

19. The connection between the Cagould and the Corvignolles has been made by a number of people, notably Parry, Philippe Bourdrel, and J. R. Tournoux.

20. ADP, PEROTIN 212-79-3-49, "Déposition de Loustaunau-Lacau, 4 février 1946."

21. Groussard, *Service secret,* 89.

22. Loustaunau-Lacau, *Mémoires d'un Français rebelle,* 115.

23. ADP, PEROTIN 212-79-3-49, "Déposition de Loustaunau-Lacau, 6 février 1946."

24. Parry, "Articulating the Third Republic," 169.

25. Loustaunau-Lacau, *Mémoires d'un Français rebelle*, 164.

26. Ibid., 361.

27. M. Cointet, *Marie-Madeleine Fourcade*, 37.

28. Archives de la Préfecture de Police (hereafter APP), GA L15, Georges Loustaunau-Lacau, report of 5 November 1941.

29. Loustaunau-Lacau, *Mémoires d'un Français rebelle*, 130–31.

30. Ibid., 362.

31. Young, *France and the Origins of the Second World War*, 77. See also Young, "Preparations for Defeat."

32. Bankwitz, "Maxime Weygand and the Fall of France," 157.

33. Ibid., 160.

34. The Archives Nationales de France has indexed the UMF with the PPF, in fact.

35. APP, GA L15, Georges Loustaunau-Lacau, report of 5 November 1941.

36. "Pacte anticommuniste," *Barrage*, no. 10 (September–October 1938): 43.

37. Ibid.

38. ANF, F7 14817, Partis et mouvements politiques, report from the governor-general of Algeria to the French minister of the interior, 20 January 1939.

39. Kalman, *French Colonial Fascism*, 135.

40. ANF, F7 14817, Partis et mouvements politiques, report from the governor-general of Algeria to the French minister of the interior, 20 January 1939.

41. Kalman, *French Colonial Fascism*, 138.

42. ANF, F7 14817, Partis et mouvements politiques, report from the governor-general of Algeria to the French minister of the interior, 20 January 1939.

43. ANF, 3W 278, Mouvement Spiralien de l'Ordre National booklet.

44. Ibid.

45. The directing committee included Loustaunau-Lacau, M. Besset, M. Hubert Bourgin, M. Marot, M. de la Raudière, M. Tristani, M. Michel-Dansac, and M. Peyre.

46. ANF, 3W 278, Mouvement Spiralien de l'Ordre National booklet.

47. Ibid.

48. ADP, PEROTIN 212-79-3-49. Note of 23 December 1938 from the Sûreté nationale about a conference given in Paris by M. Navarre (i.e., Loustaunau-Lacau).

49. ADP, PEROTIN 212-79-3-49, Mouvement Spiralien de l'Ordre National booklet, 15 April 1939.

50. ANF, 3W 278, Mouvement Spiralien de l'Ordre National booklet.

51. Ibid.

52. There were three kinds of *spirales*: *spirales de lieu*, which were based on locality; *spirales d'objets*, which were formed with specific objects of study in mind (e.g., the financial state of affairs); and *spirales indépendantes*, various groups to be formed on the initiative of the UMF.

53. ANF, 3W 278, Mouvement Spiralien de l'Ordre National booklet.

54. Ibid.

55. Ibid.

56. Ibid.

57. Ibid.

58. Ibid.

59. Ibid.

60. *Le Figaro*, 10 September 1937, 6, and 25 August 1937, 6.

61. Navarre [Georges Loustaunau-Lacau], "La conjonction des empires," *Notre Prestige*, July 1938, 3.

62. Ibid.

63. Jean Paillard, "Un nil français," *Notre Prestige*, July 1938, 18.

64. Navarre, "Allemagne: Veut-elle faire la guerre?," ibid., August 1938, 30.

65. Ibid., 29.

66. Navarre, "Lettre ouvert a M. Georges Bonnet," *Notre Prestige*, September 1938, 3.

67. Ibid.

68. Even the articles about cultural events or automobiles were usually tied to defense, sometimes explicitly military defense, other times just the defense of the French consciousness.

69. ANF, F7 14817, *Barrage*, no. 1.

70. *Barrage*, no. 3 (January 1938): 2.

71. Ibid.

72. Epstein, *Un paradoxe français*, 396.

RESISTANCE AT THE HEART OF VICHY

1. Loustaunau-Lacau, *Mémoires d'un Français rebelle*, 200.

2. Fourcade, *Noah's Ark*, 24.

3. Loustaunau-Lacau, *Mémoires d'un Français rebelle*, 206.

4. Fourcade, *Noah's Ark*, 26. Loustaunau-Lacau also testified to the fact that Pétain knew the truth about these early activities at Pétain's trial. "Déposition de M. Loustaunau-Lacau," in Pétain and Haute cour de justice, *Le procès du Maréchal Pétain*, 351.

5. Jackson, *France: The Dark Years*, 409. See also Azéma, *De Munich à la Libération, 1938–1944* (Paris: Seuil, 1979), 249, 310. He notes that in 1944 the organized Resistance counted around 500,000 people and the networks 150,000—not including occasional agents.

6. Cohen, preface to Fourcade, *Noah's Ark*, 9.

7. Fourcade, *Noah's Ark*, 74.

8. ANF, 171 Mi 35, tract written by Loustaunau-Lacau to be dropped over France.

9. Ibid., "Organisation de la Croisade."

10. Ibid.

11. Lucas was one alias of Pierre Fourcaud, who, as we will see, maintained his relationships with Loustaunau-Lacau, Groussard, and other members of the extreme Right throughout the war.

12. ANF, 171 Mi 25, "Rapport Lucas [Pierre Fourcaud]," 1940.

13. Dreyfus, *Histoire de la Résistance*, 24.

14. Jackson, *France: The Dark Years*, 181. The Protocols were ultimately stalled and not long after, in June of 1941, Vichy France lost Syria after a successful Anglo-Gaullist operation there.

15. ADP, PEROTIN 212-79-3-51, "Acte d'Accusation, 8 octobre 1941."

16. ADP, PEROTIN 212-79-3-51, "Copie de deux lettres saisies au domicile du nommé HERPIN," letter from "Granier" to "Mon cher Guillaume."

17. ADP, PEROTIN 212-79-3-51, letter from Loustaunau-Lacau to Commandant Gruillot, 6 June 1941.

18. Fourcade, *Noah's Ark*, 26.

19. Fourcade, *Noah's Ark*.

20. Jeffery, *MI6*, 390.

21. After reading Jeffery's *MI6*, I realized that perhaps some of this strain came from within SIS itself. He notes that "A.4 and A.5 represented passionately opposed French political opinions." Jeffery details some of these schisms, as both sections battled for agents and intelligence. Ibid., 397. I don't think we can split these political opinions as neatly as all that, given that many Alliance members remained hostile to de Gaulle even while working with A.5, but it is worth considering the possibility that some of the tension may have been external to the group itself.

22. Fourcade, *Noah's Ark*, 125.

23. Darlan, at the time still the vice president of Pétain's council, was in Algiers visiting his son, who was hospitalized.

24. Jackson, *France: The Dark Years*, 448.

25. Giraud ultimately did declare Vichy to be illegitimate, but not until March 1943.

26. ADP, PEROTIN 212-79-3-47, "Procès-verbal du 12 janvier 1946."

27. Ibid.

28. ADP, PEROTIN 212-79-3-49, "Synthèse n.C/I—Loustanau-Lacau [sic], l'Alliance, et ses origines," September 1944.

29. Ibid.

30. ADP, PEROTIN 212-79-3-49, "Rapport de l'Inspecteur Pierre Gervais, 16 janvier 1945."

31. ADP, PEROTIN 212-79-3-49, documents seized from Général Baston at Vichy.

32. We can only assume that the author of this document is referring to Alliance but confuses the group's name with its leader's pseudonym, Navarre.

33. ADP, PEROTIN 212-79-3-49, doc. 6.

34. ANF, 72 AJ/35, Résistance intérieure: mouvements, réseaux, partis politiques, "Témoignage de Mme Marie Madeleine Fourcade."

35. ANF, 72 AJ/231, Résistance hors de France et organes centraux de la Résistance, "Témoignage de Maurice Duclos—dit 'St. Jacques.'"

36. ADP, PEROTIN 212-79-3-51, "Procès-Verbal—11 août 1941—Capitaine de Corvette Joseph LECUSSAN."

37. Flood and Frey, "Extreme Right-Wing Reactions," 80.

38. Jackson, "General de Gaulle and His Enemies," 46.

39. ANF, 171 Mi 35, "Memorandum du Répresentant de l'Alliance à Londres, au Commandant Manuel, Chef du B.R.A.L., Londres—18 avril 1944."

40. Ibid.

41. Loustaunau-Lacau, Mémoires d'un Français rebelle, 340.

42. ADP, PEROTIN 212-79-3-48, "Liste des membres de la 'cagoule' et de ses filiales," n.d. (postwar).

43. ADP, PEROTIN 212-79-3-49, "Déclaration préalable—7 dec. 1946" (Loustaunau-Lacau).

44. ADP, PEROTIN 212-79-3-49, "Rapport de l'Inspecteur Pierre Gervais, 16 janvier 1945."

45. M. Cointet, Marie-Madeleine Fourcade, 67.

46. Ibid., 101.

47. Loustaunau-Lacau, Mémoires d'un Français rebelle, 127.

48. Kedward, Resistance in Vichy France, 23.

49. Ibid., 78.

50. Michel, "Psychology of the French Resister," 162.

51. Ibid., 164.

52. Douzou, "L'entrée en résistance," 10.

53. Wieviorka, "Structurations, modes d'intervention," 63.

54. Marcot, "Réflexions sur les valeurs de la Résistance," 84.

55. Douzou, "L'entrée en résistance," 14.

56. ADP, PEROTIN 212-79-3-49, "Procès-verbal de Marie-Alexis Mermet," 6 June 1946.

57. Wieviorka, "Pour une lecture critique," 94–95.

58. ADP, PEROTIN 212-79-3-49, "Aide-mémoire du Commandant Loustaunau-Lacau pour sa déposition devant la haute cour de justice, mai 1945."

59. Loustaunau-Lacau, Mémoires d'un Français rebelle, 68.

60. Ibid., 54.

61. Rousso, Vichy: L'événement, la mémoire, l'histoire, 359.

62. Vinen, Bourgeois Politics in France, 105.

63. "Déposition de M. Loustaunau-Lacau," in Pétain and Haute cour de justice, Le procès du Maréchal Pétain, 352, also found in Loustaunau-Lacau, Mémoires d'un Français rebelle, 339.

64. Rousso, Vichy: L'événement, la mémoire, l'histoire, 369.

65. Vinen, Bourgeois Politics in France, 114.

66. Forcade, Duhamel, and Vial, Militaires en république, 342.

67. See www.assemblee-nationale.fr/histoire/biographies/IVRepublique/loustaunau-lacau-georges-augustin-17041894.asp.

68. ANF, C/I* 618, "Procès-verbal de la Séance du Jeudi 19 juillet 1951."

69. Organizzazione per la Vigilanza e la Repressione dell'Antifascismo (Organization for Vigilance and Repression of Antifascism).

70. ANF, C/I* 618, "Procès-verbal de la 3e Séance du Jeudi 22 novembre 1951."

71. Ganser, *Nato's Secret Armies*.

72. Ibid., 87.

73. Edouard Depreux, quoted ibid., 88.

74. Augustin, *Le Plan Bleu*, 25.

75. Ibid., 67–68.

76. Ibid., 193.

77. Ibid., 220.

78. ANF, C/I* 619, "Procès-verbal de la 2e Séance du Jeudi 6 décembre 1951." Twenty-one members of the commission had voted against the ratification, fifteen for it, and there was one abstention.

79. Ibid.

80. Ibid.

81. ANF, C/I* 620, "Procès-verbal de la 3e Séance du Mardi 12 février 1952."

82. Ibid.

83. ANF, C/I* 622, "1re Séance du Dimanche 25 janvier 1953."

84. ANF, C/I* 622, "1re Séance du 26 janvier 1953."

85. Ibid.

86. ANF, 3W 278, Mouvement Spiralien de l'Ordre National booklet.

87. ANF, C/I* 618, "Procès-verbal de la Séance du Jeudi 9 août 1951."

88. ANF, C/I* 623, "Séance du 3 juin 1953."

89. ANF, C/I* 621, "Procès-verbal de la 3e Séance du Vendredi 11 juillet 1952."

90. *Le Monde*, 13–14 February 1955, 3.

91. ANF, C/I* 628, "Procès-verbal de la Séance du Vendredi 18 février 1955."

92. *Le Monde*, 13–14 February 1955, 3.

93. See www.assemblee-nationale.fr/histoire/biographies/IVRepublique/loustaunau-lacau-georges-augustin-17041894.asp.

94. APP, GA L15, Loustaunau-Lacau, Report of 13 October 1951.

95. ANF, C/I* 628, "Procès-verbal de la Séance du Vendredi 18 février 1955."

96. Ibid.

97. APP, GA L15, "Obsèques militaires et religieuses du Général LOUSTAUNAU-LACAU, Député des Basses-Pyrénées, aux Invalides."

FROM VICHY TO EXILE

1. See Duclos, *À l'ombre de Saint-Jacques*; Fourcade, *Noah's Ark*; Loustaunau-Lacau, *Mémoires d'un Français rebelle*; and Groussard, *Service secret*, among others.

2. See Belot, *Aux frontières de la liberté.*

3. The first such law was pronounced on 23 July 1940, when the government decreed that persons who had left France without authorization between 10 May and 30 June of that year would lose their nationality. A law of February 1941 targeted French citizens outside France's borders.

4. Hellman, *Knight-Monks of Vichy France,* 170.

5. Ibid., 167.

6. Service historique de la Défense (hereafter SHD), GR 8YE 88504, État des Services, Georges Groussard.

7. Loustaunau-Lacau and Groussard, *Consuls, prenez garde!,* 8.

8. *Chef d'état-major de la région de Paris.*

9. Groussard, *L'Armée et ses drames,* 14.

10. Ibid., 9.

11. Ibid., 15.

12. APP, GA G4, Groussard, Report of 31 January 1947.

13. Loustaunau-Lacau and Groussard, *Consuls, prenez garde!,* 207.

14. Groussard, *L'Armée et ses drames,* 16.

15. Loustaunau-Lacau and Groussard, *Consuls, prenez garde!,* 163.

16. Groussard, *L'Armée et ses drames,* 33.

17. Ibid., 37.

18. ANF, 3W 47, "Audition du Colonel Groussard, 5 juin 1946."

19. SHD, GR 8YE 88504, Letter from General Delmas to M. Poivre.

20. SHD, GR 8YE 88504, "Note pour la sous-direction des bureaux des cabinets—bureau correspondance et discipline générales," 14 August 1986.

21. ADP, PEROTIN 212-79-3-51, "Procès-Verbal—11 août 1941—Capitaine de Corvette Joseph LECUSSAN." Lécussan was a member of the Commissariat général aux questions juives.

22. Groussard, *Service secret,* 92.

23. Ibid., 70–71.

24. ADP, PEROTIN 212-79-3-49. "Déposition de Loustaunau-Lacau, 6 février 1946."

25. Groussard, *Service secret,* 99.

26. Ibid., 98–100.

27. Ibid., 25.

28. Ibid., 35.

29. SHD, GR 8YE 88504, "Note pour la sous-direction des bureaux des cabinets—bureau correspondance et discipline générales," 14 August 1986.

30. This is, in any case, how Groussard describes his project; many others considered it to be quite a bit less benign.

31. Groussard, *Service secret,* 78.

32. Ibid., 76.

33. ANF, 3W 47, "Procès-verbal de Georges Groussard, 14 novembre 1946."

34. Groussard, *Service secret*.

35. ANF, 3W 278, "Procès-verbal de François Méténier," 22 February 1945.

36. ANF, 3W 301, "Procès-verbal de Gabriel Jeantet, Affaire PETAIN, LAVAL."

37. ADP, PEROTIN 212-79-3-47, "Rapport sur Le Centre d'Informations et d'Etudes (1ère enquête)," 1946.

38. ANF, 3W 278, "Procès-verbal de Charles BOUDET, 30 mai 1945."

39. ANF, 3W 278, "Procès-verbal de Robert LABAT, 27 avril 1945."

40. ADP, PEROTIN 212-79-3-47, Letter from Méténier (chef des Services de Protection—GP) to M. le Docteur Knochen, 12 November 1940.

41. ANF, 3W 47, German report of 31 December 1940 on the GP, Alibert, and *cagoulards*.

42. Groussard, *Service secret*, 86.

43. Kitson, *Hunt for Nazi Spies*, 63.

44. Marcot, Leroux, and Levisse-Touzé, *Dictionnaire historique de la Résistance*, 436.

45. Paxton, *Vichy France*, 92–101.

46. Ibid., 100; Burrin, *France under the Germans*, 104.

47. Paxton, *Vichy France*, 100.

48. Groussard, *Service secret*, 141.

49. Marcot, Leroux, and Levisse-Touzé, *Dictionnaire historique de la Résistance*, 418.

50. ANF, 171 Mi 25, "Rapport Lucas [Pierre Fourcaud]," 1940. Fourcaud did not, however, doubt Groussard's intentions. In a telegram from April 1941 he wrote that "Colonel Groussard, having acting against Laval on December 13 (see my report) passes to our side. He brings us a formidable information network and the unexpected involvement of various military, police, and prefectural circles." ANF, 171 Mi 25.

51. Rémy, *Mémoires d'un agent secret*, 150.

52. Groussard describes all of this in *Service secret*; his narrative is almost identical to the one found in Passy's *Souvenirs*.

53. Groussard, *Service secret*, 302. This resistance clearly never materialized.

54. Ibid., 339.

55. Groussard went on a hunger strike virtually every time he was arrested. It certainly seemed to work for him, as he was also liberated every time.

56. Ibid., 382.

57. ANF, F1a 3729, B.C.R.A., 1942–1944, Questions militaires et paramilitaires, "Note pour Monsieur André PHILIP, Londres, le 14 septembre 1942." Philip was a member of the clandestinely regrouped SFIO and a prominent member of Libération-Sud. Upon reaching London in July 1942, he became the commissaire national à l'intérieur of the Free French.

58. In fact, de Bénouville was at the center of an internal scandal when he used his Swiss contacts from his previous *réseau*, Carte, to approach the British and American secret services in Switzerland for money for Combat. Jean Moulin was not happy to learn in 1943 that Combat had received funds from the OSS. See Marcot, Leroux, and Levisse-Touzé, *Dictionnaire historique de la Résistance*, 359.

59. Bénouville, *Unknown Warriors,* 165. Interestingly, de Bénouville was not the only person to remark on Groussard's ressemblance to Eric von Stroheim. Gilbert Renault (Rémy) also wrote upon meeting Groussard in a hotel room that "Eric von Stroheim in person welcomed us into his room. Upon closer inspection, it was not him, but the resemblance, monocle and all, was striking." Rémy, *Mémoires d'un agent secret,* 150.

60. ADP, PEROTIN 212-79-3-47, "Rapport d'ensemble sur le Service Central du CENTRE D'INFORMATION ET D'ETUDES."

61. APP, GA G4, Groussard, Report of 31 January 1947.

62. Groussard, *Service secret,* 497. Jean Luchaire was the founder of the collaborationist paper *Les Nouveaux Temps* and the minister of the interior in the German-controlled Vichy government set up in Sigmaringen in 1944 and 1945. Marcel Déat was the former socialist turned collaborator and cofounder of the RNP.

63. Loustaunau-Lacau and Groussard, *Consuls, prenez garde!,* 180. André Mornet, the prosecutor against Pétain, was already well known for having sent Mata Hari to death in 1917.

64. Groussard, *L'Armée et ses drames,* 47.

65. SHD, GR 8YE 88504, "Renseignements en vue d'un mariage, 18 décembre 1913."

66. There is no word on what happened to Groussard's first wife, but he eventually became involved with (and married) Suzanne Kohn, the sister of Antoinette Sachs, who was Jean Moulin's companion.

67. Groussard, *Service secret,* 305.

68. Ibid., 331.

69. Groussard, *L'Armée et ses drames,* 71.

70. Groussard, *Service secret,* 332.

71. Sainclivier, "Essai de prosopographie," 326.

72. Groussard, *L'Armée et ses drames,* 57–58.

73. Groussard, *Service secret,* 10.

74. Ibid., 591.

75. Ibid.

76. APP, GA G4, Groussard, Report of November 1967.

77. Ibid.

78. Belot, *La Résistance sans de Gaulle,* 204–5.

79. Ibid., 212.

80. Vergez-Chaignon, *Les vichysto-résistants,* 571.

81. Marnhan, *Resistance and Betrayal,* 221. Marnham, however, calls her a "self-confessed traitor" (221) and a "systematic liar" (245).

82. André Devigny, a resister who was celebrated for his daring escape from Montluc prison in 1943 and whose story prompted the making of a movie (*Un condamné à mort s'est echappé*), was also a member of Groussard's network and also continued to maintain Delétraz's innocence. Belot, *La Résistance sans de Gaulle,* 215.

83. Vergez-Chaignon, *Les vichysto-résistants,* 574.

RIGHTIST GAULLISM

1. Drew Middleton, "De Gaulle Repeats Democracy Pledge: His Movement Is Non-Political and Will End When France Is Free, He Promises," *New York Times*, 22 July 1943, 1.

2. Shennan, *Profiles in Power: De Gaulle*, 25–26.

3. Once French Equatorial Africa declared allegiance to the Free French, de Gaulle set about building a radio transmitter so that he could reach out without BBC interference. After November 1942 he was also able to use Radio-Algiers, which allowed him to speak to the southern part of France as well as colonial Africa.

4. National Archives (Kew), FO 371/28346, "Memo of 8 January 1941, France: treatment of Vichy government—guidance for B.B.C. and news department."

5. Douglas Johnson, "Pierre de Bénouville; French rightwinger with ambivalent resistance past" (obituary), *Guardian*, 14 December 2001.

6. Rabino, *Le réseau Carte*, 216.

7. Bénouville, *Unknown Warriors*, 13–14.

8. Ibid.

9. It should be mentioned that Deloncle was a fairly unstable character at the best of times.

10. De Bénouville, *Unknown Warriors*, 38.

11. ANF, 72 AJ/80, Résistance intérieure: mouvements, réseaux, partis politiques, "Témoignage de Mr. Dominique Ponchardier—vu par M. Michel le 25 octobre 1946."

12. De Bénouville, *Unknown Warriors*, 57.

13. Ibid., 217. The date Girard offered for when de Bénouville joined the Resistance suggests that de Bénouville's real commitment to the Resistance came only after the Germans invaded the southern, previously unoccupied zone in response to Allied landings in North Africa. Girard was perhaps suggesting that de Bénouville's resistance record was tarnished by opportunism.

14. Frenay and for a time de Bénouville were in charge of military affairs of the MUR.

15. For a brief description of the affair, see Belot, *La Résistance sans de Gaulle*, 448, in a section intriguingly titled "La Résistance trahit-elle de Gaulle?" For a much longer investigation and the only truly detailed one, Robert Belot and Gilbert Karpman's recently published *L'affaire suisse* is helpful.

16. De Bénouville, *Unknown Warriors*, 100.

17. Marcot, Leroux, and Levisse-Touzé, *Dictionnaire historique de la Résistance*, 359.

18. Belot, *La Résistance sans de Gaulle*, 217.

19. Vergez-Chaignon, *Les vichysto-résistants*, 600.

20. Ibid., 599–600.

21. See http://www.ordredelaliberation.fr/fr_compagnon/304.html.

22. ADP, 30W 0006, Cour d'Assises de la Seine.

23. ANF, 72 AJ/80, Résistance intérieure: mouvements, réseaux, partis politiques, Fiche de Renseignements, Chancellerie de 1'Ordre de la Libération, March 1963.

24. Duclos's private archives, Musée de l'Ordre de la Libération (hereafter MOL), letter from the ambassador of Uruguay to Hettier de Boislambert, the then chancellor of the Ordre, Montevideo, 3 November 1967.

25. Duclos's private archives, MOL, letter from Philippe Ditisheim to Général Simon (president, Association des Français Libres), 31 May 1987.

26. ANF, F7 14673, Armes, 1920–1939, "L'Inspecteur de Police Mobile BARBELION à M. le Commissaire de Police Mobile, Chef de la 2e Section, de l'Inspection Générale des Services de Police Criminelle, Nice le 19 janvier 1938."

27. It is impossible to know how much money Duclos was making, but his address at Place Vendôme tells us something about his financial success.

28. "M. Deloncle . . . has stopped all industrial activity to devote himself exclusively to the preparation of the plot and is helped in this task by one of his friends, a mister Duclos, importer-exporter, Place Vendôme in Paris, who is one of the people financing the affair, alongside the Comité des Forges, the banks, and the Insurance Companies." ANF, F7 14673, Armes, 1920–1939, letter from Le Préfet des Alpes-Maritimes to M. le Ministre de l'Intérieur, Nice, 25 November 1937.

29. ANF, 72 AJ/231, Résistance hors de France et organes centraux de la Résistance, "Témoinage de Maurice Duclos, recueilli par Mlle Gouineau 1949."

30. Ibid.

31. Ibid.

32. Bourdrel, *La Cagoule,* 241.

33. Ibid., 242.

34. ANF, 72 AJ/231, Résistance hors de France et organes centraux de la Résistance, "Témoinage de Maurice Duclos, recueilli par Mlle Gouineau 1949."

35. Ibid.

36. ANF, 72 AJ/80, Résistance intérieure: mouvements, réseaux, partis politiques, "Témoignage de M. Lucien Feltesse—recueilli par Mme Granet le 12 mai 1948."

37. This early mission is described in some detail in Passy, *Souvenirs,* and in Rémy, *Mémoires d'un agent secret.*

38. Philippe Bourdrel rightly points out how remarkable it was that Duclos was able to establish this network so early. He notes that the group Musée de l'Homme, often considered the first resistance network, would not even publish its first paper until mid-December 1940, one month before it was decimated by arrests. Bourdrel, *Les cagoulards dans la guerre,* 58.

39. Passy, *Souvenirs,* 159.

40. Ibid.; Rémy, *Mémoires d'un agent secret,* 158–60.

41. Vergez-Chaignon, *Les vichysto-résistants,* 74.

42. The spelling of this man's name varies from report to report.

43. Duclos's private archives, MOL, "JACK J VIA LUKE," 15 June 1941.

44. Bourdrel, *Les cagoulards dans la guerre,* 75.

45. *Nacht und Nebel* (Night and Fog) was an order signed by Hitler in 1941 to make political opponents and resistance fighters in the German-occupied countries "disappear."

46. ANF, 72 AJ/80, Résistance intérieure: mouvements, réseaux, partis politiques, war experience of Mme Marie-Anne Lefèvre-Duclos (sister of Saint-Jacques) and her daughter Monique, n.d.

47. SHD, GR13P 148, "Historique de la réseau Saint-Jacques."

48. Ibid.

49. As detailed in Bourdrel, *Les cagoulards dans la guerre*, 82–83.

50. Duclos's private archives, MOL, telegram to Saint-Jacques, 5 October 1941. The original telegram is missing the accents and I have chosen to leave it as such.

51. The *livre blanc* was an early history of the BCRA created in 1945 by Mme Vitia Hessel, M. Hessel, and M. Guillet.

52. ANF, 171 Mi*/1, "Livre blanc—partie II."

53. The first thorough study of the BCRA, by Sébastien Albertelli, is an important source for any investigation of these secret services. See Albertelli, *Les services secrets du Général de Gaulle*.

54. ANF, 171 Mi*/1, "Livre blanc—partie II."

55. Duclos's private archives, MOL.

56. Passy, *Souvenirs*, 52–53.

57. Ibid., 48.

58. Vosjoli, *Lamia*.

59. Duclos-Rostand, *À l'ombre de Saint-Jacques*, 14.

60. Ibid., 15.

61. Ibid., 26.

62. Ibid., 25.

63. Ibid., 64.

64. ANF, 72 AJ/80, Résistance intérieure: mouvements, réseaux, partis politiques, Fiche de Renseignements, Chancellerie de 1'Ordre de la Libération, March 1963.

65. ADP, PEROTIN 212-79-3-48, letter from Le commissaire divisionnaire Robin to M. le Directeur des Services de Police Judiciaire, 19 November 1945. This letter says to see an attached note about Duclos, but the note has long been lost.

66. ADP, PEROTIN 212-79-3-52, demand for provisional liberty.

67. ANF, 72 AJ/80, Résistance intérieure: mouvements, réseaux, partis politiques, "Inauguration officielle de la plaque commémorative du réseau Saint-Jacques 8 place Vendôme, Paris 14 novembre 1986, 11h30."

68. Ibid.

69. ANF, 72 AJ/80, Résistance intérieure: mouvements, réseaux, partis politiques, plans for the commemoration of 18 June in 1990.

70. Ibid.

71. The DGER was a division of the BCRA. Created in 1944, it was the forerunner to France's Service de documentation extérieure et contre-espionnage (SDECE).

72. Duclos's private archives, MOL, radiogram from Argentina to General de Gaulle, 23 December 1958.

73. Duclos's private archives, MOL, telegram from Buenos Aires, 24 April 1961.

74. Duclos's private archives, MOL, letter from the ambassador of Uruguay to Hettier de Boislambert, Montevideo, 3 November 1967.

75. Duclos's private archives, MOL, letter from Saint-Jacques to M. le Préfet, Paris, 22 June 1945.

76. Duclos's private archives, MOL, letter from Jean-Marie Pruvost to Duclos, 10 January 1966.

77. ANF, 72 AJ/231, Résistance hors de France et organes centraux de la Résistance; Duclos's private archives, MOL, "testimony of Maurice Duclos, 1949."

78. Ibid.

79. Ibid.

80. Ibid.

POSTWAR MEMORIES

1. Barasz, "Un vichyste en Résistance," 167.

2. Ibid., 168. Barasz goes on to say that examples of people who possess seemingly contradictory values present cases of cognitive dissonance.

3. ANF, 3W 301, "Audition de Gabriel Jeantet," n.d. (likely 1945). The veracity of this story is difficult to gauge. Given that Jeantet was subsequently arrested, it seems unlikely that these events took place exactly as he recounted them.

4. ANF, F7 14815, Partis et mouvements politiques, letter from the Ministère de la défense nationale et de la guerre, Etat-Major de l'armée, Cinquième Bureau (Section de centralisation des renseignments).

5. ANF, 3W 301, "Audition de Gabriel Jeantet," n.d. (likely 1945).

6. ADP, PEROTIN 212-79-3-47, "Procès-verbal d'interrogatoire et confrontations 21 jan. 1948—Paul Joseph Dungler."

7. Marcot, Leroux, and Levisse-Touzé, *Dictionnaire historique de la Résistance,* 411.

8. Jeantet seems to have provided resisters with money and false papers, and he certainly helped liberate Dungler after his first arrest in 1942. Bourdrel, *Les cagoulards dans la guerre,* 227.

9. ANF, 3W 301, "Audition de Gabriel Jeantet," n.d. (likely 1945).

10. Ibid.

11. Vergez-Chaignon, *Les vichysto-résistants,* 429.

12. ANF, 3W 301, "Audition de Gabriel Jeantet," n.d. (likely 1945).

13. ANF, F7 14880, Surveillance et répression des actes terroristes et des menées antinationales, 1940–1944, "Notes secrètes et anonymes concernant les évènements et les manifestations politiques en France 1944, Notes des agents B.P.5, D.J.5, J.P.7, L.M.4, 805 21 juin 1944."

14. Laurent and Jeantet, *Année 40,* 86.

15. ANF, 3W 301, "Audition de Gabriel Jeantet," n.d. (likely 1945).

16. Gildea, *France since 1945,* 67.

17. Rousso, *Vichy Syndrome*, 16.

18. *Resistancialist* is Rousso's term for the myth that "celebrated a people in resistance, a people symbolized exclusively by [de Gaulle]." Ibid., 18.

19. Maurice Thorez deserted and fled to Moscow in 1939, after the signing of the Non-Aggression Pact by the Nazis and the Soviets and the banning of the PCF.

20. Epstein, *Un paradoxe français*, 392.

21. Vinen, "End of an Ideology?," 374.

22. Ibid., 373–77.

23. Ibid., 377.

24. Ibid., 378.

25. Rousso, *Vichy Syndrome*, 76.

26. Furniss, *De Gaulle and the French Army*, 117.

27. Groussard, *Service secret*, 57.

28. This policy of "integration"—creating a united Franco-African community—was elaborated mostly by Jacques Soustelle, and it has become clear that Gaullists did not speak with one voice on this issue. Moreover, de Gaulle himself was likely never persuaded that such a policy would be successful. Tyre, "Gaullists, the French Army and Algeria before 1958," 99.

29. Laurent and Jeantet, *Année 40*, 28–29.

30. Ibid., 59.

31. Gabriel Jeantet died in 1978 under what Philippe Bourdrel mysteriously calls "atrocious conditions." Bourdrel, *Les cagoulards dans la guerre*, 258. What Bourdrel means by this is unknown; however, Jeantet was one of the few *cagoulards* willing to talk to Bourdrel when he was researching his book, so presumably he knows something about the circumstances of Jeantet's death. Jeantet's biography on the website of the Fondation pour la Mémoire de la Déportation de l'Allier suggests that he killed himself in 1978. www.afmd-allier.com/PBCPPlayer.asp?ID=864671.

32. Soustelle, "France Looks at Her Alliances," 129.

33. As one socialist is quoted as saying in Gildea, *France since 1945*, 26.

34. Vergez-Chaignon, *Les vichysto-résistants*, 637.

CONCLUSION

1. Fourcade, *Noah's Ark*, 232.

2. Joel Blatt, "Cagoule Plot, 1936–1937," 97–98.

3. Sainclivier, "Essai de prosopographie."

4. Handourtzel and Buffet, *La collaboration à gauche aussi*, 26.

5. Irvine, *Between Politics and Justice*; Epstein, *Un paradoxe français*.

6. This is a useful model used by Claude d'Abzac-Épezy. His article "Vichystes ou résistants?" contains a fairly elaborate table of possible intersections.

7. Semelin, "Jalons pour une histoire de la France résistante," 461.

8. See Wieviorka, "Les avatars du statut de résistant en France."

BIBLIOGRAPHY

ARCHIVES

Archives de la Préfecture de Police

GA G4. Georges Groussard.
GA H3. Pierre Hordequin.
GA L15. Georges Loustaunau-Lacau.
GA V5. Albert Vogel.

Archives de Paris

30W 0006. Cour d'Assises de la Seine, 16 January to 31 December 1948.
PEROTIN 212-79-3. Dossiers on la Cagoule.

Archives Nationales de France

72 AJ/1–2467. Papiers du Comité d'histoire de la Deuxième Guerre mondiale et fonds privés relatifs à la période 1939–1945.
171 Mi 1–208 (corresponding to the series 3AG2). BCRA Archives.
3W. Haute Cour de Justice.
C/I* 597–631. Assemblée nationale (1946–1958), procès-verbaux des séances.
F^{1a}. Ministère de l'Intérieur (administration générale / objets généraux).
F7. Police general.
Ordre de la Légion d'honneur. 19800035/27/3426.
Ordre de la Légion d'honneur. 19800035/553/63124.

Musée de l'Ordre de la Libération

Maurice Duclos (private archives).

National Archives (Kew)

FO 371. Foreign Office: Political Departments: General Correspondence, 1906–66.

Service Historique de la Défense, Vincennes

8YE 88504. Georges Groussard.

14YD 366. Georges Loustaunau-Lacau.

GR13P 145, 147, 148. Historiques des réseaux des Forces Françaises reconnus unités combattantes.

NEWSPAPERS AND BULLETINS

Barrage
Guardian
Journal des Débats Politiques et Littéraires
L'Écho de Paris
Le Figaro
Le Monde
Le Populaire
Le Temps
L'Humanité
L'Œuvre
New York Times
Notre Prestige

BOOKS AND ARTICLES

Abzac-Épezy, Claude d'. "Vichystes ou résistants? Quelques itinéraires militaires." *Guerres Mondiales et Conflits Contemporains*, no. 192 (1998): 133–49.

Adamthwaite, Anthony. *France and the Coming of the Second World War*. London: Cass, 1977.

Adereth, Maxwell. *The French Communist Party: A Critical History (1920–84)*. Manchester: Manchester University Press, 1984.

Adler, K. H. "Demography at Liberation: Using History to Forget the Past." In *Vichy, Resistance, Liberation: New Perspectives on Wartime France*, ed. Hanna Diamond and Simon Kitson. Oxford: Berg, 2005.

Aglan, Alya. "Décision individuelle et discipline collective: La résistance des réseaux." In *La Résistance et les Français: Villes, centres et logiques de décision;*

Actes du colloque international tenu à Cachan du 16 au 18 novembre 1995, 339–50. Paris: IHTP/CNRS, 1995.

Albertelli, Sébastien. *Les services secrets du Général de Gaulle: Le BCRA, 1940–1944.* Paris: Perrin, 2009.

Albertelli, Sébastien, and Johanna Barasz. "Un résistant atypique: Le général Cochet, entre vichysme et gaullisme." *Histoire@Politique: Politique, Culture, Société,* no. 5 (May–August 2008): 1–15.

Alexander, Martin S., Martin Evans, and J. F. V. Keiger, eds. *The Algerian War and the French Army, 1954–62: Experiences, Images, Testimonies.* Basingstoke, UK: Palgrave Macmillan, 2002.

Alexander, Martin S., and Helen Graham, eds. *The French and Spanish Popular Fronts: Comparative Perspectives.* Cambridge: Cambridge University Press, 1989.

Alexander, Robert. *Re-Writing the French Revolutionary Tradition: Liberal Opposition and the Fall of the Bourbon Monarchy.* Cambridge: Cambridge University Press, 2003.

Allison, Maggie. "From the Violence of War to the War against Intolerance: Representing the Resistant Woman, Lucie Aubrac." In "Murdering Marianne? Gender and Representation in French Literature and Film," special issue, *South Central Review* 19, no. 4–20, no. 1 (Winter 2002–Spring 2003): 119–34.

Ambler, J. S. *The French Army in Politics, 1945–1962.* Columbus: Ohio State University Press, 1962.

Andrieu, Claire. *Le programme commun de la Résistance: Des idées dans la guerre.* Paris: Les Editions de l'Erudit, 1984.

———. "Les résistantes, perspectives de recherché." In "Pour une histoire sociale de la Résistance," special issue, *Le Mouvement Social,* no. 180 (July–September 1997): 69–96.

———. "L'histoire de la Résistance en question." *Vingtième Siècle: Revue d'Histoire,* no. 41 (January–March 1994): 93–95.

Ansart-Dourlen, Michèle. *Le choix de la morale en politique: Le rôle des personnalités dans la Résistance.* Paris: François-Xavier de Guibert, 2004.

Augustin, Jean-Marie. *Le Plan Bleu: Un complot contre la République en 1947.* La Crèche: Geste, 2006.

Azéma, Jean-Pierre. *De Munich à la Libération, 1938–1944.* Paris: Seuil, 1979.

———. "La Milice." *Vingtième Siècle: Revue d'Histoire,* no. 28 (1990): 83–106.

Bankwitz, Philip C. F. "Maxime Weygand and the Army-Nation Concept in the Modern French Army." *French Historical Studies* 2, 2 (Autumn 1961): 157–88.

———. "Maxime Weygand and the Fall of France: A Study in Civil-Military Relations." *Journal of Modern History* 31, no. 3 (September 1959): 225–42.

Barasz, Johanna. "Les vichysto-résistants: Choix d'un sujet, construction d'un objet." In *Chercheurs en Résistance: Pistes et outils à l'usage des historiens*, ed. Julien Blanc and Cécile Vast. Rennes: Presses universitaires de Rennes, 2014.

———. "Un vichyste en Résistance, le général de La Laurencie." *Vingtième Siècle: Revue d'Histoire*, no. 94 (2007): 167–81.

Baruch, Marc Olivier. *Servir l'état français: L'administration en France de 1940 à 1944*. Paris: Fayard, 1997.

Becker, Annette. "Les Britanniques dans la Grande Guerre et l'imaginaire résistant." In *La Résistance et les Européens du Nord: Communications présentées lors du colloque de Bruxelles, 23–25 novembre 1994*, ed. Robert Frank and José Gotovitch, 9–20. Paris: IHTP, 1994.

Bédarida, François. "L'histoire de La Resistance: Lectures d'hier, chantiers de demain." *Vingtième Siècle: Revue d'Histoire*, no. 11 (July 1986): 75–90.

———. "Sur le concept de résistance." In *Mémoire et histoire: La Résistance*, ed. J. M. Guillon and P. Laborie, 45–52. Toulouse: Éditions Privat, 1995.

Belot, Robert. *Aux frontières de la liberté: Vichy—Madrid—Alger—Londres: S'évader de France sous l'occupation*. Paris: Fayard, 1998.

———. *Henri Frenay: De la Résistance à l'Europe*. Paris: Seuil, 2003.

———. *La Résistance sans de Gaulle*. Paris: Fayard, 2006.

Belot, Robert, and Gilbert Karpman. *L'affaire suisse: La Résistance a-t-elle trahi De Gaulle?* Paris: Armand Colin, 2009.

Benouville, Guillain de. *The Unknown Warriors*. Trans. Lawrence G. Blochman. New York: Simon & Schuster, 1949.

Bernadac, Christian. *Dagore: Les carnets secrets de la Cagoule*. Paris: Éditions France—Empire, 1977.

Bernard, Mathias. *La guerre des droites: De l'affaire Dreyfus à nos jours*. Paris: Odile Jacob, 2007.

Bernstein, Samuel. *Auguste Blanqui and the Art of Insurrection*. London: Lawrence & Wishart, 1971.

Blanc, Julien. *Au commencement de la Résistance: Du côté du Musée de l'Homme, 1940–1941*. Paris: Seuil, 2010.

Blanc, Julien, and Cécile Vast, eds. *Chercheurs en Résistance: Pistes et outils à l'usage des historiens*. Rennes: Presses universitaires de Rennes, 2014.

Blatt, Joel. "The Cagoule Plot, 1936–1937." In *Crisis and Renewal in France, 1918–1962*, ed. Kenneth Mouré and Martin S. Alexander, 86–104. New York: Berghahn Books, 2002.

———, ed. *The French Defeat of 1940: Reassessments*. Providence, RI: Berghahn Books, 1998.

Bourdrel, Philippe. *La Cagoule: 30 ans de complots*. Paris: Albin Michel, 1970.

———. *Les cagoulards dans la guerre*. Paris: Albin Michel, 2009.

Bracher, Nathan. "Remembering the French Resistance: Ethics and Poetics of the Epic." *History & Memory* 19, no. 1 (2007): 39–67.

Brelot, Claude-Isabelle. "Nobles français en Résistance." In *La Résistance et les Européens du Nord: Communications présentées lors du colloque de Bruxelles, 23–25 novembre 1994*, ed. Robert Frank and José Gotovitch, 2:21–28. Paris: IHTP, 1996.

Brunelle, Gayle K., and Annette Finley-Croswhite. *Murder in the Métro: Laetitia Toureaux and the Cagoule in 1930s France*. Baton Rouge: Louisiana State University Press, 2010.

Burrin, Philippe. *France under the Germans: Collaboration and Compromise*. Trans. Janet Lloyd. New York: New Press, 1996.

Clark, Linda L. "Higher-Ranking Women Civil Servants and the Vichy Regime: Firings and Hirings, Collaboration and Resistance." *French History* 13, no. 3 (September 1999): 332–59.

Cohen, Kenneth. Preface to *Noah's Ark*, by Marie-Madeleine Fourcade, 9–12. Trans. Kenneth Morgan. New York: E. P. Dutton, 1974.

Cointet, Jean-Paul. *La légion française des combattants: La tentation du fascisme [1940–1944]*. Paris: Albin Michel, 1995.

Cointet, Michèle. *Marie-Madeleine Fourcade: Un chef de la Résistance*. Paris: Perrin, 2006.

Colton, Joel. "The Formation of the French Popular Front, 1934–6." In *The French and Spanish Popular Fronts: Comparative Perspectives*, ed. Martin S. Alexander and Helen Graham. Cambridge: Cambridge University Press, 1989.

Cordier, Daniel. *Jean Moulin: L'inconnu du Panthéon*. 3 vols. Paris: J-C. Lattès, 1989.

Cornick, Martyn. "The Role of the BBC European Intelligence Department in the Propaganda War against Occupied France." In *La Résistance et les Européens du Nord: Communications présentées lors du colloque de Bruxelles, 23–25 novembre 1994*, ed. Robert Frank and José Gotovitch, 86–95. Paris: IHTP, 1994.

Cotillon, Jérôme. *Ce qu'il reste de Vichy*. Paris: Armand Colin, 2003.

Crémieux-Brilhac, Jean-Louis. "De Gaulle: L'affirmation d'une légitimité." In *La Résistance et les Français: Villes, centres et logiques de décision; Actes du colloque international tenu à Cachan du 16 au 18 novembre 1995*, 299–308. Paris: IHTP/CNRS, 1995.

Dank, Milton. *The French against the French: Collaboration and Resistance*. New York: J. B. Lippincott, 1974.

Deacon, Valerie. "Fitting in to the French Resistance: Marie-Madeleine Fourcade and Georges Loustaunau-Lacau at the Intersection of Politics and Gender." *Journal of Contemporary History* 50, no. 2 (April 2015): 259–73.

de la Gorce, Paul Marie. *The French Army: A Military-Political History*. New York: George Braziller, 1963.

Désert, Joseph. *Toute la vérité sur l'affaire de la Cagoule: Sa trahison, ses crimes, ses hommes*. Paris: Librairie des Sciences et des Arts, 1946.

Desprairies, Cécile. *L'héritage de Vichy: Ces 100 mesures toujours en vigueur*. Paris: Armand Colin, 2012.

de Vosjoli, P. L. Thyraud. *Lamia*. Boston: Little, 1970.

Diamond, Hanna. *Fleeing Hitler: France 1940*. Oxford: Oxford University Press, 2007.

———. *Women and the Second World War in France, 1939–1948: Choices and Constraints*. New York: Longman, 1999.

Diamond, Hanna, and Simon Kitson, eds. *Vichy, Resistance, Liberation: New Perspectives on Wartime France*. Oxford: Berg, 2005.

Doré-Rivé, Isabelle. *Traits résistants: La Résistance dans la bande dessinée de 1944 à nos jours*. Lyon: Libel, 2011.

Douzou, Laurent, ed. *Faire l'histoire de la Résistance*. Rennes: Presses Universitaires de Rennes, 2010.

———. *La désobéissance: Histoire d'un mouvement et d'un journal clandestins; "Libération-Sud," 1940–1944*. Paris: Éditions Odile Jacob, 1995.

———. "La Résistance et le monde rural: Entre histoire et mémoire." *Ruralia: Sciences Sociales et Mondes Ruraux Contemporains*, no. 4 (1999). http://ruralia. revues.org/88.

———. *La Résistance française: Une histoire périlleuse*. Paris: Seuil, 2005.

———. "L'entrée en résistance." In *La Résistance: Une histoire sociale*, ed. Antoine Prost, 9–20. Paris: Éditions de l'Atelier, 1997.

Douzou, Laurent, Robert Frank, Denis Peschanski, and Dominique Veillon. Preface to *La Résistance et les Français: Villes, centres et logiques de décision; Actes du colloque international tenu à Cachan du 16 au 18 novembre 1995*. Paris: IHTP/CNRS, 1995.

Douzou, Laurent, and Denis Peschanski. "Les premiers résistants face à l'hypothèque Vichy (1940–1942)." In *La Résistance et les Français: Villes, centres et logiques de décision; Actes du colloque international tenu à Cachan du 16 au 18 novembre 1995*, 427–46. Paris: IHTP/CNRS, 1995.

Dreyfus, François-Georges. *Histoire de la Résistance, 1940–1945*. Paris: Éditions de Fallois, 1996.

Duclos-Rostand, Geneviève. À l'ombre de Saint-Jacques: Une famille française dans
    la Résistance. Luçon: Hécate, 1995.

Duranton-Crabol, Anne-Marie. "'Combat' et le guerre d'Algérie." Vingtième Siècle:
    Revue d'Histoire, no. 40 (October–December 1993): 86–96.

Dutailly, Henry. Les problèmes de l'Armée de terre française, 1935–1939. Paris: Im-
    primerie Nationale, 1980.

Epstein, Simon. Un paradoxe français: Antiracistes dans la collaboration, antisémites
    dans la Résistance. Paris: Albin Michel, 2008.

Fishman, Sarah, Laura Lee Downs, and Ioannis Sinanoglou, eds. France at War:
    Vichy and the Historians. Oxford: Berg, 2000.

Fleutot, François Marin. Des royalistes dans la Résistance. Paris: Flammarion, 2000.

Flood, Christopher, and Hugo Frey. "Extreme Right-Wing Reactions to Charles
    de Gaulle's 'Mémoires de Guerre': A Scene from the French Civil War." South
    Central Review 17, no. 4 (Winter 2000): 72–83.

Fontenay, Fernand. La Cagoule contre la France: Ses crimes, son organisation, ses
    chefs, ses inspirateurs. Paris: Éditions Sociales Internationales, 1938.

Foot, M. R. D. SOE in France: An Account of the Work of the British Special Operations
    Executive in France, 1940–1944. London: Her Majesty's Stationery Office, 1966.

Footitt, H. "Women and (Cold) War: The Cold War Creation of the Myth of 'La
    Francaise Resistante.'" French Cultural Studies 8, no. 22 (1997): 41–51.

Forcade, Olivier, Eric Duhamel, and Philippe Vial, eds. Militaires en république,
    1870–1962. Paris: Publications de la Sorbonne, 1999.

Fourcade, Marie-Madeleine. Noah's Ark. Trans. Kenneth Morgan. New York: E. P.
    Dutton, 1974.

Fournier, Georges. "Contestations collectives, résistances et Résistance: Quelles
    continuités?" In Mémoire et histoire: La Résistance, ed. J. M. Guillon and
    P. Laborie, 53–60. Toulouse: Éditions Privat, 1995.

Frank, Robert. "Résistance et résistants dans la stratégie des Britanniques et
    Américains." In La Résistance et les Français: Villes, centres et logiques de décision;
    Actes du colloque international tenu à Cachan du 16 au 18 novembre 1995, 471–84.
    Paris: IHTP/CNRS, 1995.

Frenay, Henri. The Night Will End. Trans. Dan Hofstadter. London: Abelard-
    Schuman, 1976.

Funk, Arthur Layton. "American Contacts with the Resistance in France, 1940–
    1943." Military Affairs 34, no. 1 (February 1970): 15–21.

Furniss, Edgar S., Jr. De Gaulle and the French Army: A Crisis in Civil-Military Rela-
    tions. New York: Twentieth Century Fund, 1964.

Ganser, Daniele. *Nato's Secret Armies: Operation Gladio and Terrorism in Western Europe*. New York: Frank Cass, 2005.

Gildea, Robert. *France since 1945*. 1996. Reprint, Oxford: Oxford University Press, 2002.

Gordon, Bertram M. "The 'Vichy Syndrome' Problem in History." *French Historical Studies* 19, no. 2 (Autumn 1995): 495–518.

Griotteray, Alain. *1940: Qui étaient les premiers résistants?* Lausanne: Éditions l'Age d'Homme, 1999.

Groussard, Georges A. *L'Armée et ses drames*. Paris: Éditions de la Table Ronde, 1968.

———. *Service secret, 1940–1945*. Paris: Éditions de la Table Ronde, 1964.

Guillon, Jean-Marie. "Résistance et classes moyennes en zone sud." In *La Résistance et les Européens du Nord: Communications présentées lors du colloque de Bruxelles, 23–25 novembre 1994*, ed. Robert Frank and José Gotovitch, 288–99. Paris: IHTP, 1994.

Handourtzel, Rémy, and Cyril Buffet. *La collaboration à gauche aussi*. Paris: Perrin, 1989.

Harrison, Alexander. *Challenging de Gaulle: The O.A.S. and the Counterrevolution in Algeria, 1954–1962*. New York: Praeger, 1989.

Hellman, John. *The Knight-Monks of Vichy France: Uriage, 1940–1945*. Montreal: McGill-Queen's University Press, 1993.

———. "Wounding Memories: Mitterrand, Moulin, Touvier, and the Divine Half-Lie of Resistance." *French Historical Studies* 19, no. 2 (Autumn 1995): 461–86.

Hessel, Stéphane. *Time for Outrage!* Trans. Damion Searls. London: Quartet Books, 2011.

Hogenhuis-Seliverstoff, Anne. *Des savants dans la Résistance: Boris Vildé et le réseau du Musée de l'Homme*. Paris: CNRS, 2009.

Horne, Alistair. *The French Army and Politics, 1870–1970*. New York: Peter Bedrick Books, 1984.

Hutton, Patrick H. *The Cult of the Revolutionary Tradition: The Blanquists in French Politics, 1864–1893*. Berkeley and Los Angeles: University of California Press, 1981.

Huyse, Luc, and Kris Hoflack. "Life after Prison: The Purge and the Reintegration of Wartime Collaborators in Belgium, Holland and France (1944–1994)." In "1945: Consequences and Sequels of the Second World War," special issue, *Bulletin du Comité International d'Histoire de la Deuxième Guerre Mondiale*, nos. 27–28 (1995): 257–80.

Ingram, Norman. *The Politics of Dissent: Pacifism in France, 1919–1939*. Oxford: Clarendon, 1991.

Irvine, William D. *Between Politics and Justice: The Ligue des droits de l'homme, 1898–1945*. Stanford, CA: Stanford University Press, 2006.

———. "Beyond Left and Right: Rethinking Political Boundaries in 1930s France." In *The French Right between the Wars: Political and Intellectual Movements from Conservatism to Fascism*, ed. Samuel Kalman and Sean Kennedy. New York: Berghahn Books, 2014.

———. "Domestic Politics and the Fall of France in 1940." In *The French Defeat of 1940: Reassessments*, ed. Joel Blatt. Providence, RI: Berghahn Books, 1998

Jackson, Julian. *The Fall of France: The Nazi Invasion of 1940*. New York: Oxford University Press, 2003.

———. *France: The Dark Years, 1940–1944*. Oxford: Oxford University Press, 2001.

———. "General de Gaulle and His Enemies: Anti-Gaullism in France since 1940." *Transactions of the Royal Historical Society*, 6th ser., 9 (1999): 43–65.

Jaladieu, Corinne. "Les résistantes dans les prisons de Vichy: L'exemple de La Centrale de Rennes." *Cahiers d'Histoire: Revue d'Histoire Critique*, no. 89 (2002): 81–97.

Jankowski, Paul. "In Defense of Fiction: Resistance, Collaboration, and Lacombe, Lucien." *Journal of Modern History* 63, no. 3 (September 1991): 457–82.

Jeffery, Keith. *MI6: The History of the Secret Intelligence Service, 1909–1949*. London: Bloomsbury, 2010.

Jenkins, Brian. "The *Six Fevrier* 1934 and the 'Survival' of the French Republic." *French History* 20, no. 3 (September 2006): 333–51.

Judt, Tony. *Past Imperfect: French Intellectuals, 1944–1956*. Berkeley: University of California Press, 1992.

Kalman, Samuel. *French Colonial Fascism: The Extreme Right in Algeria, 1919–1939*. Gordonsville, VA: Palgrave Macmillan, 2013.

Kalman, Samuel, and Sean Kennedy, eds. *The French Right between the Wars: Political and Intellectual Movements from Conservatism to Fascism*. New York: Berghahn Books, 2014.

Kedward, H. R. *La Vie en Bleu: France and the French since 1900*. London: Allen Lane, 2005.

———. "Mapping the Resistance: An Essay on Roots and Routes." *Modern & Contemporary France* 20, no. 4 (November 2012): 491–503.

———. *Resistance in Vichy France: A Study of Ideas and Motivation in the Southern Zone, 1940–1942*. Oxford: Oxford University Press, 1978.

———. "Resisting French Resistance." *Transactions of the Royal Historical Society* 9 (1999): 271–82.

Kelly, George Armstrong. *Lost Soldiers: The French Army and Empire in Crisis,
    1947–1962.* Cambridge, MA: MIT Press, 1965.

Kennedy, Sean. *Reconciling France against Democracy: The Croix de Feu and the Parti
    Social Français, 1927–1945.* Montreal: McGill-Queen's University Press, 2007.

King, Jonathan H. "Emmanuel d'Astier and the Nature of the French Resistance."
    Journal of Contemporary History 8, no. 4 (October 1973): 25–45.

Kitson, Simon. "Arresting Nazi Spies in Vichy France, 1940–1942." *Intelligence
    and National Security* 15, no. 1 (Spring 2000): 80–120.

———. *The Hunt for Nazi Spies: Fighting Espionage in Vichy France.* Trans. Catherine
    Tihanyi. Chicago: University of Chicago Press, 2008.

———. *Vichy et la chasse aux espions nazis.* Paris: Éditions Autrement, 2005.

Koreman, Megan. *The Expectation of Justice: France, 1944–1946.* Durham, NC:
    Duke University Press, 1999.

Laborie, Pierre. "L'idée de Résistance, entre définition et sens: Retour sur un
    questionnement." *Les Cahiers de L'IHTP: La Résistance et les Français, Nouvelles
    Approches,* no. 37 (December 1997): 15–27.

———. *L'opinion française sous Vichy.* Paris: Seuil, 1990.

———. "Sur les représentations collectives de la Résistance dans la France de
    l'après libération et sur l'usage de la mémoire." In *La résistance et les Européens
    du Nord: Communications présentées lors du colloque de Bruxelles, 23–25 novembre
    1994,* ed. Robert Frank and José Gotovitch, 419–23. Paris: IHTP, 1994.

Labrosse, Diane N. "'La Dérive Bergery / The Bergery Drift': Gaston Bergery and
    the Politics of Late Third Republic France and the Early Vichy State." *Historical
    Reflections: Beyond Left and Right: New Perspectives on the Politics of the Third
    Republic* 34, no. 2 (July 2008): 66–87.

Langlois, Suzanne. *La Résistance dans le cinéma français, 1944–1994: De la Libération
    de Paris à Libera me.* Montreal: L'Harmattan, 2001.

Laurent, Jacques, and Gabriel Jeantet. *Année 40: Londres—de Gaulle—Vichy.* Paris:
    Éditions de la Table Ronde, 1965.

Lee, Daniel. *Pétain's Jewish Children: French Jewish Youth and the Vichy Regime,
    1940–1942.* Oxford: Oxford University Press, 2014.

Levisse-Touzé, Christine. "Le rôle particulier de Paris pendant la Seconde Guerre
    Mondiale." In *La Résistance et les Français: Villes, centres et logiques de décision;
    Actes du colloque international tenu à Cachan du 16 au 18 novembre 1995,* 183–98.
    Paris: IHTP/CNRS, 1995.

Levisse-Touzé, Christine, Mechtild Gilzmer, and Stefan Martens, eds. *Les femmes
    dans La Résistance en France.* Paris: Jules Tallandier, 2003.

Lieb, Peter, and Robert O. Paxton. "Maintenir l'ordre en France occupée: Combien de divisions?" *Vingtième Siècle: Revue d'Histoire*, no. 112 (2011): 115–26.

Lloyd, Christopher. *Collaboration and Resistance in Occupied France*. New York: Palgrave Macmillan, 2003.

Loustaunau-Lacau, Georges. *Mémoires d'un Français rebelle, 1914–1948*. Paris: Robert Laffont, 1948.

Loustaunau-Lacau, Georges, and Georges Groussard. *Consuls, prenez garde!* Paris: Bernard Grasset, 1952.

Machefer, Philippe. *Ligues et fascismes en France, 1919–1939*. Paris: Presses Universitaires de France, 1974.

Magraw, Roger. *France, 1815–1914: The Bourgeois Century*. Oxford: Fontana Paperbacks, 1983.

Marcot, François. "Dans quelle mesure les villes exercent-elles un pouvoir de commandement et d'orientation sur la Résistance dans son ensemble?" In *La résistance et les Français: Villes, centres et logiques de décision; Actes du colloque international tenu à Cachan du 16 au 18 novembre 1995*, 215–28. Paris: IHTP/CNRS, 1995.

———, ed. *Les résistances, miroirs des régimes d'oppression, Allemagne, France, Italie: Actes du colloque international de Besançon*. Paris: Presses universitaires de Franche-Comté, 2006.

———. "Réflexions sur les valeurs de la Résistance." In *Mémoire et histoire: La Résistance*, ed. J. Guillon and P. Laborie, 81–90. Toulouse: Éditions Privat, 1995.

Marcot, François, Bruno Leroux, and Christine Levisse-Touzé, eds. *Dictionnaire historique de la Résistance*. Paris: Éditions Robert Laffont, 2006.

Marnham, Patrick. *Resistance and Betrayal*. New York: Random House, 2000.

Michel, Henri. *Histoire de la Résistance en France (1940–1944)*. Paris: Presses Universitaires de France, 1965.

———. *Les courants de pensée de la Résistance*. Paris: Presses Universitaires de France, 1962.

———. "The Psychology of the French Resister." *Journal of Contemporary History* 5, no. 3 (1970): 159–75.

Millington, Chris. "February 6, 1934: The Veterans' Riot." *French Historical Studies* 33, no. 4 (Fall 2010): 545–72.

———. *From Victory to Vichy: Veterans in Inter-War France*. Manchester: Manchester University Press, 2012.

Milza, Pierre. *Les fascismes*. Paris: Imprimerie Nationale, 1985.

Monier, Frédéric. *Le complot dans la république: Stratégies du secret, de Boulanger à la Cagoule*. Paris: Éditions la Découverte, 1998.

Moore, Bob, ed. *Resistance in Western Europe.* Oxford: Berg, 2000.

Néaumet, Jean-Émile. *Les grandes enquêtes du commissaire Chenevier: De la Cagoule à l'affaire Dominici.* Paris: Albin Michel, 1995.

Nord, Philip G. *France's New Deal: From the Thirties to the Postwar Era.* Princeton, NJ: Princeton University Press, 2012.

Novick, Peter. *The Resistance versus Vichy: The Purge of Collaborators in Liberated France.* New York: Columbia University Press, 1968.

Ott, Sandra. "Duplicity, Indulgence and Ambiguity in Franco-German Relations, 1940–1946." *History and Anthropology* 20, no. 1 (March 2009): 57–77.

Parry, D. L. L. "Articulating the Third Republic by Conspiracy Theory." *European History Quarterly* 28, no. 2 (1998): 163–88.

Passmore, Kevin. "The French Third Republic: Stalemate Society or Cradle of Fascism?" *French History* 7, no. 4 (1993): 417–49.

———. *The Right in France from the Third Republic to Vichy.* Oxford: Oxford University Press, 2012.

Passy, Colonel André Dewavrin. *Souvenirs: 2ᵉ Bureau Londres.* Vol. 1. Monte Carlo: Raoul Solar, 1947.

Paxton, Robert O. *The Anatomy of Fascism.* New York: Alfred A. Knopf, 2004.

———. *Europe in the Twentieth Century.* Orlando, FL: Harcourt, 2002.

———. "The Five Stages of Fascism." *Journal of Modern History* 70, no. 1 (March 1998): 1–23.

———. *Vichy France: Old Guard and New Order, 1940–1944.* 1972. Reprint, New York: Columbia University Press, 2001.

Péan, Pierre. *Vies et morts de Jean Moulin.* Paris: Fayard, 1998.

Pécout, Christophe. "Pour une autre histoire des chantiers de la jeunesse (1940–1944)." *Vingtième Siècle: Revue d'Histoire,* no. 116 (2012): 97–107.

Pellissier, Pierre. *6 février 1934: La république en flammes.* Paris: Perrin, 2000.

Peschanski, Denis. "Legitimacy/Legitimation/Delegitimation: France in the Dark Years, a Textbook Case." *Contemporary European History* 13, no. 4 (2004): 409–23.

Pétain, Philippe, and Haute cour de justice. *Le procès du Maréchal Pétain: Compte rendu sténographique.* Paris: Albin Michel, 1945.

Piketty, Guillaume. " Générations résistantes à l'épreuve de la sortie de guerre." *Revue Historique* 641, no. 1 (2007): 151. doi:10.3917/rhis.071.0151.

———. "L'histoire de la Résistance dans le travail du Comité d'histoire de la Deuxième Guerre mondiale: Projets, methods." In *Faire l'histoire de la Résistance,* ed. Laurent Douzou. Rennes: Presses Universitaires de Rennes, 2010.

Plumyène, J., and R. Lasierra. *Les fascismes français, 1923–63.* Paris: Éditions du Seuil, 1963.

Pugliese, Stanislao G. "Death in Exile: The Assassination of Carlo Rosselli." *Journal of Contemporary History* 32, no. 3 (July 1997): 305–19.

Rabino, Thomas. *Le réseau Carte: Histoire d'un réseau de la Résistance antiallemand, antigaulliste, anticommuniste et anticollaborationniste.* Paris: Perrin, 2008.

Rath, R. John. "The Carbonari: Their Origins, Initiation Rites, and Aims." *American Historical Review* 69, no. 2 (January 1964): 353–70.

Read, Geoff. *The Republic of Men: Gender and the Political Parties in Interwar France.* Baton Rouge: Louisiana State University Press, 2014.

Reid, D. "Everybody Was in the French Resistance . . . Now! American Representations of the French Resistance." *French Cultural Studies* 23, no. 1 (2012): 49–63.

———. "French Singularity, the Resistance and the Vichy Syndrome: Lucie Aubrac to the Rescue." *European History Quarterly* 36, no. 2 (2006): 200–220.

Rémond, René. *The Right Wing in France: From 1815 to de Gaulle.* Trans. James M. Laux. Philadelphia: University of Pennsylvania Press, 1966.

Rémy [Gilbert Renault]. *Mémoires d'un agent secret de la France libre.* Vol. 1, *18 juin 1940–19 juin 1942.* Paris: Editions France-Empire, 1983.

Rioux, Jean-Pierre. *The Fourth Republic, 1944–1958.* Trans. Godfrey Rogers. Cambridge: Cambridge University Press, 1987.

Rossi, Mario. "United States Military Authorities and Free France, 1942–1944." *Journal of Military History* 61, no. 1 (January 1997): 49–65.

Rousso, Henry. *The Haunting Past: History, Memory, and Justice in Contemporary France.* Trans. Ralph Schoolcraft. Philadelphia: University of Pennsylvania Press, 2002.

———. *Vichy: L'événement, la mémoire, l'histoire.* Paris: Gallimard, 2001.

———. *The Vichy Syndrome: History and Memory in France since 1944.* Trans. Arthur Goldhammer. Cambridge, MA: Harvard University Press, 1991.

Sainclivier, Jacqueline. "Essai de prosopographie comparée des dirigeants de la Résistance intérieure et extérieure française." In *La Résistance et les Français: Villes, centres et logiques de décision; Actes du colloque international tenu à Cachan du 16 au 18 novembre 1995,* 321–38. Paris: IHTP/CNRS, 1995.

Sartre, Jean-Paul. *Iron in the Soul.* Trans. Gerard Hopkins. Harmondsworth, UK: Penguin Books, 1972.

Schoenbrun, David. *Soldiers of the Night: The Story of the French Resistance.* New York: E. P. Dutton, 1980.

Schwartz, Paula. "Partisanes and Gender Politics in Vichy France." *French Historical Studies* 16, no. 1 (Spring 1989): 126–51.

Semelin, Jacques. "Jalons pour une histoire de la France résistante." In *La Résistance et les Français: Villes, centres et logiques de décision; Actes du colloque international tenu à Cachan du 16 au 18 novembre 1995*, 459–70. Paris: IHTP/ CNRS, 1995.

———. *Unarmed against Hitler: Civilian Resistance in Europe, 1939–1943*. Trans. Suzan Husserl-Kapit. Westport, CT: Praeger, 1993.

Shennan, Andrew. *Profile in Power: De Gaulle*. Florence, KY: Taylor & Francis, 2014.

Siegel, Mona L. *The Moral Disarmament of France: Education, Pacifism and Patriotism, 1914–1940*. Cambridge: Cambridge University Press, 2004.

Simmel, Georg. "The Sociology of Secrecy and of Secret Societies." *American Journal of Sociology* 11, no. 4 (January 1906): 441–98.

Soucy, Robert. *French Fascism: The First Wave, 1924–1933*. New Haven, CT: Yale University Press, 1986.

———. *French Fascism: The Second Wave, 1933–1939*. New Haven, CT: Yale University Press, 1995.

Soustelle, Jacques. "France Looks at Her Alliances." *Foreign Affairs* 35, no. 1 (October 1956).

Spitzer, Alan B. *Old Hatreds and Young Hopes: The French Carbonari against the Bourbon Restoration*. Cambridge, MA: Harvard University Press, 1971.

———. *The Revolutionary Theories of Louis Auguste Blanqui*. New York: Columbia University Press, 1957.

Sternhell, Zeev. *Neither Right nor Left: Fascist Ideology in France*. Trans. David Maisel. Berkeley and Los Angeles: University of California Press, 1986.

Sweets, John. "Hold That Pendulum! Redefining Fascism, Collaborationism and Resistance in France." *French Historical Studies* 15, no. 4 (Autumn 1988): 731–58.

———. "Les historiens anglo-américains et la Résistance française." In *Faire l'histoire de la Résistance*, ed. Laurent Douzou. Rennes: Presses Universitaires de Rennes, 2010.

———. *The Politics of Resistance in France, 1940–1944: A History of the Mouvements Unis de la Résistance*. DeKalb: Northern Illinois University Press, 1976.

Szaluta, Jacques. "Marshal Petain's Ambassadorship to Spain: Conspiratorial or Providential Rise toward Power?" *French Historical Studies* 8, no. 4 (Autumn 1974): 511–33.

Taylor, Lynne. *Between Resistance and Collaboration: Popular Protest in Northern France, 1940–1945*. New York: St. Martin's, 2000.

Tombs, Robert. "From Revolution to Resistance: August 1944 in Historical Context." In *La Résistance et les Français: Villes, centres et logiques de décision; Actes du colloque international tenu à Cachan du 16 au 18 novembre 1995*, 47–58. Paris: IHTP/CNRS, 1995.

Tournoux, J. R. *L'histoire secrète*. Paris: Librairie Plon, 1962.

Tyre, Stephen. "The Gaullists, the French Army and Algeria before 1958: Common Cause or Marriage of Convenience?" *Journal of Strategic Studies* 25, no. 2 (2002): 97–117.

Ulloa, Marie-Pierre. *Francis Jeanson: A Dissident Intellectual from the French Resistance to the Algerian War*. Stanford, CA: Stanford University Press, 2007.

Valla, Jean-Claude. *La Cagoule, 1936–1937*. Paris: Éditions de la Librairie Nationale, 2000.

Vast, Cécile. *L'identité de la Résistance: Être résistant de l'occupation à l'après-guerre*. Paris: Payot, 2010.

Veillon, Dominique. "The Resistance and Vichy." In *France at War: Vichy and the Historians*, ed. Sarah Fishman, Laura Lee Downs, and Ioannis Sinanoglou Fishman. Oxford: Berg, 2000.

Veillon, Dominique, and Jacqueline Sainclivier. "La ville comme creuset de la Résistance." In *La Résistance et les Français: Villes, centres et logiques de décision; Actes du colloque international tenu à Cachan du 16 au 18 novembre 1995*, 135–50. Paris: IHTP/CNRS, 1995.

———. "Quelles différences sociales entre réseaux, mouvements et maquis?" In "Pour une histoire sociale de la Résistance," special issue, *Le Mouvement Social*, no. 180 (July–September 1997): 43–54.

Vergez-Chaignon, Bénédicte. *Les vichysto-résistants: De 1940 à nos jours*. Paris: Perrin, 2008.

Vergnon, Gilles. "Au nom de la France: Les discours des chefs d'état sur la résistance intérieure (1958–2007)." *Vingtième Siècle: Revue d'Histoire* no. 112 (2011): 139–52.

Vincendeau, Ginette. "The French Resistance through British Eyes: From 'Allo 'Allo! to Charlotte Gray." In *Je t'aime . . . moi non plus: Franco-British Cinematic Relations*, ed. Lucy Mazdon and Catherine Wheatley. New York: Berghahn Books, 2012.

Vinen, Richard. *Bourgeois Politics in France, 1945–1951*. Cambridge: Cambridge University Press, 1995.

———. "The End of an Ideology? Right-wing Antisemitism in France, 1944–1970." *Historical Journal* 37, no. 2 (June 1994): 365–88.

Walker, David A. "OSS and Operation Torch." *Journal of Contemporary History* 22, no. 4 (October 1987): 667–80.

Weber, Eugen. *Action Française: Royalism and Reaction in Twentieth-Century France*. Stanford, CA: Stanford University Press, 1962.

Weiss, Steve. "The Resistance as Part of Anglo-American Planning for the Liberation of Northwestern Europe." In *La Résistance et les Français: Enjeux stratégiques et environment social; Actes du colloque international tenu à Rennes du 29 septembre au 1 octobre 1994*, 53–66. Rennes: Presses universitaires de Rennes, 1995.

Weitz, Margaret Collins. *Sisters in the Resistance: How Women Fought to Free France, 1940–1945.* New York: John Wiley & Sons, 1998.

Wieviorka, Olivier. "A la recherche de l'engagement (1940–1944)." *Vingtième Siècle: Revue d'Histoire*, no. 60 (October 1998): 58–70.

———. *Divided Memory: French Recollections of World War II from the Liberation to the Present.* Trans. George Holoch. Stanford, CA: Stanford University Press, 2012.

———. "Les avatars du statut de résistant en France, 1945–1992." *Vingtième Siècle: Revue d'Histoire*, no. 50 (April–June 1996): 55–66.

———. "Pour une lecture critique de l'engagement résistant: L'exemple de défense de la France." In *Mémoire et histoire: La Résistance*, ed. J. Guillon and P. Laborie, 91–98. Toulouse: Éditions Privat, 1995.

———. "Structurations, modes d'intervention et prises de décision." In *La Résistance: Une histoire sociale*, ed. Antoine Prost, 55–68. Paris: Éditions de l'Atelier, 1997.

———. *Une certaine idée de la Résistance: Défense de la France, 1940–1949.* Paris: Éditions du Seuil, 1995.

———. "Vichy a-t-il été libéral? Le sens de l'intermède Flandin." *Vingtième Siècle: Revue d'Histoire*, no. 11 (July–September 1986): 55–65.

Wright, Gordon. "Reflections on the French Resistance (1940–1944)." *Political Science Quarterly* 77, no. 3 (September 1962): 336–49.

Young, Robert J. *France and the Origins of the Second World War.* New York: St. Martin's, 1996.

———. "Preparations for Defeat: French War Doctrine in the Inter-war Period." *Journal of European Studies* 2 June 1972, 155–72.

INDEX